The Military Coup d'Etat
as a Political Process

**THE JOHNS HOPKINS UNIVERSITY STUDIES
IN HISTORICAL AND POLITICAL SCIENCE
NINETY-FIFTH SERIES (1977)**

1. The Military Coup d'Etat as a Political Process: Ecuador, 1948–1966
    By John Samuel Fitch
2. William Penn's Legacy: Politics and Social Structure in Provincial
    Pennsylvania, 1726–1755
    By Alan Tully

# The Military Coup d'Etat as a Political Process

## Ecuador, 1948-1966

*John Samuel Fitch*

THE JOHNS HOPKINS UNIVERSITY PRESS ● Baltimore and London

Manufactured in the United States of America

The Johns Hopkins University Press, Baltimore, Maryland 21218
The Johns Hopkins Press Ltd., London


Library of Congress Catalog Card Number 76-47381
ISBN 0-8018-1915-6

Library of Congress Cataloging in Publication data will be found on the last printed page of this book.

# Contents

Acknowledgments      xiii

**Part One: Theory and Context**

Chapter 1:    The Military Coup d'Etat: A Theoretical Framework      3
Chapter 2:    The Ecuadorian Armed Forces      14

**Part Two: The Coup d'Etat in Ecuadorian Politics: 1948–1966**

Chapter 3:    Peace, Prosperity, and Constitutional Stability:
     1948–1960      39
Chapter 4:    The End of an Era: The Fall of Velasco Ibarra      47
Chapter 5:    The Fall of Carlos Julio Arosemena      55
Chapter 6:    The Fall of the Military Junta      65

**Part Three: Decision Criteria for Military Coups in Ecuador**

Chapter 7:    Individual Decisions to Support or Oppose a Coup
     d'Etat      77
Chapter 8:    Personal Backgrounds and Coup Decisions      89

**Part Four: The Military and the Political System: The Individual
       Components of the Coup Decision**

Chapter 9:    The Armed Forces and the Constitution      101
Chapter 10: The Influence of Public Opinion      111
Chapter 11: Anticommunism and Institutional Interests      117
Chapter 12: The Changing Role of the Ecuadorian Armed Forces      129

## Contents

**Part Five: The Coup d'Etat as a Political Process**

Chapter 13:  The Variable Political Environment                      149
Chapter 14:  The Systemic Interaction                               160
Chapter 15:  Ecuador since 1966: Testing the Model                  174


Notes                                                               187


Bibliographical References
                 Bibliography of Works Cited                        221
                 Supplementary Bibliography on Ecuador              233


Index                                                               237

# Tables

2.1    1970 Military Forces and Expenditures: Latin America and
Black Africa    22

2.2    Province/Region of Birth of Entering Army Cadets    24

2.3    Regional Shares of Population and Entering Cadets    25

2.4    Trends in Social Origins of Entering Army Cadets    26

2.5    Father's Profession of Entering Army Cadets: Ecuador and
Brazil    27

2.6    Socioeconomic Status of Military Interview Sample    28

2.7    Comparison of Monthly Salaries    29

2.8    Comparison of High Public Administration with Other
Professions    30

2.9    Military Professionalization in Latin America    31

2.10   Index of Output of New and Senior Officers    33

3.1    Factors Entering into Military Decisions: 1954    43

4.1    Factors Entering into Military Decisions: 1961    53

5.1    Factors Entering into Military Decisions: 1963    63

6.1    Factors Entering into Military Decisions: 1966    72

7.1    Characteristics of the Interview Sample    78

7.2    Factors Entering Coup Decisions of Individual Officers    78

7.3    Coup Attitudes and Summary Ratings of Government
Performance    80

7.4    Officers' Attitudes toward the Coup and Summary Ratings
of Government Performance    81

7.5    Personal Political Orientation and Attitudes toward the
Overthrow of the Government    82

7.6    Ratings of Government Performance on Socioeconomic
Reforms and Attitudes toward the Overthrow of the
Government    83

| 7.7 | Multiple Regression of Coup Positions on Ratings of Government Performance on Individual Decision Criteria | 84 |
|------|------|------|
| 7.8 | Simple and Partial Correlations among Decision Criteria Ratings: 1961 | 85 |
| 7.9 | Standardized Regression Coefficients: Individual Coup Decision Criteria | 86 |
| 7.10 | Multiple Regression of Attitudes toward Coup on Decision Criteria: Combined Sample | 87 |
| 8.1 | Coup Decisions and Rank at Time of Coup | 91 |
| 8.2 | Military Family Background and Anticommunism: 1963 | 92 |
| 8.3 | Military Family Background and Attitudes toward the Military Junta: 1966 | 92 |
| 8.4 | Region of Birth, Primary Schooling, and Political Orientation | 93 |
| 8.5 | Branch of Service and Military Coup Decisions | 95 |
| 9.1 | Correlations of Constitutionality Ratings and Coup Positions | 101 |
| 9.2 | Open-ended Responses Mentioning/Stressing Constitutional Norm | 103 |
| 9.3 | Open-ended Responses Mentioning/Stressing Public Disorders | 105 |
| 9.4 | Correlations of Ratings on Public Disorders and Attitudes toward Coup | 106 |
| 9.5 | Public Disorders, Communist Threat, and Coup Attitudes: 1963 | 107 |
| 9.6 | Military Responses to Public Disorders | 109 |
| 10.1 | Open-ended Responses Mentioning/Stressing Public Opinion | 111 |
| 10.2 | Correlations of Coup Attitudes with Ratings of Public Opinion | 112 |
| 10.3 | Editorial Opinions and Military Perceptions of Public Opinion | 115 |
| 11.1 | American Military Training and Attitudes toward 1963 Coup | 118 |
| 11.2 | Uncued Rationales for Military Anticommunism | 120 |
| 11.3 | Correlations of Attitudes toward the Coup and Ratings of Government Responsiveness to the Military's Institutional Interests | 121 |
| 11.4 | Average Annual Increase in Defense, Education, and Public Works Budgets | 122 |
| 11.5 | Ratings of Government Responsiveness to the Institutional Needs of the Armed Forces | 123 |

| | | |
|---|---|---|
| 11.6 | Average Distribution of Central Government Budget: 1950–1966 | 124 |
| 12.1 | Definitions of the Role of the Armed Forces among Ecuadorian Officers | 129 |
| 12.2 | Abstract Role Definition and Attitudes toward the 1961, 1963, and 1966 Coups | 133 |
| 12.3 | Correlations of Decision Criteria Ratings and Coup Positions among Proponents of the Same Role Definition | 135 |
| 12.4 | Formal Role Definitions and Perceptions of Civilian/ Military Capability to Govern | 137 |
| 12.5 | Foreign Training and Formal Role Definition | 140 |
| 13.1 | Rate of Growth of Exports | 151 |
| 13.2 | Changes in the Geographic Distribution of Population: 1938–1962 | 152 |
| 13.3 | Balance of Payments: 1964, 1965 | 158 |
| 14.1 | Weighting of Political Outcomes in Coup Decisions | 161 |
| 15.1 | Military Appraisal of the Political Situation: 1970–1976 | 180 |

# Figures

1.1    A Minimal Framework for the Analysis of Military Coups    4
4.1    Public Disorders: 1961    54
9.1    Perceptions of Public Disorders    108
12.1    Trends in Role Definition among Ecuadorian Officers 1954-1966    136
13.1    Modernization, Participation, and Populism    153
13.2    Export Growth, Economic Welfare, and Military Coups    159
14.1    Frequency Distribution of Attitudes toward Coup    166
14.2    Stabilization by Coup d'Etat: Combined Editorial Analysis Scores: 1961, 1963, 1966    172

# Acknowledgments

Any manuscript with a gestation period as long as this one has had must begin with a note of appreciation for the numerous intellectual midwives who guided the work through its formative stages, nursed it through a variety of labor pains, and gave so generously of their time and insight to see it through into the light of day. Special thanks are due to Alfred Stepan for his patient guidance and ceaseless encouragement and to my wife, Marty, for her tolerance of my long, bigamous relationship with this research project. Douglas Chalmers, Martin Shubik, Juan Linz, Anthony Maingot, William Foltz, Alfred Clubok, Richard Sutton, Rene Lemarchand, Daniel Lerner, and Abraham Lowenthal all offered valuable advice at various stages along the way, as did the members of the Continuing Seminar on Political Development, particularly Harold Lasswell, Garry Brewer, Raymond Hopkins, Ronald Brunner, and Bill Ascher. Henry Tom and Jacqueline Wehmueller also deserve thanks for their assistance with the book. Needless to say, none of those cited above can be held responsible for any failure on my part to put to good use their willingness to contribute comments and criticism.

I also gratefully acknowledge the permission given by the Free Press to use material from my article "Toward a Model of the Coup d'Etat in Latin America," which appeared in *Political Development and Change: A Policy Approach,* edited by Garry D. Brewer and Ronald D. Brunner (Copyright © 1975 by The Free Press, a Division of the Macmillan Publishing Co., Inc.), the computer and writing time provided by the University of Florida, and, above all, the support of the Henry and Grace Doherty Foundation, which enabled me to conduct field research in Ecuador during 1970 and 1971. That research led directly to an earlier version of this manuscript—my doctoral dissertation at Yale University.

Nevertheless, all the efforts of the persons and institutions acknowledged here might have come to naught but for the generous cooperation of former officers of the Ecuadorian armed forces. If previous studies of civil-military relations in the developing countries share any single characteristic, it is that they have generally been based on relatively informal contacts with a handful of members of the military institutions in question. Because it has historically been quite difficult to secure systematic interviews with Latin American military officers on the politically sensitive questions that lie at the heart of our theoretical concerns, most political scientists have considered it impossible to study the military through the research techniques normally used with other political elites.[1] Thus the real credit for this study belongs to the eighty military officers and nineteen political leaders who kindly gave of their time and patience in more than one hundred interviews to share their knowledge of the Ecuadorian armed forces and the various civil-military crises that are the subject of this volume. Under the terms of the interviews, most of the interview material will not be publicly attributed to any individual respondent.[2] I would therefore like to acknowledge here all those who participated in this study.

Dr. Francisco Acosta Yépez
Coronel Jaime Aguilar Paredes
General Jorge Aguinaga Meneses
Dr. Manuel Augustín Aguirre R.
Tnte. Coronel Galo Almeida Urrutia
Sr. Gonzalo Almeida Urrutia
Coronel Colón Alvarado Mejía
General Rafael Andrade Ochoa
Coronel Galo Andrade Salas
Tnte. Coronel Luis Araque
Sr. Otto Arosemena Gómez
Dr. Carlos Julio Arosemena Monroy
General Andrés Arrata Macías
Coronel Carlos Arregui Viteri
General Víctor Aulestia Mier
General Gustavo Banderas Román
General José Banderas Román
Dr. Guillermo Bossano
General Luis Cabrera Sevilla
Capitán de Navío Alejandro Cajas Vallejo
Contralmirante Gonzalo Calderón Noriega
General Enrique Calle Solano
Lic. Carlos Carrión Aguirre
Contralmirante Ramón Castro Jijón
Tnte. Coronel Bolívar Cevallos Zapata
Coronel Jorge Chiriboga Donoso
General Gonzalo Coba Cabezas
Coronel Gustavo Corral Ruilova
Mayor Luis Darquea Romero
General Luis del Pozo Lagos
Coronel Aníbal Duarte Narváez
Coronel José Endara Erazo
Tnte. Coronel Víctor Espinosa M.

General Julio Espinosa Pineda
Coronel Guillermo Freile Posso
Dr. Camilo Gallegos Toledo
General Marcos Gándara Enríquez
Coronel Jaime García Naranjo
Coronel Jorge García Negrete
Coronel Marcos González Espinosa
General Jorge González González
General Rigoberto González Zurita
Mayor Wagner Holguín Sevilla
Coronel Gustavo Izurieta Ugarte
General Héctor Jácome Castillo
General Luis Larrea Alba
Sr. Patricio Lasso Carrión
Coronel Alfonso Littuma Arízaga
General Carlos López Ozaeta
General Leopoldo Mantilla Ante
Coronel Víctor Medina Angulo
Dr. Milton Molina Calle
Coronel Telmo Moncayo Vélez
Coronel Rafael Monge Merino
General Víctor Montero Maldonado
Contralmirante Carlos Monteverde G.
General Luis Mora Bowen
General Antonio Moral Moral
Coronel Eudoro Naranjo Abarca
General Aurelio Naranjo Campaña
Contralmirante Manuel Nieto Cadena
Coronel Jacinto Ochoa Merchán
Sr. Luis Orrantia González
Ing. Federico Páez
Coronel José Patiño Zárate
Coronel Luis Pineiros Pastor

Dr. Camilo Ponce Enríquez
Mayor Carlos Puga Arroyo
Tnte. Coronel Carlos Quiroz Maldonado
Coronel Luis Ramos Paredes
Coronel Jesús Reyes Quintanilla
General Antonio Rivas Hidalgo
Coronel Genaro Rivera Brito
Lic. Luis Robles Plaza
Lic. Jorge Rosas
Coronel José Sáenz Arellano
Capitán de Navío Sergio Sáenz
Lic. Francisco Salazar Alvarado
General Jorge Salgado Murillo
Coronel Jorge Salvador y Chiriboga
Coronel Alberto Serrano Alvarado

General Víctor Suárez Haz
Dr. Mariano Suárez Veintimilla
Tnte. Coronel Francisco Tamariz P.
Coronel Gonzalo Tamayo Herrera
Tnte. Coronel Jorge Valdivieso G.
Tnte. Coronel Reinaldo Varea Donoso
General Telmo Vargas Benalcázar
Coronel Angel Vega Avilés
Coronel Jaime Veintimilla Morán
Dr. José María Velasco Ibarra
Coronel Pedro Vélez Morán
General Nilo Alfredo Villagómez Viteri
Capitán de Navío Jorge Wolf Franco
Tnte. Coronel Francisco Zambrano
General Angel Zurita Paz y Miño

Special mention should also be made of General Guillermo Rodríguez Lara, former director of the Colegio Militar Eloy Alfaro, and General Carlos Aguirre Asanza, former acting director of the army war academy, for their permission to utilize the archives of these institutions in this research, and for the kind assistance rendered by the staffs of both institutions. To all those who participated in the study and to my many Ecuadorian friends, I express my deepest gratitude. With so many distinguished persons contributing their knowledge to this study, the responsibility for any errors of fact or interpretation must be mine alone.

*part one*

# Theory and Context

# chapter one

# The Military Coup d'Etat: A Theoretical Framework

Since the end of the Second World War every Latin American country except Mexico has experienced at least one military coup d'état. In the region as a whole, the forcible overthrow of the government by the armed forces is a relatively commonplace event. In Latin America, as in Africa and Asia, military intervention in politics is the rule, not the exception. Extensive scholarly analysis of this phenomenon during the past fifteen years has mostly resulted in the proliferation of untested, often conflicting hypotheses.[1] Securing systematic empirical data on the political behavior of military officers is always difficult, but the major obstacle to theory-building in the study of the coup d'état has been the lack of a comprehensive analytical framework to link the complex set of causal processes that shape the military decision to overthrow or support the government in power.

Considering only the coup d'état (one of several forms of military intervention in politics), a minimal analytical framework must logically include at least four elements. First of all, it is apparent that even in countries with frequent military coups, not every government is overthrown, nor do coups occur randomly. This raises two questions: Why this government and not that one? Why now and not before? The first logical element of a theory of military intervention is, therefore, the specification of the decision criteria by which the armed forces judge whether at any point a particular government should be supported or overthrown in a coup d'état (figure 1.1, Class A explanatory variables). These decision criteria identify those elements of the political and socioeconomic situation of the country that military officers consider relevant to their decision to support or oppose the government. Only by specifying these decision criteria and, through them, the changing political scene to which the military responds,

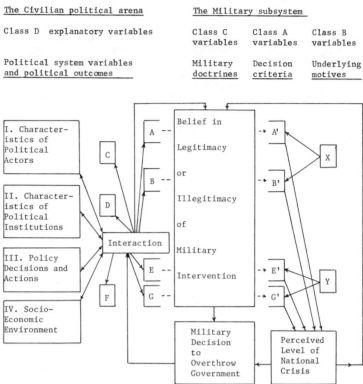

The Civilian political arena      The Military subsystem

| Class D explanatory variables | Class C variables | Class A variables | Class B variables |
| Political system variables and political outcomes | Military doctrines | Decision criteria | Underlying motives |

Where:

I–IV = subsets of variables directly or indirectly causing variations in political outcomes monitored by the military, e.g., weak political institutions, economic stagnation, etc.;

A, B, ... G = political outcomes, e.g., antigovernment riots, civilian willingness to enter conspiracies, etc.;

A', B', ... G' = perceived political outcomes deemed relevant to military coup decisions, e.g., "communist" infiltration of the government;

X, Y = underlying variables determining which outcomes are monitored by military, e.g., personal greed, professional development, class or ethnic identifications, which cause the military to be concerned with A, B, E, G, but not with C, D, F outcomes.

Figure 1.1. A Minimal Framework for the Analysis of Military Coups

can we explain why the Chilean armed forces decided to permit Salvador Allende to be installed as president, resisted various conspiracies against him for three years, yet finally intervened in one of the hemisphere's bloodiest coups. One could simply postulate the decision rule that the generals take over whenever the president cuts the military budget,[2] or, abandoning single-factor explanations, attempt to define the variety of political situations that contribute to military perceptions of a "national crisis" requiring military action.

The second logical component of a comprehensive analysis of the coup d'état is the specification of what determines which political outcomes are deemed relevant ingredients of a decision to overthrow the government (Class B explanatory variables). Why does the military dislike certain political outcomes while remaining indifferent to others? Why do most military officers react negatively to cuts in the military budget but not to cuts in the education budget, to the threat of communism but not the threat of fascism? One answer, favored by novelists and television writers, is simply that personal greed (underlying motive) leads to military coups against governments that threaten the power and privileges of the officers in charge (coup decision rule).

However, in the same sense that the decision to intervene cannot be abstracted from the situational context in which it occurs, neither can it be abstracted from the attitudes and beliefs that condition the military's appraisal of external events and their calculation of the appropriate response to them. Hence the third component of the analysis must be the specification of military attitudes toward the political role of the armed forces and the relationship of these attitudes to the behavior of military officers in crisis situations (Class C variables). In its simplest form, this may be a question of the military's belief in the legitimacy of irregular changes of government as a response to political crises.[3] More generally, what is required is a typology of military role definitions capable of explaining the military's dissimilar responses to similar political crises at different times or in different countries. Assuming a rough equivalence in situational stimuli—a long, unsuccessful, and unpopular war abroad, coupled with dissent and disorder at home—why was the response of American officers in Vietnam so different from that of many French officers in Algeria? Why did the American military make no equivalent effort to overthrow their government?

Finally, a comprehensive theory of military intervention in politics must identify the determinants of political outcomes that are deemed relevant to military coup decisions. If military coups are generally responses to political crises, why are such crises much more common and more severe in some countries than in others, or in certain periods within the history of a single country? Samuel Huntington's theory of political development is perhaps the best known example of this type of explanation of military intervention (Class D variables). According to Huntington, political systems with a low level of "institutionalization" relative to the level of socioeconomic modernization recurrently generate the kinds of political outcomes (corruption, violence, ineffective government) that lead to military decisions to overthrow the government.[4]

These four kinds of explanations for military intervention are not particularly novel, nor do they exhaust the list of possibilities. What has been lacking to date is an understanding that a comprehensive theory of the coup d'état must include all of these elements. Consider the case of those political systems where no military coup has occurred. This may be the result of any of the following factors: a lack of military motivation to be concerned with political events; a belief in doctrines precluding military intervention as a legitimate response, even to crises viewed with concern by military officers; or a strong political system, perhaps one blessed with a favorable socioeconomic environment, that consistently avoids political situations that might lead to a withdrawal of military support for the government. Conversely, a minimal explanation for any successful coup d'état must logically include the perceived events that led to the decision to overthrow the government, the underlying rationale by which these events were considered objectionable by the military, the attitudes and beliefs by which the military had a "duty" to intervene in such cases, and the direct and indirect causes of the precipitating events.

With the aid of this analytical framework, we can now introduce the major questions posed in this study of the political behavior of the Ecuadorian armed forces. The first conclusion that may be drawn from the preceding arguments is that the armed forces act as the ultimate judge of whether an existing government shall continue in office or be replaced in a coup d'état. The information necessary to make the decision to support or overthrow the government is obtained mostly by monitoring the political situation outside of the military itself. As one experienced Argentine observer put it, "the armed forces study the national scene and, if the situation arises, have the right and duty to intervene when, in their judgment, important national objectives are threatened. As interpreters of the national interest, they have an unavoidable responsibility to replace a government when necessary to protect national objectives."[5] The critical question, then, becomes one of specifying under what conditions the armed forces will consider "the national interest" or "important national objectives" to be threatened. Previous studies of the Latin American military suggest six kinds of political events that significantly influence the military's appraisal of the level of political crisis and therefore the degree to which the military feels a need to intervene.

One of the factors most commonly cited as leading to military coups is the pressure of civilian groups hostile to the government calling on the military to do "its patriotic duty" and "save the country from ruin" by removing the government in power.[6] According to Edwin Lieuwen, "The militarism of the postwar period, like that of the 1930s has been primarily a reflection of the demands made upon the armed forces by antagonistic forces—by the traditional order attempting to maintain the *status quo* and by new social forces attempting to alter it."[7] The importance of civilian pressures in the coup d'état process and the general support of civilians for a nonsubordinated military are such that John Johnson, in choosing a descriptive label for Latin American civil-military relations, rejected "militarism" in favor of "civil-militarism."[8] As Venezuela's former president, Dr. Rafael Caldera, ruefully noted, "Venezuelans are so accustomed to make the army the arbiter of their political conflicts that at any moment the most varied groups seeking the most dissimilar ends try to involve the army in new adventures to change our political reality."[9] Thus the first coup decision criterion suggested is the degree of civilian opposition to the government—"the pressure of public opinion."

High levels of hostility toward the government among working class groups (if they are politically relevant) may also incite a coup d'état. Such hostility frequently leads to antigovernment demonstrations, strikes, and riots by these groups, who usually lack direct access to the military.[10] "If public order threatens to break down as a result of growing opposition to the policies of the incumbent government, then the military feels a constitutional duty to intervene."[11] Egil Fossum finds that of the seventy-eight Latin American coups between 1907 and 1966 for which he has information, there were prior public disorders in sixty-one cases.[12] This follows in part from the military's constitutional role as the guardian of internal order; more important is the fact that the military is forced to pass judgment on the government, since it is usually the army that is called upon to suppress the disorders, a police role not popular with the military.[13] Use of the army by an unpopular government to suppress internal disorders affects the public image of the armed forces and, as Samuel Finer notes, in most Latin American cases "the armed forces are morbidly concerned with their popularity."[14] Therefore the level of public disorders may also be a major factor influencing coup decisions.

Another student of the Latin American military observes that "because people wear a uniform they do not cease to be subject to the determinants of political attitudes which act upon civilians."[15] Given the role of the military as the ultimate guardians of the national interest, how that interest will be defined in a particular situation is of crucial importance. The relevant personal political attitudes of military officers have never been clearly identified, but it is likely that the officer corps will be recruited from one or another social stratum and informed through kinship ties of the pro- or antigovernment sentiments of that stratum. José Nun argues that Latin American military officers are in close contact with their civilian peers in political and social life, thanks to the absence of wars and the large number of retired officers.[16] Given the lack of substantive hypotheses about the personal attitudes of military officers, one can only postulate that when the civilian sector with which the military identifies becomes hostile to the government, the military will also feel that the government is acting "contrary to the national interest."

It is also apparent that in practice the armed forces often define the public interest in such a way as to make it in large measure equivalent to the institutional interests of the military establishment. By military logic, since the armed forces are the guardians of the national interest, the national interest requires that the military itself be diligently protected. "Perversion of the governing function includes, in the eyes of the military, any actions inimical to the interests of the armed forces such as any humiliation, material weakening, or moral undermining of the armed forces establishment."[17] Neglect of the military in the distribution of government resources enhances the perceived level of na-

7

tional crisis. On the other hand, increases in the military budget may act as an incentive for the military to be tolerant in judging whether the political situation really requires a coup d'état.

A related situation frequently leading to military intervention is the perceived threat of a communist or extreme left government. In part this is a consequence of the military's role as defender of the constitutional order and of national sovereignty and in part it reflects the influence of U.S. anticommunist, counterinsurgency doctrines, conveyed through military assistance and officer-training programs.[18] Nevertheless, other evidence suggests that the military's implacable opposition to communism is based largely on the conviction that a communist or Castro-style government would destroy the army and replace it with a civilian militia.[19] The fate of the old military in the Cuban revolution is seen as a clear indication that Castro-inspired movements present the ultimate threat to the military institution—a challenge to its continued existence.

Finally, it has been noted that military coups often occur in connection with elections, with the military intervening to prevent elections from being held or to veto the electoral results. Between 1945 and 1964, 42 percent of the coups in Latin America occurred within the twelve months before or four months after a presidential election.[20] Most often this involved persons or parties previously deposed by the military whose prospective return to office both threatened the careers of the officers involved in the previous action and reactivated their previous objections to that individual or party. Thus the proximity of a threatening election may also enter into coup decisions.

Given the dearth of empirical data on the political behavior of military officers, previous studies provide little assurance that these are in fact the criteria by which the military measures the level of "national crisis." On the basis of the existing evidence, one cannot assert with confidence that other, equally significant, decision criteria have not been omitted. Moreover, in the descriptive literature from which these initial hypotheses have been culled, one generally finds only the assertion that these political outcomes are causally related to military coups without any further specification of the relationship. The argument that the military tends to overthrow governments that cut the military budget, for example, does not specify whether military officers care equally about the operating (salary) and equipment budgets, how large a cut or how small an increase will be considered objectionable, or under what conditions military budget demands might vary. The existing literature also fails to provide any indication of how many or what combinations of these coup-motivating events would have to be present to assure the successful overthrow of the government.

The first set of questions posed in this study, therefore, concerns the accuracy of this initial list of coup decision criteria, the specification of the relationships between these political events and the decision to intervene, and the identification of the sufficient conditions for a successful coup. The period from 1948 to 1966 in Ecuador provides especially fertile ground in which to seek answers to these questions. Between 1948 and 1960, despite one major attempted coup, freely elected governments completed their full four-year terms for the first time in Ecuadorian history. Yet in the next six years, three successive governments—two civilian and one military—were overthrown by the armed forces. During this period all of the coup-motivating political outcomes postulated above were present in varying frequency and intensity. This permits a systematic analysis of the manner in which these events were perceived by military officers and the way in which these perceptions of their political environment shaped the positions taken by Ecuadorian officers in four rather dissimilar crises. Through an extensive analysis of historical materials and interview data from the major participants in each of these coups, the initial list of coup decision criteria will be amended and further specified as to what political outcomes are monitored by the armed forces, the manner in which these events are perceived, and their individual and cumulative impact on military perceptions of a "national crisis."

Nevertheless, by my previous argument, military perceptions of a political crisis are not in themselves sufficient to cause a coup d'état. The decision to support the military overthrow of the government also requires a concomitant belief in the legitimacy of military intervention in politics. Within Latin America it is frequently argued that the armed forces are the legitimate guardians and interpreters of the national interest. Most Latin American constitutions give the military the responsibility not only for securing national defense but also for maintaining internal order and guaranteeing the constitution and the constitutionally established powers.[21] These constitutional provisions tend to legitimize the belief common among both civilians and officers that the ultimate responsibility of the armed forces is to the national interest, even if this requires acting against the established government. On the other hand, the contrary tendency has also been noted by various analysts: the desire of Latin American military officers to conform to the apolitical, "professional" image of the modern officer diffused through American and European training missions.[22] According to these arguments, professional bureaucratic norms encourage resistance to politicization of the military. Military intervention in politics must be deemed undesirable, since it inevitably introduces political considerations into purely military affairs and leads to presidential meddling with promotions and garrison assignments as a means of self-defense.[23]

Previous discussions of the attitudes of military officers toward their political role raise a number of questions about the Ecuadorian military. Do the two opposing currents of opinion noted above in fact adequately describe the range of role definitions held by Ecuadorian officers? For example, Alfred Stepan has described the emergence of new doctrines in Brazil according to which military professionalism is not thought to be incompatible with extensive involvement in politics.[24] Secondly, what is the relationship between these military doctrines and the political behavior of officers who espouse them? Is it simply a question of differential resistance to military intervention or do these attitudes also influence other aspects of the decision to intervene? Finally, what accounts for the substantial shifts in role definitions among Ecuadorian officers from the "constitutionalist" military of the 1950s to more interventionist doctrines, culminating in the installation of a military government in 1963 and again in 1972?

As indicated in the discussion of coup decision criteria, the military's concern for these particular political outcomes has been ascribed to a variety of personal, political, class, institutional, and patriotic motives. The question of the relative significance of these underlying motives as determinants of military behavior has been perhaps the most enduring controversy among students of civil-military relations.[25] In the early literature, both Johnson and Janowitz stressed the importance of the socioeconomic origins and status of the military in developing countries[26] —in direct contrast to Lieuwen's emphasis on institutional interests.[27] More recently the controversy has centered around José Nun's thesis that the Latin American military is predominantly middle class in origin and has reflected middle-class interests and values in its political behavior,[28] a view strongly denied in Stepan's analysis of the Brazilian military.[29] Writing on the African military, Robert Price has added another argument, stressing reference group identifications with foreign military elites by African officers who have received their military training abroad.[30]

In part the debate has been obscured by the lack of agreement on two prior questions: What political events are relevant to coup decisions? What is the relative salience of these events to the military? These questions are treated in detail in chapter 7, which is followed by a statistical analysis of the influence of personal background characteristics on the pro- or antigovernment positions of Ecuadorian officers in the various crises. Yet the crux of the controversy concerns the psychological underpinning of military behavior, particularly the personal identity structure of the individual military officer. Chapter 11 addresses itself directly to the thesis of the "middle-class military," and argues that a primary identification with the military institution itself underlies the decision criteria employed by Ecuadorian officers to judge government performance. The evolution of this identity structure in the Ecuadorian military and its basis in the military socialization process are described in chapter 2.

Of the various types of explanations of military coups, none evokes less scholarly consensus than the attempt to identify the systemic sources of the situational crises leading to military intervention. While most analysts share Huntington's view that Latin America's endemic political instability is part of a larger pattern of political underdevelopment,[31] there is little agreement as to its underlying causes. The generally "praetorian" character of Latin American political systems has been variously ascribed to Hispanic political culture,[32] high/low political participation,[33] high/low modernization,[34] weak political institutions,[35] ethnic composition,[36] economic development/underdevelopment,[37] a rigid/amorphous class structure,[38] foreign penetration, and U.S. imperialism,[39] as well as various combinations thereof. Given the complexity of Latin American politics and the substantial variations from country to country, one can find sufficient evidence to make a plausible case for many of these arguments. Yet the multiplicity of often conflicting claims suggests that much empirical research remains to be done.

Most recently, cross-national statistical analysis has been used in an attempt to determine empirically the systemic sources of instability and military intervention in Latin America and other Third World areas.[40] This approach to the problem is both theoretically and methodologically suspect. If we assume that a coup d'état is the outcome of a complex interaction, over a period of time, of many elements of the social, economic, and political context of the particular country in question, the cross-national approach is theoretically inappropriate, since it is basically static and acontextual.[41] In addition, the standard regression model used in such analyses requires the use of several assumptions already shown to be inconsistent with the complex nature of the coup process.[42] Largely as a result of these inconsistencies, the cross-national aggregate-data approach typically ends in the "Argentina paradox" illustrated in John Johnson's comment on political instability in the post-Perón era: "That such should be the case in one of the most technologically advanced, urbanized, racially homologous, and literate republics, with . . . positive middle sector participation in public affairs is somewhat surprising, but also in large part understandable when viewed historically."[43] As the statement suggests, understanding military intervention in politics requires a "historical view," that is, a focus on the processes by which a political system changes over time.

Thus the more productive route to an understanding of the systemic sources of military coups lies through an understanding of the coup itself. Tracing backward from the political outcomes leading to military intervention, one can show that the greater frequency of such events in the latter years of the 1948–1966 period resulted primarily from changes in the international economy. With the end of the banana boom and the increase in participation it stimulated, the inability of Ecuadorian political institutions to mobilize support independently of the international economic cycle led to a series of crises pitting weak populist and reformist governments (civilian and military) against the established economic elites and ending in three successive coups. The dynamics of these variations in the military's political environment and their basis in the structure of Ecuadorian politics and society are explored in chapter 13.

In addition to answering the questions posed above about coup decision criteria, underlying motives, military role definitions, and the systemic causes of military coups in Ecuador, this study advances three major arguments. The first is the necessity of integrating the partial explanations of military coups offered by coup participants, case studies of individual coups, general essays on civil-military relations, and global theorizing about Latin American politics, each of which tends to focus on only one or two of the questions above. In the absence of a comprehensive analytical framework, the general tendency during the past decade has been to focus on competing partial explanations—on some single factor or subset of factors—rather than on the entire complex of factors shaping the decision to intervene. In Ecuador, during the period in question, there have been important changes in all of the four areas identified above; each in turn resulted in significant changes in military behavior. The framework proposed here, by clarifying the relationship among the various partial perspectives, should reduce the number of sterile debates among their proponents.[44] As such, it is a necessary first step toward a coherent theoretical model of the coup d'état as a political process.

Nevertheless, one essential element of a comprehensive theory of the coup d'état is still lacking. The demonstrated ability of even the most rudimentary military organizations to execute a coup d'état must not obscure the key role of institutional characteristics in shaping military behavior. Despite the essentially political nature of the coup d'état process, it will be shown that institutional variables influence every aspect of the military's interaction with its political environment. In subtle but important ways, the social and regional bases of officer recruitment, the extent and nature of foreign military training, and the size and structure of the armed forces affect military perceptions of the political scene, beliefs about military roles, and the style of collective decision-making in crisis situations. More important, the level of military professionalization (defined institutionally in terms of technical development and complexity) directly affects the psychological makeup of military officers as well as their attitudes toward intervention in politics. Together with the nature of the larger political system, the degree of military professionalization is a cornerstone underlying the different patterns of civil-military relations encountered in pre-war and postwar Ecuador. Given the intermediate level of development of the Ecuadorian military—between the more highly professionalized militaries of the larger South American countries and the less professionalized African militaries—the Ecuadorian experience also suggests that institutional variables are an important factor in cross-regional differences in the coup d'état as a political process.

Finally, it will be argued that the coup d'état plays an important role in Ecuador's continued inability to escape the "praetorian syndrome." Like most Latin American political systems, Ecuador's has, in a basic sense, changed very little during the past quarter-century, despite a high level of surface political instability. The basic economic structure remains intact and the political system continues to lack legitimacy and strong institutions. The absence of more profound change is only partially a result of military fears of radical social forces or of the generally non-radical orientation of the military in power. In large part, this conservative bias is built into the political system by the institutionalization of the coup d'état as a political process. By providing a means of resolving the periodic crises stemming from weak political institutions and a fluctuating, externally dependent economy, the coup d'état ensures the stability of the underlying structural deficiencies. As a mechanism for the release and limitation of socioeconomic discontents, the institutionalized coup d'état exerts a profoundly conservative influence in Latin American politics. As such, the coup d'état is much more than a mere symptom of political underdevelopment.

# chapter two

# The Ecuadorian Armed Forces

The impact of military structure and organization on military politics has been a favorite point of debate among students of civil-military relations, though the trend in recent years has been to denigrate the importance of institutional variables. Samuel Huntington has stated the latter argument quite forcefully. "Military explanations do not explain military interventions.... The most important causes of military intervention in politics are not military but political and reflect not the organizational characteristics of the military establishment but the political and institutional structure of the country."[1] While it is true that military coups have been staged by some of the world's most primitive military organizations as well as by some of the largest and most professionalized, the simple fact of intervention or nonintervention in politics is not the only issue. Indeed, it is perhaps not even the most important one.

In a wide range of other questions—such as which governments are overthrown and which supported, the reasons for such military actions, the manner in which the coup occurs, what happens afterward—institutional characteristics often do play a key role. Thus the hitherto common practice of treating "the military" as an amorphous, largely abstract entity[2] ignores the considerable differences in the military institutions of such countries as Brazil, Ecuador, or Cuba. Ignoring these institutional differences leads in turn to the de facto neglect of a major source of variation in the political behavior of the armed forces. In Ecuador, the importance of these institutional variables is particularly apparent. Each of the major shifts in civil-military relations since that country's independence from Spain can be shown to have originated in changes taking place within the armed forces. Each of the three distinct patterns of civil-military interaction since 1830 corresponds to a certain stage in the institutional development of the armed forces.[3]

The period from independence until 1916 was the era of the military caudillos. During this time, a succession of military strong men dominated the country's political life, largely because the nation created by the Constitution of 1830 existed only on paper. The disintegration of the Spanish empire[4] left the country for more than twenty years with no real national administration except that provided by various Spanish armies and the 6,000-member Gran Colombian Army of the South, which in 1830 became the Ecuadorian Army and the power base of Ecuador's first president, General Juan José Flores. At the local level, the basic social and economic structure remained the hacienda, whose owners assumed de facto authority over a fairly large Indian population.[5] At the national level, however, no principle of authority commanded general assent or obedience, and several armed revolts broke out even as the new constitution was being written. Nevertheless, through a series of tacit agreements between the old aristocracy and the new breed of military leaders, the basic aristocratic socioeconomic structure was preserved, even though at the national level it was not possible to establish a stable political order based on the land-owning class.[6]

In this way the foundations were laid for a pattern of political conflict that persisted, with some variations, well into the twentieth century. This pattern of "hidalgo politics"[7] was characterized by a high level of conflict (generally by force of arms) over control of the state (virtually the only significant source of wealth other than large landholdings in a primitive economy) among a small number of participants drawn predominantly from the highest strata of the existing social order.[8] Thus the first half-century of Ecuadorian history is largely a tale of a series of generals—Flores, Urbina, Veintimilla—who dominated Ecuadorian politics for relatively long periods of time, interspersed with civil wars in which various military leaders contested to establish their personal hegemony.[9]

In the last two decades of the nineteenth century, this pattern was altered somewhat by the enormous expansion of cacao exports that brought hitherto unknown levels of prosperity to the land-owning and commercial families of the coast.[10] The growth and consolidation of the coastal plutocracy and the accompanying rise in the influence of nineteenth-century liberal ideas on the coast led to increasingly serious challenges to the traditional political pre-eminence of the interior. Through its sponsorship of irregular Liberal armies, the new coastal elite sought a political position commensurate with its new status as the dominant economic force and source of a large share of the government's revenues. While the essential elements of hidalgo politics remained the same, in 1895 General Eloy Alfaro occupied Quito and took control of the government, thus beginning a thirty-year period of Liberal hegemony in Ecuadorian politics.

As the Liberal-Conservative wars gradually died down, Alfaro and his successor, General Leonidas Plaza, made the first efforts to professionalize the national army. In 1901 a new Escuela Militar began operation for the training of military officers. Military laws were codified, battlefield promotions were prohibited, and a decree was issued prohibiting soldiers from belonging to parties or electoral clubs.[11] However, the effect of these reforms was partially lost in the 1910–1916 wars between Generals Alfaro and Plaza, a conflict that was no less bitter for the fact that there were no perceptible doctrinal differences between them.[12] Despite the eventual victory of General Plaza and a brief period of relative stability based on his alliance with a powerful Guayaquil banking clique, the age of the military caudillos was drawing to a close. With the sudden collapse of the cocoa boom in 1922, plutocratic rule became increasingly oppressive, until three years later a group of junior officers overthrew the Liberal regime in Ecuador's first modern coup d'état.[13]

Despite the exaggerated level of political instability that followed the "July Revolution," military officers generally played a distinctly secondary role vis-à-vis the civilian politicians. After the 1925 coup, power was handed over to a junta of reform-minded civilians and later to a civilian dictator, who ruled until 1931. Even though in the next seventeen years seventeen governments came and went, only three were headed by military men and only one of these stayed in office for as long as a year.[14] Unlike previous periods of political instability, this one did not end with the emergence of a strong president whose accession to power and political dominance was based on military support.

To understand this change, it is important to emphasize the distinction between the power of military officers as individuals and the power of the military as an institution.[15] Military men were prominent among Ecuador's dominant personalities from 1830 to 1916, but this does not demonstrate that the army as an institution ever exercised any great power. Although the frequent recourse to civil war to resolve political disputes gave a decided edge in the political struggle to those with military skill and a following in the army, the standing army was in fact defeated on at least three occasions by ad hoc opposition forces. Indeed, it is difficult to even speak of civil-military relations in the nineteenth century, since there was little or no distinction between the two spheres. The dominant figures of the nineteenth century were political and military figures at the same time, and there is little evidence of military self-awareness or self-identification.

The turn-of-the-century attempts to professionalize the military did imply some differentiation of political and military spheres. The newly created military institution clearly emerged second-best in this process. The presidency ceased to be the final step in a military career, while the level of technical and bureaucratic development of the armed forces was only marginally improved. At the end of the 1910–1916 civil wars, the standing army was sharply reduced in numbers, military budgets were slashed, and military salaries began to lag seriously behind those of their civilian counterparts.[16] There is also abundant evidence that during this period senior Ecuadorian officers were hired and fired largely on the basis of their political loyalty to the president. The armed forces were either unable or not inclined to reject their civilian-defined mission to defend whatever government was in power at the time.[17] That these governments, none of which was strong enough to stay in office a full four years, should nevertheless be able to impose their will on the armed forces does not support the accepted image of the Ecuadorian military as a politically powerful and autonomous organization.

Two critical factors lie behind this change in civil-military relations from the nineteenth-century pattern of military-political caudillos to the early-twentieth-century pattern of a minimally professionalized military largely subordinated to civilian political control: a shift in the social recruitment base of military officers and a shift in the content of the basic socialization process. Although no concrete data exist on the social origins of the nineteenth-century officers, it appears that most were either sons of military families, sons of impoverished gentry, or ambitious sons of poorer families who had advanced through the ranks.[18] Whether by upbringing or by aspiration, nineteenth-century officers tended to consider themselves socially equal to civilian politicians.[19] In addition, they received their basic military socialization through their apprenticeship in politico-military affairs in the barracks and on the battlefield. Not until after the 1925 revolution was the Escuela Militar established as the primary source of recruitment for the officer corps.[20] As a result, the nineteenth-century officer generally shared a similar social background with the civilian politician, and was probably equally well versed in political affairs. Even though his particular expertise lay in armed conflict rather than in pamphleteering or in constitution-writing, the nineteenth-century general could claim that in the end his skill was the one that really counted and that he had equal, if not greater, claim to govern when he was on the winning side.

In contrast, during the first years of the twentieth century, the military came increasingly to be recruited from the urban middle strata, while the military educational establishment replaced the civil war battleground as the primary socialization agent. According to the earliest data available, in the years from 1928 to 1930, 38 percent of the *cadetes* entering the Escuela Militar came from land-owning or professional families, 57 percent were sons of employees, military officers, or merchants, and 4 percent were sons of workers or tradesmen.[21] Of the 38 percent from the upper–upper-middle strata, few seem to have come from families belonging to the national elite, and in most cases these did not continue in a military career. Thus the large majority of the officer corps was recruited from a numerically small "middle class"—from families at best subordinate in social status, economically vulnerable, and in many cases dependent on the upper strata for social mobility or a continued place in the middle strata. In addition, the education requirements for admission to the Escuela Militar effectively blocked the entry of ambitious or aggressive sons of working-class families.[22] As the political leaders of the country continued to come mainly from the traditional elites or from among university-educated professionals, the status of the military officers no longer equaled that of the politicians. Moreover, as the Escuela Militar became the primary means of socialization into the military career, the price of the claim to a special military expertise in the new "professional" army was the loss of expertise in political affairs, now mostly the prerogative of the civilian politician, by virtue of his political apprenticeship and specialized education in law, commerce, or engineering.

For the purpose of our discussion of postwar Ecuadorian politics, it is important to note that the transition to a minimally professionalized military largely subordinate to civilian domination occurred *despite* the failure to develop any civilian political institutions capable of establishing even a modicum of political order. While contemporary Liberals and Conservatives like to trace the conflict between them to the beginning of the Republic, the available evidence indicates that even rudimentary party organization did not emerge until around the time of the 1895 Liberal Revolution.[23] Although the Radical Liberal, Conservative, and Socialist parties began to hold conventions in the 1920s, the actual level of party development remained quite low. Strong parties were hardly necessary, since the electorate was highly restricted and free elections were rather infrequent prior to 1948.[24]

Given the low level of party development and the absence of constitutional traditions, the economic collapse of the coastal plutocracy and the end of Liberal hegemony in 1925 ushered in the longest period of political instability in Ecuadorian history. Despite the high rate of civilian instability, the role of the military in the politics of this period was minimal. While individual officers were co-opted into a variety of civilian intrigues and occasionally into the presidency, most often the armed forces were reduced to a political tool of the government in power. In practice, the military was subordinated to the civilian political elite, even though the debility and fragmentation of the civilian leadership precluded any stable system of civilian control.

This period in the development of Ecuadorian civil-military relations is especially important, because it runs directly counter to the usual North American assumption that the military has played a key role in Latin American politics ever since the wars of independence. According to this view, the Latin American military has always been a powerful and autonomous political force. If the military does not intervene directly in politics, the absence of military intervention is attributed largely to military self-restraint. Conversely, when the military does intervene, such intervention is seen as a reassertion of the old historical pattern. These arguments assume that there is some substantial continuity between the political power wielded by nineteenth-century generals and the (occasionally unexercised) power of the contemporary armed forces. In the case of Ecuador, this assumption is clearly incorrect.

With the creation of a minimally professionalized military institution, the political power of military officers was sharply reduced. With the accompanying shift in the social base of the army to a dependent middle class, most officers appear to have accepted the generalized claim to deference made by the traditional elites who continued to provide most of the nation's political leaders. Since basic military training was now provided in the classrooms of the Escuela

Militar rather than on the civil-war battlefield, the military also gave up its claim to equivalent political expertise. Minimal professionalization thus contributed to the political subordination of the armed forces, with individual officers being generally reduced to secondary roles in the clienteles of civilian leaders, whether of the government or of its opposition.

The defeat of the Ecuadorian armed forces in the 1941 invasion by Peru marks a second turning point in Ecuadorian civil-military relations. Younger officers in particular were outraged by the Arroyo government's decision to withhold troops from the front lines, by the woeful lack of military preparedness, and by the government's acceptance of the Rio Protocol, which ceded to Peru an area equal to nearly half the national territory.[25] Among this generation of officers there was a deep belief that the fundamental cause of the 1941 defeat was Ecuador's long history of military interference in politics and political interference in purely military affairs.[26] Although the younger officers were in the forefront of the revolt that overthrew Arroyo in 1944,[27] this same group of officers, now mostly captains in provincial commands, played a key role in the 1947 counter-coup that prevented the defense minister, Colonel Carlos Mancheno, from assuming power after he had deposed President Velasco Ibarra in a coup stemming largely from a personal feud between Velasco and his minister.[28]

The thrust of the 1941 generation's attitude toward civil-military relations was not the removal of the military from politics in the broad sense of the term, but toward keeping the armed forces out of partisan politics, while at the same time limiting government interference with the military.[29] In its new relationship to politics, the military was to be more removed, more autonomous. The end of the era of military subordination was at hand. The crucial factor was not, however, the shift in military attitudes toward civil-military relations as much as it was the subsequent changes in the institutional characteristics underlying the previous pattern of military subordination.

As the generation of officers forged in the bitter defeat of 1941 began to reach positions of power within the armed forces, they began a rather sweeping program of military reforms and reorganization. The most important changes involved the expansion of the military educational system and the insistence after 1950 that all officers be graduates of their respective service academies. Whereas previously the subordinate social origins and status of military officers had contributed to the subordination of the military to the civilian political elite, the effect of these military reforms was ultimately to reduce the impact of social origins on the military's political behavior. Over time the extension and strengthening of the military socialization process led to the development of a new sense of corporate military identity superseding identifications derived from the civilian social structure.

Since the 1941 war, the basic institutions for socialization into the various branches of the armed forces have been the three service academies: the Escuela

Aerea in Salinas on the coast, the Escuela Naval, now also located in Salinas after many years in Quito, and the Colegio Militar in Quito. The air and naval schools are four-year military courses for high school graduates. The Colegio Militar, on the other hand, is a five-year program, with the first three years corresponding to the last three years of high school, followed by two years of purely military courses.[30] In the army, then, the impact of military socialization is heightened by the relatively early age at which most officers begin their military careers. During the years 1936–1940, when most of the 1941 generation was entering the army, the Colegio Militar contained all six secondary grades, and nearly half of the new cadets were less than sixteen years old.

While the typical cadet spends much of his time completing his secondary education and learning about military regulations and organization, the most important part of his training is his socialization to believe in the special professional and moral responsibilities of the military officer, which set him apart from the ordinary civilian. The "special idealism" of military life is a typical theme in this socialization process. "The military college, Eloy Alfaro, is the crucible in which the spirits of the future defenders of sovereignty and national integrity are tempered to the rugged life of constant striving, of self-sacrifice, and of permanent dedication to the fatherland and its great eternal values."[31] The self-abnegation and patriotism of the career officer are likewise constantly emphasized. "The labor of the soldier is a series of silent acts of self-sacrifice on the altar of the fatherland."[32] Throughout his training the cadet is also reminded of the vital role of the military officer in the survival and well-being of his country. "The professional armed forces have been throughout the history of all time and in all countries of the world the basic column which sustains the integrity, honor, and progress of nations. For this reason the Ecuadorian armed forces understand that they do not defend individual men, but ideals and institutions created to serve the fatherland."[33]

Although explicit political indoctrination is generally limited to learning the current constitutional definition of the military's assigned roles, implicit in the statements cited above are the elements of a political doctrine, which, despite its vague rhetorical character, informs the political behavior of the Ecuadorian officer throughout his military career: the loyalty of the military officer to the fatherland rather than to any particular government; the indispensable role of the armed forces in the survival of the country; and the special identity of the military officer, apart from and, in some respects, above the rest of society.[34]

Further opportunities for reaffirmation of these attitudes exist in the series of military schools within each service, which an officer must complete before attaining promotion to the next higher rank. In addition, most officers receive some foreign training, most often short, largely technical courses in the United States or in the Canal Zone. In part because of the Ecuadorian military's traditionally close ties with the United States, and in part because the Ecuadorian war academy was closed from 1952 until 1956, 80 percent of the officers interviewed had received at least some of their military education abroad.[35]

The capstone of the military educational system is the two-year war academy and general staff school. Until recently only the army had its own academy, and, prior to 1956, the army course lasted only one year. Navy officers generally went to the Chilean naval war academy for two years, although in the mid-sixties the navy established its own academy in Guayaquil. Air force officers continue to go abroad, in most cases to the United States or Brazil, for a one-year course. In addition, one or two army officers a year, by virtue of their academic ranking in the war academy, win the right to attend a superior war college, usually in Brazil or Argentina, since Ecuador did not have such a school or an equivalent (such as the center for higher military studies—CAEM—in Peru).[36] Aspirants to the rank of lieutenant colonel are required by law to be graduates of their respective war academy courses. The war academy is and has been almost exclusively devoted to training senior officers in purely military areas. Generally the only nonmilitary subjects taught have been geopolitics and international and constitutional law.[37] Although during the mid-fifties a small number of captains and majors received permission and encouragement to study international law at Central University, this practice was soon discontinued.

Since the mid-fifties Ecuadorian military officers have generally received rather extensive military training compared to the training offered in previous decades. Whereas previously direct promotions from noncommissioned officer to officer were not uncommon,[38] after 1950 direct promotions were strictly limited, and by 1961 the Colegio Militar was legally established as the exclusive source of officer recruitment.[39] In comparative terms, the professional socialization process is now clearly more extensive than is common in many of the new African armies. To take only one example, "out of the 19 officers and non-commissioned officers who sat on Burundi's Conseil Suprême de la République in 1972, 10 had undergone a 6-month training program at Arlon Infantry School; only one (a major) had gone to St. Cyr for a 3-year training period."[40] On the other hand, the Ecuadorian military lags behind most of its counterparts in the larger Latin American countries, where even more extensive programs have been in effect for a number of years. Moreover, the basic military education is still at the secondary level in Ecuador and, equally important, without a superior war college, Ecuadorian officers have generally received little, if any, university-level preparation in nonmilitary subjects.

A similar pattern emerges with regard to the size and organizational structure of the postwar armed forces. Although the exact magnitude of force levels and total military expenditures is highly classified, it appears that between the late forties and mid-fifties total military manpower nearly doubled, to between 17,000 and 19,000 men, while defense expenditures, excluding major purchases of military equipment, climbed from $7 million in 1950 to $17 million in 1955.[41] Since 1955, total manpower seems to have remained more or less constant, with army effectives just under 13,000 men and the remaining 6,000 to 7,000 men split evenly between the navy and air force.[42] Military spending has increased only slightly in absolute terms, falling from 22 percent of total government expenditures and 2.7 percent of the gross national product in 1955 to 13.5 percent and 2.1 percent, respectively, by 1965.[43]

In both size and expenditures, the substantial improvements in the position of the Ecuadorian military during the mid-fifties merely served to restore Ecuador to an intermediate international position, far behind the larger military institutions of the more developed South American countries, but still ahead of

Table 2.1 1970 Military Forces and Expenditures:
Latin America and Black Africa

| Total Forces in Thousands (Total expenditures in million US $) | | | | | | | | |
|---|---|---|---|---|---|---|---|---|
| South America | | | Central America and Caribbean | | | Black Africa | | |
| Brazil | 225 | ($1017) | | | | | | |
| Argentina | 144 | ($514) | | | | | | |
| | | | Mexico | 71 | ($224) | Nigeria | 70 | ($91)* |
| Chile | 64 | ($167) | | | | | | |
| Colombia | 55 | ($97) | | | | | | |
| Peru | 50 | ($196) | | | | | | |
| Venezuela | 31 | ($204) | | | | Ethiopia | 45 | ($41) |
| | | | | | | Zaire | 38 | ($60) |
| | | | | | | Sudan | 28 | ($116) |
| ECUADOR | 17 | ($26) | Dominican Republic | 19 | ($30) | Ghana | 15 | ($44) |
| Bolivia | 17 | ($19) | | | | | | |
| Uruguay | 16 | ($44) | | | | | | |
| Paraguay | 13 | ($11) | | | | | | |
| | | | Guatemala | 9 | ($29) | Tanzania | 10 | ($17) |
| | | | Nicaragua | 6 | ($12) | Somali | 8 | ($9) |
| | | | El Salvador | 6 | ($11) | Uganda | 6 | ($19) |
| | | | Honduras | 5 | ($7) | + 20 countries with military forces of less than 6,000 men. | | |
| | | | Haiti | 5 | ($7) | | | |

*1968 figures

SOURCE: United States Arms Control and Disarmament Agency, *World Military Expenditures 1971* (Washington, D.C.: Bureau of Economic Affairs, 1971), pp. 11–13.

NOTE: Most of the figures are provisional estimates.

the similarly small, poor countries of Central America and all but a few of the new militaries of the tropical African nations, most of which consist of less than 6,000 men. While it is clear that by South American standards the Ecuadorian military is still relatively small and poor, the expansion and reorganization of the mid-fifties did represent a considerable increase in the organizational complexity of the armed forces compared to that of the prewar period.

Within the organizational structure of the military established by the reorganization of 1956, the supreme authority is the president, who holds the title of commander-in-chief. Execution of presidential policies is entrusted to the minister of defense, who has, traditionally, been a civilian.[44] He in turn is advised on military matters, especially military politics, by the subsecretary, a high-ranking active duty officer.[45] Below the minister of defense are the chief of the general staff and the commanding generals of the army, navy, and air force, who jointly constitute the high command. As Ecuador has only recently followed the precedent of other Latin republics in establishing a joint command,[46] the three services have tended to be largely self-contained. The chief of the general staff, usually the senior active duty officer, enjoys the status of *primus inter pares* but has no hierarchical authority over the force commanders. Coordination between the three services is provided largely by the defense ministry and the three subdirectors of the armed forces general staff, one for each service. Below the subdirectors are the heads of the six general staff departments, who by virtue of their location in the national capital and their policy-making positions are generally active figures in military politics.

The general command of the army in turn has its own staff with various departments paralleling those of the armed forces general staff. Below the commanding general are the chiefs of the three military zone commands: Quito, Cuenca, and Guayaquil. Within the first and second military zones there are in turn nearly a dozen separate politically strategic infantry, armored, and artillery units in or around Quito and Guayaquil. The third military zone, based in Cuenca, the country's third-largest city, contains the garrisons of Cuenca and Loja and the division of El Oro. In the internal politics of the military the latter unit, with about 50 percent of the army's troop strength deployed along the Peruvian frontier, retains considerable importance, despite the distance separating it from the centers of power. Another politically important unit is the war academy in Quito, whose status as an institution of study close to the centers of power makes its staff and students particularly sensitive to national and institutional problems. The war academy, the Escuela de Perfeccionamiento, the Colegio Militar, the paratrooper school, and the military geographic institute, all in or around Quito, are technically part of the general staff, but all have tended to act as independent units in times of political crisis.

In the air force, besides the commanding general, the important figures are the second zone commander in Guayaquil, the commander and pilots of the air base at Taura near Guayaquil (containing the bulk of the country's combat aircraft), and, to a lesser extent, the commander of the air transport base in Quito. In the navy, the only politically important figures are the commanding general and the squadron commander in Guayaquil. Since neither the navy nor the air force controls significant ground forces, their political role has been much less important than that of the army, and in the unlikely event of a strict confrontation along service lines, their role would be even further reduced by their inability to defend their own bases.

In political terms the expansion and reorganization of the armed forces had at least one important but little-noticed consequence: a subtle change in the process of military decision-making during political crises, specifically, the emergence of the institutional military coup d'état and the disappearance of the *cuartelazo,* the isolated barracks revolt, as modal patterns of military behavior. The proliferation of military units along with the increased number of staff officers reduced both the degree of any individual officer's control over any important unit and the weight of any individual unit in the final institutional decision to support or overthrow the government. Although as the following chapter indicates, civilian politicians were slow to grasp the significance of these changes, the net effect was a sharp reduction in the utility of political strategies based on personal co-optation of individual military leaders.[47] While still small enough not to require anything like the institutionalization of intramilitary politics in Brazil's Clube Militar or Argentina's secret military lodges,[48] the organizational structure of the Ecuadorian military by the mid-fifties included enough politically significant nodes to substantially decrease the effectiveness of purely clientelistic modes of control by the government[49] or penetration by the opposition. As a result, coup decisions at the aggregate level increasingly came to depend on the rough consensus of opinion within the officer corps at large.

On the other hand, there were only minor changes in the social origins or status of military officers. In geographic terms the Ecuadorian officer corps was and still is primarily recruited from the inter-Andean provinces of the sierra. Despite the origins of the professional army in the Liberal armies of the 1890s, for the last half-century between 80 and 90 percent of all army officers have been natives of the interior.[50] Since most of the senior officers who were active

Table 2.2  Province/Region of Birth
of Entering Army Cadets

| Years | Northern interior | Pichincha | Central interior | Southern interior | Coast |
|---|---|---|---|---|---|
| 1916–1919 | 7.7% | 30.8% | 24.6% | 20.8% | 16.1% |
| 1921, 1924–1929 | 14.4% | 42.8% | 21.7% | 7.2% | 13.3% |
| 1930–1939 | 10.7% | 36.9% | 25.2% | 7.9% | 19.4% |
| 1940, 1943–1949 | 17.8% | 32.6% | 25.9% | 15.1% | 9.0% |
| 1951–1957 | 15.6% | 36.4% | 28.5% | 9.8% | 9.6% |
| 1960–1966 | 18.4% | 39.2% | 23.8% | 8.8% | 9.7% |

SOURCE: *Libro de solicitudes de ingreso,* annual series (Archive of the Colegio Militar Eloy Alfaro).

during the period from 1948 to 1966 entered the army between 1930 and 1939, the recruitment patterns prevailing at that time are perhaps more significant for this study than are those of later years. During that decade more than 35 percent of the cadets entering the Colegio Militar came from the single province of Pichincha, almost all from the capital city of Quito. Another 35 percent came from the largely rural sierra provinces to the north and south of the capital. The southern sierra provinces provided 8 percent of the cadets, while the coastal provinces, containing the nation's largest city and a third of the total population, contributed less than 20 percent of the entering officers.

Perhaps the most striking feature of the army's geographic recruitment pattern has been its failure to respond to the major demographic shifts of the past thirty years. Recruitment from the coastal provinces has, in fact, decreased substantially at the same time that the coast's share of the total population has been rapidly growing—exceeding that of the sierra by the mid-1960s. In 1963, Guayas province, the commercial and financial capital of the country, with a fifth of the nation's population, provided less than 1 percent of the new cadets. While comparable data are not available for the other services, it seems that, in contrast to the pattern in Peru and Argentina, recruitment of both navy and air force officers is also disproportionately from the interior highlands.[51] Relative to other Latin American militaries, the apparently similar biases in recruitment patterns have probably helped minimize potential political cleavage along service lines.

Table 2.3 Regional Shares of
Population and Entering Cadets

| Region | % Population 1950 census | % Cadets 1951 | % Population 1962 census | % Cadets 1963 |
|---|---|---|---|---|
| Northern interior | 7.0% | 26.9% | 5.9% | 19.7% |
| Pichincha (Quito) | 12.1% | 34.9% | 13.0% | 36.6% |
| Central interior | 21.3% | 19.2% | 18.4% | 27.6% |
| Southern interior | 17.6% | 6.7% | 14.8% | 9.0% |
| Guayas (Guayaquil) | 18.2% | 8.7% | 21.2% | 0.9% |
| Other coast | 23.8% | 3.8% | 26.6% | 6.2% |
| Total Sierra | 58.0% | 87.7% | 52.1% | 92.9% |
| Total Coast | 42.0% | 12.5% | 47.8% | 7.1% |

SOURCE: *Libro de solicitudes de ingreso,* annual series (Archive of the Colegio Militar Eloy Alfaro); Pedro Merlo, "Crecimiento de la población del Ecuador," *Indicadores Econó- micos* 1, no. 3 (July 1967): 35.

NOTE: In both the census and recruitment data, the small percentages representing the Amazon provinces have been included with the coast.

Determining the social bases of recruitment of the officer corps is somewhat more difficult. Using data provided on application forms regarding father's occupation (cross-checked where possible against information on birth certificates), cadets entering the Colegio Militar can be classified as originating from one of three broad social strata. The first consists of the property-owning upper-class and upper-middle-class professionals. The second consists of the middle layer of the middle class—of such occupations as public or private employees, military officers, teachers, and most merchants. The third group is composed of working-class and lower-middle-class occupations—small merchants, artisans, noncommissioned officers and soldiers, and workers.[52]

Even in the earliest years for which data are available, the middle-middle stratum provided the majority of the entering cadets. In the decade 1930–1939, when the top army officers of the 1948–1966 period were entering, 61 percent came from the middle-middle group, 34 percent from the upper- and upper-middle strata, and 5 percent from the lower- and lower-middle strata. In the years since then, the most significant change has been the gradual

Table 2.4 Trends in Social Origins
of Entering Army Cadets

| Years | Upper, Upper-middle | Middle-middle | Lower-middle, Lower |
|---|---|---|---|
| 1928–1929 | 44.4% | 55.6% | 0 |
| 1930–1939 | 33.8% | 61.5% | 4.7% |
| 1951–1957 | 20.1% | 63.5% | 16.4% |
| 1960–1966 | 16.5% | 62.2% | 21.3% |

NOTE: During the years 1940 to 1950, "father's occupation" was omitted from the Colegio Militar application form.

displacement of the upper-status recruits by cadets from the lower-middle and lower social strata, which, since 1960, have constituted around 20 percent of the total.[53] Given the natural tendency to exaggerate on "father's occupation" questions,[54] this trend is undoubtedly less recent and more pronounced than these figures indicate.

In comparative terms, the Ecuadorian officer corps seems somewhat less narrowly recruited from the middle class than are Brazilian army officers. While a trend toward "democratization" is apparent in both countries, with Ecuador lagging somewhat behind Brazil, the size of the middle-strata majority is substantially smaller in both time periods in Ecuador. A more striking difference appears in the degree of internal recruitment. Sons of military officers constituted approximately 20 percent of the cadets in both countries in the late thirties and early forties, but in Ecuador the percentage has remained constant, despite the growing number of sons of sergeants and corporals since 1956. In Brazil, on the other hand, over a third of all new cadets in the early sixties were sons of officers. While the tendency toward inbreeding may only have been

Table 2.5 Father's Profession of
Entering Army Cadets: Ecuador and Brazil

|  | Upper, Upper-middle | Middle- middle | Lower-middle, Lower | Sons of officers |
|---|---|---|---|---|
| *Brazil 1941–1943 | 19.8% | 76.4% | 3.8% | 21.2% |
| Ecuador 1937–1939 | 40.1% | 57.1% | 2.8% | 16.5% |
| *Brazil 1962–1966 | 6.0% | 78.2% | 15.3% | 34.9% |
| Ecuador 1962–1966 | 16.6% | 59.8% | 23.6% | 16.4% |

*Figures for Brazil recalculated from Alfred C. Stepan, *The Military in Politics: Changing Patterns in Brazil* (Princeton, N.J.: Princeton University Press, 1971), pp. 32–33, 40.

deferred in Ecuador,[55] to the extent that the political behavior of sons of military officers is distinctive,[56] this difference in recruitment patterns in recent years may be quite significant. In any case, if previous studies of the more highly modernized countries have not already done so, the clear evidence that even in Ecuador the officer corps is and has been since the late 1920s predominantly recruited from the middle class should definitively lay to rest the myth of the high-status origins of Latin American military officers.

Finally, although the common soldier and noncommissioned officer have had only a negligible impact on the political behavior of the army, it is worth noting that since 1950 a major shift has occurred in the pattern of recruitment of enlisted men. Whereas soldiers were previously "mostly peasant draftees . . . drawn from Indian villages,"[57] most of them illiterate, soldiers now come predominantly from the burgeoning urban lower class, and there seems to be an informal rule of thumb that no more than 10 to 15 percent illiterates will be accepted into any given unit,[58] despite a national illiteracy rate of around 40 percent. (In some provinces, the figure is nearly twice that.)[59] Given that conscripts only serve for eleven months, the economic rationale for preferring literates is obvious. The obligatory military service law does not in practice apply to the middle or upper classes, since the requirements may be satisfied through payment of a relatively small fine or by receiving premilitary training in the larger high schools and universities.[60]

Thus the prevailing recruitment patterns for both officers and soldiers sharply limit the potential contribution of the armed forces to national integration.[61] Instead of transcending societal divisions through the incorporation of diverse social elements into an institutional environment free of ascriptive criteria, Ecuadorian military recruitment reflects existing regional and class divisions. The majority of the nation's population now lives on the coast, yet this region is barely represented in the officer corps. In a similar manner, the de facto exemption of the middle and upper classes from military service reproduces—in the strong rank distinctions between regular officers, noncoms, and conscripts—the societal divisions between the middle, lower-middle, and lower classes.

Regardless of his social origins, the Ecuadorian military officer considers himself and is considered by others a part of the middle class. When asked as part of a series of personal background questions, over 90 percent of the officers interviewed for this study identified themselves as middle-class or upper-middle-class.[62] None identified themselves as less than middle-class, despite the fact

Table 2.6 Socioeconomic Status of
Military Interview Sample

| Interviewer-rated economic status* | | | Self-rated class status | | |
|---|---|---|---|---|---|
| | N | % | | N | % |
| Upper | 5 | 7.4 | Upper | 4 | 6.8 |
| Upper-middle | 47 | 69.1 | Upper-middle | 7 | 11.9 |
| Middle | 16 | 23.5 | Middle | 48 | 81.4 |
| Lower | 0 | 0 | Lower | 0 | 0 |
| Total | 68 | 100 | | 59 | 100 |

*Rated on the basis of neighborhood of residence, wealth evidenced in the residence and its furnishings, and age and type of automobiles.

that at least a small proportion were undoubtedly from lower-middle- or lower-class families. Nevertheless, while the overwhelming majority identified themselves as middle-class rather than upper-middle-class, a large majority enjoyed a better than middle-class standard of living. The discrepancy reflects the moderate inconsistency in the economic and social status of Ecuadorian officers.

Basic salaries for the various grades of officers are very low by any international standard, around $200 a month for generals, but still quite high for a country with a per capita income of $251 annually.[63] However, in addition to his basic salary, the Ecuadorian officer receives various kinds of bonuses.[64] Although the details of the bonus system are classified, it appears that these commonly range from 50 percent of basic salary for lower-ranking officers up to

Table 2.7 Comparison of Monthly Salaries
(In current sucres)

| Officers | | | Teachers | | |
|---|---|---|---|---|---|
| Basic | Total | Rank | Education | Basic | Total |
| 5100 | 10800 | General | Doctor of Education | 2655 | 6185 |
| 4100 | 8185 | Colonel | Master of Education | 2415 | 5145 |
| 3600 | 6900 | Lt. Col. | Academic Degree | 2195 | 3920 |
| 2600 | 4500 | Major | High School degree | 1995 | 3140 |
| 2100 | 3540 | Lieutenant | High School degree | 1815 | 2855 |
| 1800 | 3000 | Second Lieut. | Rural school | 1650 | 1980 |

SOURCE: "Tabla de sueldos básicos y functionales del magisterio," Departamento de Planeamiento, Ministerio de Educación Pública; "Aprobó el senado," *El Universo*, 25 September 1969, p. 3.

100 percent for generals. Total salaries, then, are rather high within the Ecuadorian context. In a comparison of basic and total salaries for school-teachers and military officers, the advantages of the officers are clear, since the top salary in the educational hierarchy is still less than that of a lieutenant colonel, although the educational peak can apparently be reached in less time. Of the three services, air force officers are by far the best paid; flight pay for pilots is often equivalent to one or more steps in rank. In addition to the excellent salaries, the military enjoys low-cost medical care and an Ecuadorian-scale PX system.

The pension and severance pay systems are also quite generous. Time in service is calculated from the year of entry into the Colegio Militar, and an officer can retire at full pay after thirty years of service, often before age fifty. Officers with as little as thirteen years' service can retire with 40 percent pay, generally around age thirty. It appears that the pension is in fact calculated on the basis of the basic salary plus at least some of the bonuses and that there are certain bonuses toward "time in service" for participation in combat, flying hours, and other special duties.[65] Officers also receive a sizable severance allowance (*cesantía*), consisting of a deduction taken from other officers' salaries and a contribution from the government. Depending on rank and length of service, retiring officers may receive up to $10,000.[66] This payment is often used to acquire an agricultural or other income-producing property or to set up a small business. Of the retired officers interviewed in this study, almost all have taken a new job or profession and nearly 70 percent seem to fall easily into the upper-middle-income bracket, with another 7 percent—mainly engineers in civil practice—in the upper-income bracket.

The economic attractions of the military profession partially compensate for its lack of social prestige. The small and declining percentage of cadets originating in the upper- and upper-middle strata has already been noted. In general it seems that the higher social strata regard the military profession as a career of low prestige. Even though only the air force has its own country club, there are no military members in either the Club de la Unión in Guayaquil or the Guayaquil country club and only two or three military members in the Quito tennis club.[67] Another indication of the low prestige of the military career comes from a survey of upper-level bureaucrats who were asked to rank a list of occupations as more prestigious, less prestigious, or equal in prestige to their

Table 2.8 Comparison of High Public
Administration with Other Professions

|  | Prestige greater | Prestige equal | Prestige less | Prestige index |
|---|---|---|---|---|
| University professor | 60 | 16 | 8 | 1.62 |
| Medical doctor | 50 | 29 | 3 | 1.57 |
| Engineer | 49 | 29 | 5 | 1.53 |
| Business executive | 40 | 37 | 3 | 1.41 |
| Lawyer | 32 | 42 | 9 | 1.28 |
| Dentist | 25 | 35 | 20 | 1.06 |
| Hacienda owner | 12 | 27 | 39 | .65 |
| Military officer | 11 | 29 | 38 | .65 |
| Store owner | 5 | 15 | 59 | .32 |

SOURCE: Freeman Wright, *The Upper Level Public Administrator in Ecuador* (Institute of Administrative Studies, Central University. Quito, Ecuador: Editorial "Fray Jodoco Ricke," 1968), p. 17.

own profession. The relationship of university training to social prestige seems fairly clear; the military's problem is that the basic military education remains at the high school level. The vast majority of the political elite appears to come from the five highest-ranking professions on the list. According to Ecuadorian lore, the sharpest-witted and least-scrupulous member of the family becomes a lawyer; the shyest and weakest becomes a priest; the least intelligent becomes a military officer; and the laziest and most audacious becomes a politician and the pride of the family![68]

If we define military professionalization in the strict sense of the level of technical development of the military profession,[69] a number of factors indicate that, despite the considerable advances of the last twenty years, the overall level of professionalization of the Ecuadorian armed forces remains significantly lower than that of most other South American militaries. First there is the relatively small number of military journals published by the Ecuadorian armed forces. Any highly developed and complex profession requires regular means of communication for the diffusion of new technology and the discussion of common problems, both among its practitioners at large and among the various technical specializations within the profession. While the list of regularly published Latin American military journals in table 2.9 is undoubtedly incomplete—Ecuador has at times had three journals, at times only one—there can be little doubt that Ecuador's position is far behind that of any other South American countries except Bolivia and Paraguay.

Table 2.9  Military Professionalization in Latin America

| Number of regularly published military journals* | | Military expenditure per soldier† 1966 | | (1970) | Gross National Product (million US $) 1966† | |
|---|---|---|---|---|---|---|
| Argentina | 23 | Venezuela | $6555 | ($6581) | Brazil | $25,790 |
| Brazil | 20 | Argentina | $3526 | ($3569) | Mexico | $21,770 |
| Peru | 19 | Brazil | $2777 | ($4520) | Argentina | $16,240 |
| Colombia | 13 | Peru | $2660 | ($3920) | Venezuela | $ 7,940 |
| Mexico | 10 | Mexico | $2435 | ($3155) | Colombia | $ 5,457 |
| Venezuela | 8 | Chile | $2167 | ($2609) | Chile | $ 4,867 |
| Chile | 7 | Colombia | $1917 | ($1764) | Peru | $ 3,547 |
| Uruguay | 6 | Dominican R. | $1682 | ($1579) | Uruguay | $ 1,565 |
| Guatemala | 5 | Guatemala | $1667 | ($3222) | Guatemala | $ 1,388 |
| Honduras | 5 | El Salvador | $1667 | ($1833) | ECUADOR | $ 1,245 |
| El Salvador | 3 | ECUADOR | $1474 | ($1529) | Dominican R. | $ 996 |
| Bolivia | 3 | Honduras | $1400 | ($1400) | El Salvador | $ 845 |
| Paraguay | 3 | Uruguay | $1294 | ($2750) | Bolivia | $ 661 |
| Dominican R. | 2 | Bolivia | $1000 | ($1118) | Honduras | $ 536 |
| ECUADOR | 2 | Paraguay | $ 933 | ($846) | Paraguay | $ 463 |

NOTE: Cuba was disregarded as a noncomparable case. Nicaragua, Costa Rica, Panama, and Haiti were excluded because of incomplete data.

*Data on journals were recompiled from Luigi Einaudi and Herbert Goldheimer, "An Annotated Bibliography of Latin American Military Journals," *Latin American Research Review* 2, no. 2 (Spring 1967):95–120.

†Expenditure and GNP figures were provisional estimates taken from the United States Arms Control and Disarmament Agency, *World Military Expenditures 1971* (Washington, D.C.: Bureau of Economic Affairs, 1971), pp. 11, 19, 35. The figure for 1966 per soldier expenditure for Colombia is calculated from the figures originally given in the 1966 volume of the same publication.

A second, though somewhat imperfect,[70] indicator of the Ecuadorian military's relative degree of professionalization is the relatively low level of military spending per member of the armed forces. Within Latin America, the model of the "modern" military is clearly the image, diffused through American military missions and assistance programs, of a force well equipped with technologically sophisticated and expensive weapons systems. At least within this particular context, high professionalization implies a capital-intensive military and a high level of military expenditure per soldier.[71] Again, the

Ecuadorian military ranks slightly behind even most of the Central American militaries and far below the larger South American countries.[72]

Finally, perhaps the most clear-cut indication of the limited professionalization of the Ecuadorian military was its consistent inability during the 1948–1966 period to resist governmental intromission of purely political criteria into the internal affairs of the armed forces, despite the lessons of the 1941 war. Jacques Lambert has noted that, in most Latin American countries, "the Armed Forces themselves determine their strength, equipment, and the percentage of the budget to be earmarked for defense and they impose on the government the Defense Minister of their choice."[73] Clearly, the Ecuadorian military has never demanded or received the degree of professional autonomy implied in Lambert's statement.[74] As indicated previously, the defense minister has normally been a civilian. Members of the high command have generally been chosen because they enjoy the confidence of the president. Most often they have been men with known political loyalties or a special reputation for being antipolitical. Higher-ranking officers without the right political qualifications are normally retired or sent abroad as military attachés. (Not surprisingly, in contrast to Peru or Brazil, where promotion to the highest rank is closely related to academic achievement in the war academy,[75] in Ecuador over the past decade, army members of the high command have shown a pronounced tendency to rank in the middle of their graduating class.)[76] Moreover, through the high command, assignments to the politically strategic zone commands in Quito and Guayaquil and even unit commands in Quito have been made on the basis of political reliability. When not sent abroad or asked to resign, politically unreliable officers are generally assigned to desk jobs, often in the general staff, or to command posts far from the centers of power. As one military group complained, "Both junior and senior officers are continually expelled from active service, at times massively, in an arbitrary and illegal manner. . . . The principles of hierarchy and seniority are continually insulted for unmentionable political motives."[77] Yet at no point was the military able to put an end to practices that were a clear violation of professional norms and a widely recognized impediment to the professional development of the armed forces.[78]

This demonstrated lack of solidarity in defense of the professional integrity of the armed forces appears to have its origins in several of the institutional characteristics described above. In the first place, given the generous provisions of the pension and severance pay systems, the officers affected by these purges have relatively little incentive to be active in their own defense.[79] With thirty years of service (and sometimes less), they will have pensions equal or close to their regular salaries,[80] while an unsuccessful protest could result in a court-martial and possible loss of both the pension and the *cesantia*.[81] Moreover, a challenge by the affected officers would, most likely, lack credibility, since most of them could be shown to have benefited in the past from the very practices they were now attacking. For those officers not tapped for forced retirement, the urge to solidarity is weakened by the promise of more rapid promotion, which also carries with it a guarantee of a higher pension and *cesantía* at retirement.

Secondly, reflecting the low level of technical-professional development, there has been no rational planning in recruitment and promotion policies to assure a reasonable balance between the number of qualified candidates for promotion and the number of vacancies available. Indeed, the wide fluctuations in the number of officers graduated from the military college and the war academy have made it virtually inevitable that periods of rapid promotion alternate with long periods of slow promotion. The lack of a system like that of

Table 2.10 Index of Output of
New and Senior Officers

| Year | Index of the total number of officers graduating from: | |
| | The Colegio Militar | The army war academy |
|---|---|---|
| 1958 | 100 | 100 |
| 1959 | 183 | 200 |
| 1960 | 161 | 213 |
| 1961 | 122 | 137 |
| 1962 | 78 | 225 |
| 1963 | 106 | 113 |
| 1964 | 44 | 163 |
| 1965 | 0 | 163 |
| 1966 | 0 | 113 |
| 1967 | 93 | Not available |

Brazil, where officers qualifying for promotion are given the salary and perquisites of the higher grade without the rank if no openings are available, further increased the reluctance of officers with a long time in grade to come to the defense of their superiors.[82] The intermittent existence of the war academy during the 1950s also clouded the issue somewhat by creating situations where those officers who were most qualified in terms of seniority were often not as well trained and professionally prepared as less senior officers, particularly those who had studied abroad.[83] As a result of these and, perhaps, other factors, the Ecuadorian military was not able to resist political practices by civilian governments that clearly would not have been tolerated by the more highly professionalized military institutions of Peru, Brazil, or Argentina. Overall, the level of professionalization of the Ecuadorian military appears to be rather low, at least by Latin American standards.

Nevertheless, during the 1950s the Ecuadorian armed forces did reach a level of technical development and complexity clearly superior to that of the prewar period of minimal professionalization. With the growth in the size and complexity of the armed forces, the efficacy of clientelistic strategies of civilian penetration was correspondingly reduced. While recruitment patterns remained largely unchanged, the expansion of military training and consequent intensification of institutional socialization promoted and strengthened the individual officer's identification with the military institution itself, thereby decreasing the significance of his social origins. It is also important to note that, as a result of these organizational changes, the level of military "institutionalization"[84] was now at least approximately equivalent to that of other Ecuadorian institutions.[85] Moreover, despite its low initial starting point, the trend in military professionalization was clearly upward during the 1950s and '60s, whereas the socioeconomic and political transformations occurring at this time combined to ensure that there was no parallel strengthening of civilian political institutions.

It is to those political events—the interaction of the armed forces with its political environment—that we must now turn to begin our analysis of the new pattern of civil-military relations that emerged in the postwar period.

*part two*

# The Coup d'Etat in Ecuadorian Politics: 1948-1966

According to the analytic framework elaborated in the first chapter, the logical starting point for the analysis of the military's new role in politics is the specification of the criteria by which military officers decide to support or overthrow the government at a particular time. What political events, what kind of situations lead to a decision to intervene? Answering that question is a complex task, partly because only one of the Ecuadorian coups in question has been studied in detail, but also because an adequate political history of the postwar period has yet to be written. Without pretending to fill that void, this section reconstructs the major events leading up to each coup, military reactions to these events, and the process of intramilitary decision-making culminating in the successful or unsuccessful attempt to overthrow the government. Information on military perceptions of and response to antecedent events was derived from interviews with military and civilian leaders, including most of the key military participants in each of these crises. In each case, explicit attention is devoted to the occurrence or nonoccurrence of the six types of political outcomes which, according to previous studies, lead to military intervention. As a first step toward identifying the coup decision criteria actually used by the Ecuadorian military, the description of each crisis concludes with the participants' explanations of the factors that entered into their decisions to support or overthrow the government. Nevertheless, since these chapters constitute the only record of several crucial events in Ecuadorian history, I have tried to leaven the social scientist's concern for discerning order in societal forces with some of the historian's appreciation of the historically capricious and of the individual acts through which social forces must find expression.

# chapter three

# Peace, Prosperity, and Constitutional Stability: 1948-1960

In its focus on the political outcomes leading to a military coup, the analysis of coup decision criteria has much in common with descriptive case studies of individual military coups that typically explain a coup d'état in terms of its relation to a larger sequence of events. Such explanations are, however, subject to criticism on the grounds that the occurrence of these events prior to the coup does not prove that, in the absence of some or all of them, the coup would not have occurred anyway, or that the same events have not occurred before, perhaps frequently, without resulting in the overthrow of the government.[1] The difficulty is compounded by the tendency of postcoup military manifestos to include all possible justifications for the military's actions, rather than merely those that were in fact salient to the military. The obvious solution to the problem is also to study the nonoccurrence of coups and coups that were unsuccessful. Indeed, Ecuador was selected for this study partly because its recent history contains a twelve-year period (from 1948 to 1960) in which, despite a major crisis in 1954, three successive governments completed their full four-year terms.

At least initially, the stability of this period was due, in part, to the reaction of civilian and military leaders against the exaggerated rate of government turnover that had plagued the country since 1931. In accordance with the political pact that ended the 1947 succession crisis, presidential elections were held in June 1948.[2] Largely as a result of an innovation in the 1946 constitution that gave the armed forces responsibility for guaranteeing free elections,[3] these proceeded without government interference for only the third time in twentieth-century Ecuadorian history. Backed by a loose coalition of independents, Liberals, and Socialists, Galo Plaza was declared the victor by a narrow margin over the candidate of the Conservative parties and a third ticket representing Liberal and Socialist dissidents.[4] The son of the last great Liberal military caudillo and a member of one of the principal land-owning families of the sierra, Plaza stressed his unique qualifications for bringing an end to the political strife that had produced four different presidents in 1947. Calling for national unity in the face of renewed border conflicts with Peru[5] and a devastating earthquake in the central sierra, Plaza managed to create "an atmosphere of peace and a certain mystique around the idea of finishing his constitutional period in office."[6] To facilitate his political stabilization efforts, Plaza adopted a thoroughly nonaggressive posture, incorporating all major political groups into his cabinet and downgrading politics in order to concentrate on revitalizing the economy. Through generous government bank credits and the opening of new coastal roads to increase the area under cultivation, the value of agricultural exports nearly doubled during the Plaza administration. With American-owned plantations in Central America devastated by plant diseases and hurricanes, Ecuador soon became one of the world's largest producers of bananas. For the "productive classes"—especially landowners—it was a time of considerable prosperity.[7]

Nevertheless, there were several minor attempts to overthrow Plaza's government. The most serious threat came shortly after temporary economic difficulties, including a balance of payments problem and a rise in the cost of living, led to a government defeat in the 1950 congressional elections. A month later, Carlos Guevara Moreno, leader of the Concentration of Popular Forces (CFP), a newly formed populist party based primarily in the Guayaquil lower class, attempted to launch a popular revolt. With the backing of an infantry battalion, an irregular force of civilians and members of the civil guard seized control of radio and telephone facilities and of the Guayaquil airport. The local military command remained loyal to the government, however, and with the aid of nearby tank and cavalry units quashed the revolt in less than twenty-four hours.[8] The expected mass support never materialized; press and party support for the government was unanimous. Despite the opposition majority in both houses, Congress voted against three deputies implicated in the plot, stripping them of their legislative immunity. The Plaza government likewise insisted on stiff penalties for military insubordination; the rebel officers were dishonorably discharged and, along with Guevara, sentenced to a year in prison. Similarly, in 1952, when the lack of money for arms or maneuvers led to war academy complaints that the country was not prepared to confront a threat from Peru, Plaza closed the academy and sent the younger officers abroad for their general staff training.[9] Military resentment against the government's "false concept of pacifism"[10] simmered below the surface, but none of the attempts to stir up barracks revolts managed to sway the constitutionalist convictions of the younger officers. On 31 August 1952, Galo Plaza completed his fourth year in office and turned power over to his elected successor—the first Ecuadorian president to do so in twenty-eight years.

Plaza's successor in the presidential palace, Dr. José María Velasco Ibarra, provided a more stringent test of the country's newly formed commitment to constitutional procedures. Despite his 36,000-vote margin in a four-way race [11] (resulting largely from the backing of the CFP in Guayaquil), Velasco had twice before come to power riding a wave of popular acclaim[12] only to be deposed after attempting to seize dictatorial powers. A spellbinding orator and a man of exceedingly volatile temperament, Velasco was at the same time an austere intellectual known for his books expounding his own rather eclectic political philosophy.[13] The new administration was almost immediately plunged into a crisis when fifty field-grade officers, retired by Velasco for their part in his overthrow in 1947, appealed unsuccessfully for a hearing before Congress. Less than two months later, the government announced the smashing of a conspiratorial movement with the arrest and deportation of Guevara Moreno and other CFP leaders. Shortly thereafter, the president's political about-face was completed when the Liberals who had nominated him in the election withdrew their support. Velasco promptly formed a new cabinet with the Conservatives and Social Christians, and thus maintained government control of Congress. Another crisis ensued when the new minister of the interior, Camilo Ponce Enríquez, closed two opposition newspapers in Guayaquil for illegal possession of firearms after their employees fired on a mob of progovernment demonstrators who were stoning the newspaper building. Following a series of small demonstrations and the temporary closure of the major Quito daily, *El Comercio,* a flare-up of the border dispute led both sides to moderate their differences. As a gesture for unity, the government arrested the head of the militant conservative group, *Acción Revolucionaria Nacionalista Ecuatoriana* (ARNE), because of its violent attacks on the opposition. The government suffered moderate losses in the midterm congressional elections, but another record year for exports helped bring a lull in the political battles. Although government-decreed 10 to 40 percent wage increases sent consumer prices up, real per capita income jumped by nearly 6 percent for the year.[14] With the Conservatives sharing in the government and the coastal oligarchy riding the crest of the export boom, one observer noted, "The legislative meetings [August–October 1954] have been unusually quiet; none of the opposition leaders has chosen to make an attack on the administration."[15] A half-hearted attempt to censure the minister of the interior for the government's attack on freedom of the press was soundly defeated.

Without warning, three days before Christmas an internal conflict erupted within the military that almost led to the overthrow of the government. In late 1953, when Carlos Julio Arosemena was fired as minister of defense, Velasco decided to give that position to the subsecretary, a young army major, Reinaldo Varea Donoso, who was promoted to lieutenant colonel and then retired. Despite an impressive record in the Colegio Militar and advanced training in the United States, Varea's meteoric rise was based primarily on a close personal association with Velasco dating back to the Revolution of 1944.[16] Varea soon won a strong position within the cabinet by keeping the military loyal to the government during the 1953 controversies. At the same time, he promoted to key posts in the general staff a small group of young army majors who had recently returned from general staff school in Peronist Argentina.[17] Better trained and considerably more aggressive than their superiors (among whom they were thoroughly resented), this group of officers set out to reorganize and re-equip Ecuador's "ailing military institutions." Velasco responded with promises of generous funding for military projects.[18]

Meanwhile, the growing personal rivalry between Varea and Ponce for primacy within the cabinet came to a head over remarks made by Economics Minister Jaime Nebot, who questioned the wisdom of deficit spending and use of scarce foreign reserves for the military.[19] Sensing a weakening of his position with the president, Varea offered his resignation. Angered by Nebot's "anti-military" attitude, Varea's followers demanded that Varea's resignation be rejected and that Ponce and Nebot be dismissed. The next day, after a meeting with the general staff, the high command passed on to the president a more delicately worded petition, defending Varea's work in behalf of the armed forces. Infuriated at the news of the meeting, Velasco replied, "Tell them that the constitution gives me the right to name ministers as I please."[20] A meeting that afternoon with Varea ended in a shouting match. During the night, as the hard-liners moved to organize support within the Quito garrison, Velasco, forewarned by a military aide, fled by car to Guayaquil, where he arrived at dawn.[21] After being called to the governor's palace, the commander of the second zone unexpectedly encountered the president, who explained that the minister of defense had launched an attempt to overthrow him. Pledging his own support, Lieutenant Colonel Almeida quickly called together the officers at his command. Still ashen from his narrow escape from Quito, Velasco commented as he entered the gathering that he had virtually ceased to be president, and he asked only to be treated with consideration. Showing Velasco to the presiding seat, one officer spoke for the rest as he said, "Dr. Velasco, you are still the constitutional president of the country."[22]

With the assurances of support from Guayaquil, attention focused on the division of El Oro, where the bulk of the army's forces were gathered on the Peruvian border—commanded by a young officer who had been briefly imprisoned and discharged for rejecting Velasco's seizure of dictatorial powers in 1946. After receiving a telegram from Quito denouncing the replacement of Varea as treason, Lieutenant Colonel Aulestia[23] convoked an assembly of battalion commanders, announcing, "I have defended the constitution before. I defend it now, and this is our position even if we have to support it with force."[24] Placing his troops on alert, Aulestia communicated to Quito and Guayaquil the division's decision to oppose any unconstitutional political movement.[25]

Meanwhile, Velasco's unexpected flight to Guayaquil thoroughly confused Varea's supporters in Quito. Some unit commanders thought they were acting to force Velasco to reject Varea's resignation, while Varea's followers on the general staff seized the opportunity to transform the movement into a coup d'état.[26] No one was more confused than Varea himself, caught between the desires of his friends and supporters for a Peronist-type coup and his own loyalties to Velasco and constitutionalist principles. An attempt to negotiate ended with the arrest, release, and rearrest of several of the movement's ringleaders. Varea subsequently abdicated leadership of the movement formed in his behalf and went home, still unable to resolve his internal conflicts.[27] While the subsecretary of defense tried to rally the procoup forces,[28] the vice-president and a number of older officers who had been pushed aside by the Varea group energetically worked to recapture control of the Quito units. By the morning of the twenty-fourth, the crisis was ended and Quito submitted to the authority of the vice-president and the new minister of defense.[29]

Among the principal military participants in the crisis, the major reasons given to explain individual decisions to support or oppose the attempted coup d'état were the undisputed constitutionality of the Velasco government in the face of the Quito rebellion and the strong personal feelings most officers had toward Lieutenant Colonel Varea.[30] A number of the officers interviewed mentioned Varea's highly effective work in behalf of the renovation of the

Table 3.1 Factors Entering into
Military Decisions: 1954

| Explanations | Cited | Most stressed |
|---|---|---|
| Personal feud of Varea with Velasco and/or Ponce | 17 (89%) | 0 |
| Constitutional status of government | 13 (68%) | 9 (47%) |
| Personal loyalties/antipathies to Varea | 13 (68%) | 8 (42%) |
| Work of Varea benefitting/corrupting the Institution | 8 (42%) | 2 (11%) |
| Government corruption | 1 ( 5%) | 0 |
| Velasco's temperament | 1 ( 5%) | 0 |
| | N = 19 | |

armed forces, while others argued that Varea and his group of majors were destroying the institution through utter disregard for seniority rules. Nearly all of the respondents mentioned the personal conflicts between Varea, Velasco, and Ponce, although, as in subsequent crises, this type of response was given as an explanation of the crisis rather than to explain individual positions taken in the coup.

The failure of the 1954 coup attempt is entirely consistent with our initial hypotheses specifying the types of political outcomes leading to military willingness to overthrow the government. In the first place, there were no public pressures for military intervention. Despite their connections with the opposition Liberal party, the major newspapers of Quito and Guayaquil[31] appear to have expressed the consensus of the politically articulate public in condemning the pro-Varea movement in unequivocal terms.

> The role of the armed forces (especially its leaders) is exactly that defined by the president: administration and training of their specialized services and defense of the national integrity and honor. A deliberative position or, worse yet, imposition, in matters that are not military affairs but pertain to the competence of the president, cannot be admitted or tolerated.[32]

> The nation has to resolve definitively to live within the rule of the constitution, because only in this way can it guarantee its existence as an organized entity and maintain the respect of other members of the American community. . . . Happily, there exists a firm conviction that the constitutional order must be maintained at any price.[33]

The personal political opinions of officers toward the government are more difficult to gauge. Only the complaint against government corruption would seem to fit this category. If we take the editorial opinion of the Quito daily *El Comercio* as the closest available gauge of feelings among the sierra middle class, the balance of public opinion for the six weeks prior to the coup was, on the whole, favorable to the government. Of the thirty-four editorials commenting on government policies or performance, 53 percent were in favor of the government position. There were no prior events—strikes or demonstrations—that could be interpreted as public disorders, and obviously no threat of a communist takeover or unacceptable election results existed. The only previously postulated conditions present in the 1954 case were Nebot's alleged insult to the military and the question of institutional interests. Even here, there was no agreement within the military as to whether Varea was a benefactor or malefactor of the institution. Given the strong constitutionalist reaction of the younger officers to the consequences of previous military involvement in political affairs, the procoup forces were largely limited to Varea's personal followers. In the absence of the necessary external justifications, the coup failed, despite the fact that Varea's supporters held most of the strategic posts in and around the capital city.

Although pleased by various manifestations of support (including a large rally in defense of the president and the constitution), Velasco nevertheless carefully set out to improve his relations with the military. Nebot and Ponce were soon eased out of the cabinet. Loyal constitutionalists were promoted and assurances were given that plans to reorganize and re-equip the armed forces would go forward with the complete support of the government.[34] Despite declining exports and a generally stagnant economy, 1955 was uneventful except for a railroad strike and a brief flurry of student unrest. In the maneuvering prior to the 1956 elections, the *velasquista* movement and ARNE nominated a popular ex-mayor of Quito, but as the campaign progressed, Velasco virtually ignored the official candidate, endorsing instead his former minister, Camilo Ponce Enríquez. Ponce was the nominee of the Conservative party and his own Social Christian movement (MSC), actually the more aristocratic and conservative wing of the Ecuadorian right. Aided by a close split in the coastal provinces between Guevara Moreno of the CFP and the candidate of the Liberal-Socialist coalition, Ponce emerged the victor by 3,000 votes, with 29 percent of the total vote.[35] After the electoral tribunal rejected charges of fraud in several provinces, Liberal leaders began looking for military backing in an attempt to prevent the seating of the first Conservative government since 1895, but a barracks revolt in the Liberal stronghold of Manabí—instigated by Galo Plaza's brother—encountered neither military nor civilian support and was quickly suppressed.[36]

Declaring the principal objective of his administration to be "the moral and economic recuperation of the country,"[37] Ponce quickly called for a political truce. He gave the Liberal party equal representation in his cabinet and excluded only the Socialists, who shortly thereafter declared their "belligerent" but largely ineffectual opposition to the government. With the aid of a modest recovery in export earnings after the stagnation of 1955-1956, the first two years of the Ponce administration were relatively crisis-free. Even Richard Nixon, in contrast to his reception elsewhere in Latin America, was received in Ecuador with polite applause. Despite a total freeze on military spending, the armed forces contented themselves with Ponce's willingness to let them run their internal affairs on the basis of seniority and merit,[38] pointing with pride to their contribution to the new era of political stability. "After an agitated political life which rocked the very foundations of the *patria,* we now have had a decade of true, constructive, and fruitful peace; but this peace we owe exclusively to the uncontrovertible fact that the armed forces no longer take an active part in the politics of the country. The country has achieved political maturity as its armed forces have achieved professional maturity."[39] Almost imperceptibly at first, that oft-proclaimed maturity began to come under increasing pressure.

Falling world prices for coffee and cacao held export earnings at a virtual standstill in 1958 and 1959. To protect foreign reserves and avoid inflation, Ponce applied the classic conservative remedies—restricting the growth of bank credit and cutting the government budget deficit in order to restrict the growth of demand for imports. Monetary stability was preserved and consumer prices actually declined slightly from 1955 to 1960,[40] but the net effect was to reproduce the stagnation of exports in all sectors of the economy. Despite rapidly growing unemployment and falling corporate profits, there were no immediate political repercussions. The first indication of the growing malaise came in July 1959 in Manabí, after an enlisted man shot and wounded his commanding officer and then committed suicide. A riot ensued in which the officer was killed and a small barracks was burned by an angry mob of civilians.

News of the incident immediately sparked two days of widespread anomic rioting and looting in Guayaquil. Declaring the entire country under martial law, Ponce immediately delegated his powers as commander-in-chief to the chief of the general staff, who subsequently directed military operations to forcefully suppress the disorders, which left more than forty dead and one hundred fifty persons hospitalized.[41] Frightened by the virulence of the fighting, the government moved to relax its curbs on spending for public works and education in hopes of stimulating employment. Three months later a minor incident during Guayaquil's Independence Day parade again sparked riots and looting at the cost of four more lives, but as the year ended, attention was increasingly focused on the upcoming presidential elections.

Despite the social unrest, the decade ended without alteration of the military's political quiescence—the first decade in twentieth-century Ecuadorian history not punctuated at least once by the forcible overthrow of the government, and the longest period of peaceful succession in office since the *paz bancaria* of 1916–1925. At the simplest level of explanation, this achievement can be largely attributed to the nonoccurrence of political outcomes that would lead to military perceptions of a crisis requiring military intervention. As far as can be ascertained, these three governments always maintained the support of at least one of the two traditional elite groups and never sharply antagonized either of them. Within the rather limited participant public, "public opinion" seems to have been generally favorable or at worst mildly critical, except perhaps during Velasco's 1953 attacks on the press. At no point did any major social group call for the overthrow of the government, its impeachment, or even its resignation. Except for the 1959 riots, which were anomic rather than politically directed (and in any case willingly suppressed by the military), public disorders were limited to isolated economic strikes and an occasional student protest. There were no parties or candidates under military veto, and radical movements were virtually nonexistent. The military's institutional interests were not well looked after except by Velasco, but the army's dissatisfaction on this score was not sufficient to overshadow its negative memories of past political incursions and its gradually growing pride in its new role as defender of the constitution.

# *chapter four*

# The End of an Era: The Fall of Velasco Ibarra

Despite the constitutional stability of the previous decade, the political environment was beginning to change. In an atmosphere of increasing social and economic tensions, Velasco Ibarra appeared as a candidate for an unprecedented fourth, nonconsecutive term as president. Liberals, Socialists, and independents revived the *Frente Democrática Nacional* to support the candidacy of Galo Plaza, while the Conservatives, the *Movimiento Social Cristiano,* and ARNE backed Dr. Gonzalo Cordero Crespo. A splinter socialist faction allied with the Communists to support a fourth candidate, Dr. Antonio Parra. Velasco launched an electrifying populist campaign, promising large-scale government programs to benefit the dislocated and increasingly politicized masses created by the wave of migration to the coast and the cities during the 1950s. Even the conservative candidate felt compelled to promise a "white revolution" of nonviolent social and economic reforms,[1] but none of the candidates could come close to matching Velasco's gift for arousing the emotions of those who came by the thousands to hear his fiery attacks against the corrupt, immoral oligarchy and the outgoing Ponce government. The emotional fervor of the campaign brought a new wave of political violence resulting in several civilian deaths.[2] When the votes were counted, Velasco had won easily with nearly 400,000 votes, more than had been accumulated by his Liberal and Conservative opponents combined. Deeply angered by Velasco's campaign attacks on his government, Camilo Ponce resigned the presidency on his last day in office rather than preside over Velasco's inauguration.[3]

After taking power in September 1960, the Velasco government did little to satisfy the popular expectations raised in the election campaign. Characteristically, after naming the new cabinet, Velasco issued a decree forcing sixty high-ranking officers into retirement.[4] Protests from the affected officers led Velasco's hotheaded minister of government to denounce the sixty as traitors to the *patria*. Although Velasco eventually asked for his minister's resignation, the decree was not revoked.[5]

The first three months of the new administration were largely devoted to castigating the previous government and restaffing the bureaucracy with *velasquistas*. In January 1961 President Velasco reached a high point of public support; massive progovernment demonstrations followed his declaration of the "nullity of the Rio Protocol," which had ended the 1941 war with Peru by ceding, under American pressure, an enormous territory to Peru. United States policy toward Cuba and the refusal of the United States to consider the nullity thesis soon resulted in serious outbreaks of violence between the pro-Castro left, led by university and secondary students, and the anticommunist right, led by the Conservatives and ARNE with the support of the Catholic church and the CIA.[6]

Meanwhile, the economic situation worsened. A drought and falling export prices led to a sharp decrease in foreign exchange reserves, which was further aggravated by the flight of speculative private capital. A deliberately manipulated 20 percent devaluation in what for a decade had been one of Latin America's most stable currencies brought immense windfall profits to the Guayaquil economic elite and government insiders[7]—and rising prices to the general public. A new sales tax to finance pay raises for the military, police, and teachers added to economic unrest.[8] With exports down, the real GNP rose by only 1.5 percent in 1961, and per capita income fell. Estimated unemployment increased from 150,000 to 200,000, and consumer prices increased more during a single year than in the previous four. Velasco's popular base, the Guayaquil working class, was particularly hard hit.[9]

In addition to the growing opposition from party and labor groups, Velasco soon faced another problem as the government party underwent a serious internal schism. The 1960 election victory had been so overwhelming that not all claims to shares in the spoils, particularly government jobs, could be filled. In areas where *velasquistas* controlled the provincial government, *velasquista* legislators often found themselves excluded from the government circle. When the 1961 congressional session convened, many joined in denouncing government insiders as more interested in personal enrichment than in socioeconomic reform.[10] Velasco's vice-president, Dr. Carlos Julio Arosemena Monroy, in his capacity as president of the National Congress, became the leading spokesman for the opposition faction. After a confrontation with Velasco over an invitation to visit Eastern Europe, Arosemena openly broke with the government in July 1961. The defection of the Arosemena faction gave the opposition a legislative majority and the opening months of the 1961 Congress were largely devoted to attacks on the government's economic and foreign policies.[11] At the end of the government's first year in office, after ten changes of ministers, only four members of Velasco's original cabinet remained.[12] In other areas the government's record in promoting change was less impressive.

The confrontation began in earnest in October 1961 when the Confederation of Ecuadorian Workers, backed by the political opposition, called a twenty-four-hour general strike to demand an immediate 30 percent wage hike and elimination of all new taxes decreed by the Velasco government. At the same time, the Chambers of Commerce and the sierra Chamber of Agriculture, representing the merchants and sierra landowners respectively, issued their own attacks on government economic policy. The strike effectively closed down most of the country and provided the occasion for widespread antigovernment riots, which were contained only by full-scale employment of army troops at the cost of three civilian deaths. During the rest of October, riots and demonstrations continued in Tulcán, Ibarra, Esmeraldas, and Cuenca, as well as in Quito and Guayaquil. In Congress, the opposition formed a Frente Popular to protest the temporary arrest of two deputies accused by the government of conspiring to overthrow the president, while Vice-President Arosemena called upon the government to change direction or perish. Relations with Congress deteriorated even further with government packing of congressional galleries. This led to a series of incidents, including one full-scale shootout between legislators and progovernment spectators.[13]

On 3 November, ignoring the advice of his military high command and the petitions of local organizations, the president decided to go to Cuenca to attend the celebration of the anniversary of that city's independence. Even with a heavy military escort, Velasco barely managed to enter the city.[14] In the ensuing disorders two persons died, including a university student, sparking new riots in Quito and in Guayaquil, where another student was killed.

Three days later, amid continued protests against the deaths in Cuenca and Guayaquil, a delegation from the Federation of University Students appeared before Congress to denounce as unconstitutional the installation of a military governor in Cuenca without congressional consent. Declining the invitation to go into the streets and demonstrate, Vice-President Arosemena explained over the nationwide radio network carrying the special afternoon session, "In this moment when the constitution has been broken . . . I must represent the law in the name of the National Parliament."[15] Loyal *velasquista* legislators reported to Velasco in Guayaquil that Arosemena had openly declared himself president.[16] Infuriated, the president left immediately for Quito and decided to order the arrest and deportation of the vice-president. All four members of the high command opposed the decision to arrest Arosemena as a breach of the constitution that would cause serious division within the armed forces, arguing that the end of the congressional session was less than twenty-four hours away.[17] Velasco insisted, declaring, "There cannot be two presidents, one elected by 400,000 votes and another by Congress," and threatened to resign if the order was not carried out.[18] Nevertheless, the president's explanation of the need for the arrest was coolly received during a tour of military units in Quito. Finally the high command, with the aid of the minister of defense, convinced Velasco to countermand the arrest order, only to learn that the vice-president had already been taken prisoner along with his military aides and several members of Congress.[19] As Arosemena awaited the deportation order in an air force plane, the president hesitated, acting against military advice that now his only hope was to carry out his original plan. Visibly tired, Velasco finally ordered Arosemena's detention in the Penal García Moreno pending presentation of charges before the Supreme Court, concluding, "It is not the time for a dictatorship."[20]

Meanwhile, in the engineering battalion "Chimborazo," which had been repeatedly employed in putting down opposition disorders in Quito, the news of the vice-president's arrest and the sudden replacement of the unit's commander for his opposition to the arrest order caused new discontent.[21] Major Jorge Valdivieso, now in command, discussed the charges against the vice-president with the other officers. Having heard Arosemena's speech on radio, they concluded that, while inflammatory, it in no way justified his unconstitutional arrest. With little or no dissension, the unit decided to revolt in favor of the vice-president and in opposition to the attempted dictatorship.[22] During the night the barracks were fortified and a few reinforcements recruited from the military geographic institute. Emissaries sent to seek support from other Quito units met with little success, and transmission of the unit's manifesto was blocked by police occupation of radio and television stations.[23]

At dawn, as members of the high command arrived at the barracks to investigate reports of suspicious activities, Army Commander General Del Pozo was taken prisoner. Another car, containing the chief of staff, narrowly escaped capture. While General Aulestia informed the president, Subsecretary Naranjo organized the suppression of the insurrection, surrounding the barracks with artillery, cavalry, and paratrooper units. At seven o'clock, when the rebels refused a negotiated surrender, both sides opened fire. After about two hours of fighting, which killed four and exhausted the battalion's ammunition, the rebel officers decided to surrender to their prisoner, General Del Pozo, accepting his word that there would be "neither victors nor vanquished."[24] As the progovernment forces departed, hostile crowds of spectators jeered and threw rocks and garbage.[25]

The same morning, the news of the vice-president's arrest and the Chimborazo revolt sparked two more movements against the government. Air Force Commander Suárez, who had almost been removed for his opposition to the arrest order, refused to order an air attack against the Chimborazo barracks and, after consulting with other air force officers, sent a delegation to demand that the vice-president be freed. Velasco reluctantly accepted the ultimatum, but when the agreed-upon hour passed with no results, the conviction grew within the air force command that the dictatorship was now a fact.[26] Meanwhile, at the main air base at Taura near Guayaquil, the officers decided at a general meeting not to attack the Chimborazo rebels but to support a constitutionalist position.[27] While gaining time through another ultimatum to the president, General Suárez managed to avoid his own arrest and slipped out of Quito with the rest of the air force planes, landing at Taura and taking command of the constitutionalist forces.[28]

Manifestos began to fly from all sides. The Congress in emergency session resolved "to remind all members of the armed forces that Article 157 of the constitution establishes the obligation of the armed forces to maintain the constitution and that any attempt to deny the authority of the Congress or of its president [Arosemena] constitutes a violation of the constitution and consequently an attempt to establish a dictatorship."[29] An air force communiqué also invoked the oath of the Ecuadorian soldier to uphold the constitution and called for the immediate convocation of an extraordinary Congress as the legally competent authority to rule on the constitutionality of the acts of the president and vice-president.[30]

The second movement against the government came from the army war academy. An open meeting of professors and students decided to issue a proclamation calling on all officers to refuse any order to attack another unit and resolved to send a delegation headed by the director, General Villacís, to ask Velasco to resign.[31] In a noon meeting with the president, the most senior of the academy's students bluntly told him, "The country needs peace and tranquility for progress, so that the people can work. Wherever you go, there are arrests, disorders, and deaths."[32] Slumped in his chair, Velasco replied that he was already considering resignation, but asked to be allowed to do so the next day before the Council of State, rather than resign before a hostile Congress.[33] Later that afternoon Velasco abandoned the Presidential Palace for parts unknown, possibly thinking of repeating his successful 1954 escape to Guayaquil.

However, in Guayaquil the constitutionalist group at Taura was gaining support. After receiving an air force delegation, the navy, led by its squadron commander, refused to accept any further orders from the navy commanding general in Quito and declared its support for the constitutionalist position.[34] Patrol boats were quickly sent to guard the river-crossing facing the air base at Taura from possible army attack, and the rest of the fleet was put to sea.[35] In Guayaquil itself, despite pressure from opposition politicians, the commander of the second army zone remained unenthusiastically loyal to the high command. But by the night of 7 November, many of the units in his zone had begun declaring their support for the constitutionalist cause. That same night, the Taura group received the support of the powerful division of El Oro.[36]

In Quito, a general meeting of all officers was called to discuss the new situation presented by Velasco's abandonment of power. In the discussion of possible successors, opinions were divided, with the high command particularly opposed to the succession of the vice-president. One group of officers proposed to designate the chief of general staff as interim president, but when he refused to accept the position, a weak compromise was reached with the decision to turn power over to Dr. Camilo Gallegos Toledo, president of the Supreme Court. [37] The support for Gallegos came primarily from those officers who had supported Velasco, on the argument that if Velasco had broken the constitution by arresting the vice-president, Arosemena had done so by his ill-concealed campaign to overthrow the government; thus only the judicial power was left unblemished. [38] Gallegos, who was known to many officers through six years' service on the National Defense Board, was asked by the chief of staff and the three commanding generals [39] to accept the presidency on an interim basis until new elections could be called. Gallegos reluctantly accepted the position when he was told that this was the only means to avoid civil war. With promises that the armed forces would unite behind him, Gallegos set about forming a cabinet, designating General Villacís of the war academy as minister of government and General Aulestia as minister of defense. [40]

While Gallegos was busy organizing his government, the vice-president of the Senate, retired Lieutenant Colonel Reinaldo Varea, managed to secure Arosemena's release from the Penal García Moreno. [41] Congress was hastily called into session despite the troops surrounding the Legislative Palace, and at midnight, as its official mandate expired, Congress declared Dr. Carlos Julio Arosemena Monroy the constitutional president of the Republic. [42] After receiving delegations from the war academy the morning of the eighth, the remaining provincial garrisons declared for the succession of the vice-president [43] and Gallegos supporters, including General Villacís, began defecting. [44] Colonel Vega of the war academy group broke the loyalists' hold on the Quito garrison by winning over the cavalry battalion "Yaguachi" and other units. [45] When he learned of the congressional resolution and the continued division within the armed forces, Gallegos immediately resigned. [46] Seeing that further resistance could only lead to useless bloodshed, the loyalist commander of the first zone ordered all troops to return to barracks, as air force jets from Taura fired warning shots over the tanks retiring from the Legislative Palace. [47]

Among the major military participants in the 1961 crisis, the constitutional question was again clearly the leading issue, although there was no agreement as to the import of the constitutional norm in this particular situation. The majority argued that Velasco had broken the constitution by arresting the vice-president, while half as many officers countered that Dr. Arosemena was equally guilty of violating the constitution. Three officers defended Velasco as the legally constituted authority, regardless of the arrest. Half of the respondents cited the month-long wave of civil disorders and deaths preceding the government's fall as well as public hostility toward Velasco. Again a number of officers mentioned personal attachments to or complaints against the government, with three members of the high command citing their personal loyalty to

Table 4.1  Factors Entering into
Military Decisions: 1961

| Explanations | Cited | Most stressed |
|---|---|---|
| Violation(s) of the constitution | 23 (92%) | 13 (52%) |
| Public disorders against the government | 14 (56%) | 4 (16%) |
| Public opinion against the government | 12 (48%) | 0 |
| Personal loyalties/antipathies to Velasco or Arosemena | 10 (40%) | 3 (12%) |
| Opposition efforts to overthrow the government | 9 (36%) | 4 (16%) |
| Economic problems | 4 (16%) | 0 |
| Political purges of military | 2 ( 8%) | 1 ( 4%) |
| Avoid civil war | 2 ( 8%) | 0 |
| Velasco's personality | 1 ( 4%) | 0 |
| | N = 25 | |

Velasco as the most important factor in their decision. Others attributed Velasco's fall wholly or in part to the efforts of Arosemena to bring down the government.

In sharp contrast to the previous decade, by November 1961, three of the postulated coup-motivating conditions were present simultaneously. While there were no publicly expressed appeals for military intervention prior to the vice-president's arrest, student-backed demands for Velasco's resignation were gaining force and impeachment by the opposition majority in Congress was a possibility hindered only by the approaching end of the congressional session. Clearly Velasco had alienated virtually every segment of public opinion. The traditional land-owning elite of the sierra had been protesting against government economic policy since the devaluation. Even the Guayaquil financial and export interests that had benefited from the devaluation had, judging by the editorial stance of *El Universo,* withdrawn their support. In the month preceding the coup, fifteen of the twenty editorials dealing with government policy or performance were critical of the government, most very strongly so. Again taking *El Comercio* editorial comment as the only available indicator of sierra middle-class opinion, in the six weeks prior, only two out of nineteen editorials dealing with the Velasco administration were even partially favorable.

The hostility toward the government among the organized and participating sectors of the urban lower class is most dramatically revealed in the high and rising tide of public disorders. Figure 4.1 provides a simple index of public disorders based on reported instances of strikes, antigovernment demonstrations, riots, and bombings from June to November 1961. Individual event scores reflect the number of people involved, whether the event occurred in the two major urban centers or elsewhere, its duration, whether it was accompanied by violence, whether the army was involved in its suppression, and the extent of property damage, injuries, or deaths. These individual scores are then summed to give the raw scores for each two-week period preceding the coup. Assuming that military perceptions of particularly tense periods of disorder carry over until gradually they are forgotten, a score reflecting the cumulative impact of present and past disorders in each time period has also been calculated.[48] If scores for the minor strikes and demonstrations of the previous summer can be considered to represent "normal" levels, by late October public disorders were running at roughly five times the normal rate, giving the cumulative impression of an explosion of opposition to the government.

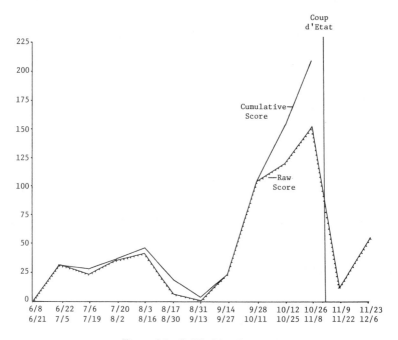

Figure 4.1. Public Disorders: 1961

Neither electoral nor communist threats were involved in the 1961 coup, and neither the military pay raise nor Velasco's forced retirement of senior officers figure prominently in military self-explanations of what factors entered into their decisions. Despite the absence of these factors, even before the vice-president's arrest, the level of public hostility toward the government and the perceived level of political crisis appear to have been approaching the threshold at which the accumulated inhibitions against military intervention were no longer a sufficient constraint. Nevertheless, it seems clear that, in the final decision to withdraw military support from the government, the most important factor was an event not included in the initial hypotheses—the arrest of the vice-president and the attendant loss of the government's claim to constitutional legitimacy.

# *chapter five*

# The Fall of Carlos Julio Arosemena

The strong popular support for the coup against Velasco and the victory of the constitutionalist forces over those attempting to impose Gallegos as his successor produced a brief mood of national euphoria. The problems of a declining economy, the polarization of left and right sparked by the Cuban revolution, and the character of the man who had led the fight against Velasco all faded into the background as joyous pro-Arosemena demonstrations and parades filled the streets of Quito and Guayaquil. In his inaugural address, Arosemena called for national unity; subsequently he named a cabinet composed of men of excellent reputation from all of the major parties, including three Conservatives, three Liberals, and two moderate Socialists. In a move to allay doubts created by his trip to the Soviet Union and his expressions of sympathy for Fidel Castro, Dr. Arosemena dispatched ex-President Galo Plaza to Washington to assure the American government of his administration's commitment to the goals of the Alliance for Progress and the principles of the inter-American system.

The moderately well-to-do son of a prominent Guayaquil banking family, whose father had overseen the return to a constitutional regime after the anti-Velasco coup in 1947, Carlos Julio Arosemena Monroy began his political career as a lawyer working with the embryonic trade-union movement in the port city. Abandoning the traditional Liberal affiliations of the Guayaquil elite, Arosemena had linked his political fortunes to those of Velasco Ibarra in one of the most volatile alliances in Ecuadorian political history. The two clashed in 1953, leading to Arosemena's ouster as minister of defense and a short-lived attempt to encourage a military coup against his mentor.[1] The relationship was re-established after Velasco's return for the 1960 campaign, only to disintegrate again over the issue of the direction of the fourth Velasco administration.

Like Velasco in that he was a brilliant man with a gift for biting oratory, Arosemena nevertheless had a different kind of personal charisma, based on an earthy *machismo,* that contrasted dramatically with Velasco's aloof and austere paternalism. Although he was a strong nationalist in his university days, during a brief period of service in the Ecuadorian Embassy in Washington, Arosemena apparently acquired a deep, personal sense of the inequalities behind the façade of inter-American diplomacy[2] and a distaste for U.S. policies in Latin America.

Appropriately enough, it was the American government's efforts to organize support for its campaign to isolate Cuba from the Organization of American States that brought an abrupt end to Arosemena's political honeymoon, less than two months after his inauguration. A delegation headed by the Cuban undersecretary of foreign affairs was hastily dispatched from Havana to seek Ecuador's support in the Punta del Este Conference of Foreign Ministers, which had been called to consider U.S. demands that Cuba be expelled from the OAS and subjected to collective sanctions. (In an eyebrow-raising scene given wide press coverage, the somberly dressed Cuban diplomat was received on the beach by the Ecuadorian president, who was wearing bathing trunks and sunglasses and carrying a drink in his hand.) After the brief meeting, President Arosemena, backed by a vote of the cabinet, announced Ecuador's support for the principle of nonintervention and the rule of law in hemispheric relations, and particularly for the OAS charter, which contains no provision for expulsion of a member nation. At the conference, Foreign Minister Francisco Acosta Yépez abstained along with the representatives of five other members on the critical votes "excluding" Cuba from OAS participation, for which he was promptly expelled from the Social Christian movement.

The question of whether to maintain diplomatic relations with Cuba led to increased mobilization of both the left and right. The Communist party (PCE), the Confederation of Ecuadorian Workers (CTE), the Federation of University Students (FEUE), the Revolutionary Union of Ecuadorian Youth (URJE), and the Revolutionary Socialist party (PSR) banded together in a pro-Castro Popular Revolutionary movement, which was soon countered by a National Anti-communist front composed of the Conservative party, the MSC, and ARNE.

Having actively promoted the anticommunist cause during the Velasco administration, the U.S. Central Intelligence Agency station began to step up its campaign of anticommunist propaganda, support for right-wing groups, and infiltration of pro-Castro forces. In addition, the agency employed a variety of "dirty tricks" to increase the pressure on the government to break with Cuba and purge "leftist sympathizers" from government ranks.[3] Demonstrations and counterdemonstrations, marked by occasional violent clashes, competed for attention with frequent manifestos and editorials that mostly favored the severance of diplomatic relations. As the situation polarized, the government was increasingly caught in the middle. Only a month after defending his foreign policy before a large anticommunist demonstration, Arosemena faced a large demonstration of his own supporters who were demanding more money for the universities. Right-wing provocateurs, chanting "More universities and less army" turned the rally into an antimilitary protest.[4] The demonstration was publicly denounced by the military high command as the work of "international communism,"[5] and Arosemena's improvised defense of military expenditures was only partially successful in countering the negative impression created by the presence of two of his cabinet ministers among the protest leaders.

The issue of diplomatic relations with Cuba also became the focal point of military concern over government inaction in controlling local communists. After various military suggestions in favor of a break with Cuba were brushed off by the president, the high command and general staff resolved to send a delegation to present him with a two-volume "White Paper" documenting the role of the Cuban Embassy in disseminating pro-Castro propaganda and its support for URJE and other revolutionary groups.[6] As Colonel Arrata and his delegation entered, President Arosemena said coolly, "When I heard you were coming, my first reaction was to receive you with a copy of the constitution and military laws in one hand and an order for your arrest in the other."[7] Nevertheless, Arosemena promised to reconsider his position after his upcoming meeting with President Kennedy, during which Ecuador's international position might be an important bargaining point. Despite assurances from the high command that the problem would be solved within regular channels, two young officers in Cuenca, both recently returned from a course in counterrevolutionary warfare in Argentina, secured the aid of the third zone commander, Colonel Naranjo, in an effort to force a confrontation.[8]

On March 29, a large anticommunist demonstration was organized by ARNE and the Conservative party to coincide with a meeting of senior officers from the third zone in which it was resolved to issue a public ultimatum asking for a break in relations with Cuba and the dismissal of "cryptocommunists" in the government, including the minister of social welfare. Despite pressure from his nonmilitary supporters on the right, Colonel Naranjo refused to lead a coup against the government, hoping the June congressional elections might solve the problem. No move was taken to occupy Cuenca.[9] The Cuenca ultimatum produced a flurry of supporting and opposing demonstrations in Quito and Guayaquil and a hurried tour of military commands by the minister of defense and members of the high command. They reported no sentiment in favor of moving against the government, but strong support for "a break in relations with Cuba . . . from the minister of defense down to the last conscript."[10] Press reaction to the crisis was moderately cool to the idea of a military ultimatum, but favored the break with Cuba.[11] Infuriated, President Arosemena denounced the ultimatum as "audacious insubordination."[12] But when it was not withdrawn, he reluctantly accepted the resignation of the welfare minister along with those of the remaining Conservatives in his cabinet. In an unexpected countermove, Arosemena announced he would call a national plebiscite on the question of maintaining relations with Cuba. The idea of a plebiscite was, however, opposed, even by the parties backing the government. The Supreme

Electoral Board quickly killed the idea by refusing to administer the election, deeming it both unconstitutional and impractical. In the end, the president was forced to admit defeat in order to solve the cabinet crisis brought about by the withdrawal of Conservative and MSC support for the government. The old Plaza alliance of the Liberal and Socialist parties, the National Democratic front (FDN), offered to form a new government in exchange for acceptance of the Cuenca ultimatum and five cabinet posts. Reluctantly, Arosemena accepted, and on 2 April, diplomatic relations with Cuba, Poland, and Czechoslovakia were officially severed.

Even as Fidel Castro denounced Arosemena as a coward and a habitual drunkard,[13] a group of forty-seven would-be guerrillas, mostly members of URJE, tried to establish a *foco* in the densely forested banana plantation area northwest of Quito. Although the group was quickly rounded up by the army without a shot, military anxieties were spurred by the later revelation that part of the small arsenal held by the guerrillas had been provided by an army lieutenant, Lenín Torres, and several other members of the paratrooper school. By order of the president, the guerrillas were brought to Quito and turned over to civilian authorities for trial on charges of sabotage.[14]

After a weak effort to reassert its authority through the transfer of the army and air force commanders (resulting in the resignation of both, along with the minister of defense), the Arosemena government began a long period of drifting, without any real direction from the president. Personally disillusioned by the defeat of his neutralist foreign policy, hemmed in by the "anticommunist psychosis sweeping the country,"[15] and hamstrung by the lack of any real party base other than his miniscule National Arosemenista Movement, Arosemena increasingly withdrew from leadership of the government, concentrated on his personal affairs, and indulged in more frequent drinking spells. The June congressional elections were a major defeat for the government, as the FDN lost ground to the Conservatives in the sierra and to the Concentration of Popular Forces on the coast. Despite a series of strikes by schoolteachers, bank employees, hospital workers, and transport workers, the economy began a slow recovery from the Velasco debacle as the balance of payments and monetary reserves improved under the government's austerity program. A congressional attempt to censure the president for personal incapacity to govern failed, and some measure of surface calm returned when Congress lost itself in an investigation of a military equipment scandal in which the new vice-president and several top officials of the Velasco administration were charged with responsibility for the purchase of useless military vehicles from a U.S. arms dealer.

Meanwhile, stories of new drinking scandals circulated through the country. After a strongly regionalist speech by the president in Guayaquil, the Conservatives openly presented a motion to impeach Arosemena. The motion failed again when, in secret negotiations, the Liberals and Conservatives each insisted on one of their own as the next President.[16] Both the government and the opposition subsequently lost prestige within the military, as obstruction on both sides prevented congressional approval of the annual military promotion list before its term expired, thus directly alienating twenty-four senior officers as well as numerous junior officers waiting for vacancies higher up. This incident was followed in December by the most serious drinking scandal yet, which took place at a Guayaquil airport reception for Chilean President Jorge Alessandri. Arosemena was unable to hold himself up, much less read his welcoming speech. However, in the confusion of the December holidays, a Conservative petition to call a special session of Congress to reconsider impeachment failed to get the necessary number of signatures. Thereafter the legalist mentality of the armed forces began to wane.[17]

At the end of Arosemena's first year in office, only the economy offered any moderate cause for optimism. Perhaps aided by the government's neglect of demands for new socioeconomic programs, government expenditures were reduced slightly in real terms and the budget deficit was cut by more than a third. Inflation was held to less than 3 percent and, with the aid of restrictions on imports and a recovery in banana and coffee production, the balance of payments for 1962 showed a substantial surplus, restoring Central Bank reserves to 1960 levels. Per capita income rose by 1.5 percent over the previous year, [18] although per capita consumption remained virtually unchanged.[19] Despite the modest economic recovery, the uncertain political climate pushed free market exchange rates higher[20] and dollar assets held by Ecuadorians in U.S. banks increased sharply.[21]

As the new year began, numerous military officers, mostly in the army, began plotting the overthrow of the government. Colonel Naranjo continued working with Conservative politicians, even though his subsequent transfer to an office job in Quito considerably reduced his political influence. Another conspiratorial group sprang up around Colonel Carlos Arregui, the former army commanding general who had been fired after the events in Cuenca. Composed largely of a group of moderately reformist university professors and army officers who had been studying part-time at Central University, the Arregui group aimed its efforts at an August coup, which would be followed by an interim government headed by the president of the Supreme Court that would promulgate a series of socioeconomic reform laws and reinstate the liberal Constitution of 1945.[22] Velasco's former chief of staff, General Víctor Aulestia Mier, and several other officers who had been forced into retirement in 1961 began soon afterward to organize a movement against Arosemena under the name Nuevo Orden Nacional (NON). NON began recruiting active-duty officers and formulating a detailed plan of government. The NON program envisioned, among other things, the creation of a superior war college similar to Peru's CAEM to train a new civil-military political elite; the establishment of a government party; administrative, agrarian, and tax reforms; and industrial profit sharing.[23] The group's military recruiting efforts were fairly successful; by June they had won the adhesion of Colonel Marcos Gándara, the director of the war academy, as well as members of the general staff and lower-ranking officers scattered around the country. NON also received a promise of instant support from the commander of the 9,000-man division in El Oro. Despite NON's professed devotion to the objectives of "social justice, economic independence, and national security,"[24] the most prominent civilian members of the movement were ex-*velasquistas* and moderate conservatives.[25]

All of the anti-Arosemena movements received warm support and encouragement from the American military attaché, Colonel Charles Pratt, who, in his intelligence-gathering activities, gave the strong impression that the U.S. government was actively working for Arosemena's overthrow.[26] While Dr. Arosemena has subsequently accused the U.S. government of being the prime force behind the 1963 coup, an authoritative source in the embassy at the time has denied that there was any conscious policy of trying to foment a coup.[27] Although one of the officers interviewed admitted that he received American money to underwrite his antigovernment efforts, the amounts involved appear to be small—probably nothing more than the usual CIA payments to its large network of political informants. Reliable sources in the Arosemena government and in the CIA station indicate that Ambassador Bernbaum was not aware of CIA or U.S. military activities in support of the overthrow of the government.[28] In any case the issue is moot, since most high-ranking Ecuadorian officers believed that the United States favored an early anti-Arosemena coup.

Characteristically, President Arosemena did nothing to stop the spread of these opposition movements, remarking sardonically, "In contrast to its predecessor, my government has been distinguished by its total respect for individual liberties, including the illicit liberty of conspiracy."[29] In the absence of any real effort by Arosemena to defend himself, his military supporters were reduced to arguing that for all his faults, Arosemena was still the constitutional president, and that "to intervene to overthrow the government would lead to a loss of institutional prestige."[30]

On the political front, the various Chambers of Commerce, Agriculture, and Industry representing the country's economic elites began a strong campaign of opposition to a new corporate tax law and to proposals being studied by the government for agrarian and tax reform. As all segments of public opinion turned increasingly hostile toward the government, the Liberal party split over the costs of continued collaboration, and the moderate Socialist party withdrew to an "independent" stance. Both the Communists and Revolutionary Socialists gave up their support of the government in favor of direct action, but in practice a variety of ideological and personal disputes between the followers of Moscow and Peking seriously impaired the ability of the extreme left to undertake a program of any kind. Nevertheless, a rash of small-scale terrorist incidents and publication of "secret communist plans," allegedly confiscated from returning

East European travelers,[31] led to new demands for a government crackdown on subversive groups.

In June, for the first time, conservative spokesmen and various newspaper and magazine articles began openly to call for a military takeover. In the 7 June issue of the weekly magazine *La Calle,* an editorial called on the armed forces "to be aware that the communists are at war with democracy . . . . We remind the armed forces of their constitutional obligation."[32] The next issue warned the military that "the hour for institutional action is here."[33] *El Universo* of Guayaquil began running an almost daily series of major editorials predicting an imminent communist attempt to take over the government and denouncing Arosemena's failure to take action. In a column entitled "Which dictatorship do you prefer? " its chief political writer argued, "There are two alternatives . . . either appeal to the armed forces to comply with their historic mission to give a new direction to the country or convert Congress to a national assembly to elect a new president."[34] Choosing the first alternative, the 3 July editorial warned, "If Ecuador manages to survive . . . it will be because the armed forces are complying with the duty of service to the fatherland and are no longer subject to political interests, because the armed forces have become the guardians of the national interest."[35] A Conservative party statement denounced communist attacks on the armed forces as "treason to the fatherland" and declared that "the Conservative party stands ready to realize a joint action with the armed forces to save the country from communism"[36] The Confederation of Ecuadorian Workers countered with a threat to meet any attempted coup with a nationwide general strike, and the PSR, URJE, and student groups promised to fight any military takeover in the streets.

The night of 10 July, buoyed by the recent addition of Colonel Gándara to their ranks, the leaders of Nuevo Orden Nacional decided that, despite their minority position among active-duty officers, the general discontent in the armed forces was sufficently strong that a revolt against the government would receive the support of those officers still not committed to the movement. The date of the coup was set for 18 July. Colonel Gándara was formally slated to become the new president with General Aulestia as his minister of defense. The existing high command was to be retired, since it was thought to be too closely associated with Arosemena. Ironically, that same night the commanders of the three services were attending a state banquet given by the president for the visiting president of Grace Lines, with the Quito diplomatic community in attendance.[37] Arosemena arrived late in an advanced state of intoxication and, after the first course had been served, arose to give an impromptu speech in which he sharply attacked the U.S. government for exploiting Latin America and, particularly, Ecuador.[38] When the American ambassador attempted to defend U.S. policies, Arosemena indicated his displeasure by turning his back and abruptly walking out.[39] Immediately after the dinner's sudden end, Army Commander Cabrera, Air Commander Freile, and Navy Commander Castro met in the home of the vice-president and agreed that something had to be done, despite some hesitation by Castro and Cabrera. After a brief discussion of various alternatives (including elevation of the vice-president, convocation of Congress, or imposition of a military government), the meeting concluded with an agreement to consult a general assembly of all the officers who could reach Quito by the next morning.[40]

At 9:00 A.M., 11 July, in the Ministry of Defense, several hundred officers listened as Colonel Cabrera explained in detail what had occurred the night before. Naval Commander Castro, presiding over the session, then called on Colonel Gándara, who spoke in favor of an immediate military takeover, arguing that, from his experience as functional representative of the armed forces in the Senate, nothing positive could be expected from Congress and that the politicians there would only exploit the situation for their personal and political gain.[41] Starting with Colonel Freile, one by one the senior officers present denounced the drunken behavior of the president and stressed the need for action against the communist threat. All called for an immediate takeover by the three service commanders, warning that, if the commanders hesitated, lower-ranking officers would not.[42] No one stood up to defend Arosemena or oppose the creation of a military government. News of the high command's decision to take over was quickly communicated to all military garrisons, who responded immediately with declarations of support, the first being that of the El Oro division, whose commander thought he was supporting the coup of the Nuevo Orden Nacional.[43]

At noon, the military's decision was officially announced to the nation, and troops were dispatched to seize the Presidential Palace. A momentary delay caused by an exchange of gunfire with leftist youths outside the Palace[44] was followed by a longer delay when President Arosemena, brandishing his pistol, barricaded himself in his apartment and refused to resign.[45] Eventually disarmed by an aide, Arosemena was quickly deported to Panama, where he was joined by the vice-president, who was arrested when he tried to convene an emergency session of Congress.

Among the principal military participants in the overthrow of Arosemena, the primary and nearly universal complaints were the scandals created by the president's excessive drinking and the feeling that the government was condoning by inaction, if not covertly encouraging, the upsurge in pro-Castro or "communist" activities. Many officers also cited civilian appeals for military action to depose Arosemena. An equal number of officers mentioned the constitutional question, although some of these were in fact questioning the government's legitimacy. Finally, a smaller number complained that the president's constant drinking left the government with no real leadership, especially in the area of social, economic, and administrative reform.

In terms of our initial hypotheses, the 1963 coup involved a different constellation of antecedent crisis conditions than that which led to the

Table 5.1 Factors Entering into
Military Decisions: 1963

| Explanations | Cited | Most stressed |
|---|---|---|
| President's excessive drinking | 33 (94%) | 18 (51%) |
| International repercussions | 4 (11%) | 0 |
| Communist threat | 31 (86%) | 12 (34%) |
| Public pressures for intervention | 14 (40%) | 0 |
| Constitutional considerations (10+, 4−) | 14 (40%) | 0 |
| Socioeconomic crisis—*desgobierno* | 7 (20%) | 3 ( 9%) |
| Personal ties/antipathies to the president | 7 (20%) | 1 ( 3%) |
| Arosemena's antimilitary attitudes | 4 (11%) | 0 |
| Public disorders | 3 ( 9%) | 0 |
| American or oligarchical reaction | 3 ( 9%) | 1 ( 3%) |
| | N = 35 | |

overthrow of Velasco in 1961. The president's personal behavior is, perhaps, the most obvious difference in the two situations, but, as an essentially unpredictable variable, this is also the least interesting theoretically. Moreover, to the extent that Arosemena's drinking became the focus for other kinds of discontents, its significance is probably overrated in the military self-explanations. Aside from that factor, as Martin Needler has observed, the 1963 coup was quite similar to the wave of conservative military coups throughout Latin America in the early 1960s, in which the fear of communism and threats to the military's institutional interests played a major role.[46] Although the latter was not stressed in the self-explanations of military coup decisions in 1963, it is, nevertheless, clear that military budget restraints, the handling of the promotions bill, and the antimilitary attitudes of Arosemena's radical supporters gave ample cause for institutional resentment.[47] If we include the complaints against the *desgobierno* of the Arosemena administration, the important antecedent political outcomes were, in 1963, primarily in the area of government policy. In contrast, the major complaints in 1961 centered on the short-term consequences of hostility toward Velasco, rather than on any particular policies. In that sense, the 1963 coup was based more on the military "push" than on the "pull" of an unstable civilian political arena—the reverse of the 1961 situation. Recast in terms of the types of decision criteria employed in military coups, the debate between explanations of military intervention stressing the military "push" or alternatively the "pull" of civilian instability[48] is unresolvable, since both have a valid empirical basis, each in different historical contexts. Both sides are incorrect, however, in trying to generalize a fixed rather than a variable mix in the types of events leading to military intervention.

Moreover, even in 1963, there was a substantial civilian pull in the form of direct appeals for military action that were far more explicit than in any of the other three crises studied.[49] Not surprisingly, opposition from the traditional elites was particularly intense. In the month preceding the coup, every *El*

*Universo* editorial dealing with the government was critical, while editorial reaction to the coup was enthusiastic. In the six weeks prior to the coup, only three out of fifteen relevant *El Comercio* editorials offered positive comments on the Arosemena government, and, after an initial expression of regret that it had not been possible to resolve the problem constitutionally, *El Comercio* also endorsed the junta, based on its promise to undertake a constructive program of socioeconomic reform. Public disorders were relatively minor and not an important factor in coup decisions, except in the sense that the threats of mass mobilization in behalf of the government lacked credibility, given the visible indifference of the lower classes to the Arosemena administration. After the imposition of martial law, leaders of the CTE and other groups that had promised to fight the coup quickly went into hiding. Except for a small demonstration by students in Quito and another in Guayaquil by followers of the CFP mayor, Asaad Bucaram, the public reception of the junta was entirely favorable. According to one of the more moderate political columnists, "Because of the circumstances surrounding and provoking the coup d'état, we can affirm that the immense majority of Ecuadorians accepted this as the only possible solution."[50] Finally, it should be noted that military self-explanations do not support the assertion that the coup was connected to Velasco's announcement of his intention to return for the 1964 elections.[51] Indeed, in none of the interviews were the 1964 elections even mentioned as a factor in the decision to either overthrow Arosemena or install a military government.

## *chapter six*

# The Fall of the Military Junta

Having made the decision to form a military government—Ecuador's first since 1938—the three service commanders moved into the Presidential Palace. Shortly thereafter they received from the students and staff of the war academy a formal request that Colonel Gándara be added to the junta in recognition of his personal prestige and intellectual merits.[1] Recognizing, in addition, that Gándara had actively worked for a coup and that he, more than they, was prepared to get on with the business of proclaiming and organizing the new government, the commanders accepted the request.[2] The expanded junta then decided to refuse similar requests on behalf of the Conservative favorite Colonel Naranjo, vacationing General Staff Chief Arrata, and Subsecretary of Defense Morochz. Arrata and the few remaining Arosemena sympathizers in the military were forcibly retired. Naranjo and Morochz had to be content with the Ministries of Defense and Public Works; Colonel Luis Mora Bowen, commander of the strategic first zone and brother of a prominent Liberal politician, became minister of government. The remaining positions in the cabinet were filled with political independents, except for the Ministry of the Economy, which went to a Conservative from Guayaquil.

Despite the generalized desire for institutional unity that led to adoption of the junta form of government, the junta was in fact composed of four officers of rather dissimilar temperament and political orientation. None of the four was especially prepared by training or prior experience to take on the task of running the government. Ramón Castro Jijón, the president and official spokesman of the junta and its only member from the coast,[3] had been a personal friend and frequent social companion of Arosemena, and approached the FDN brand of moderate democratic reformism. Trained in Chile and in the United States, Castro had also spent part of his military career in Western Europe, as a naval attaché. In contrast, Colonel Luis Cabrera Sevilla, a product of the central sierra town of Ambato, was a staid and somber old-line troop commander with a decidedly apolitical, if not antipolitical, orientation. Cabrera's only real experience abroad came during three years at the war academy in Chile. Marcos Gándara Enríquez, the most intellectually inclined of the four, received the bulk of his military training in Spain and Italy, where he became a specialist in hydraulic engineering. Although he shared Castro's concern for social reforms, Gándara's political views ran closer to those of the right-wing nationalist ARNE. The junior member of the junta in both years and rank was Guillermo Freile Posso, a distinguished pilot who had trained in England and in the United States, and the only one of the four who was a native of Quito. By nature something of an "operator," Freile possessed more innate political ability than the rest, tending toward a conservative authoritarian populism like that of Rojas Pinilla in Colombia or that of Pérez Jiménez in Venezuela. Despite their differing political tendencies, the members of the junta approached the problems of government from an essentially pragmatic (albeit somewhat bureaucratic) perspective, rather than from one informed by any well-defined political orientation. Nevertheless, to avoid any personal or service rivalries, the junta agreed in the beginning to require unanimous consent on all major decisions.

The military government spent its first weeks arresting "communists," purging the bureaucracy of Arosemena's supporters, and turning down requests from various political groups that had proclaimed their support and wanted important government posts for their leaders. Provincial administration was placed under the authority of the ranking military officer in each province and the municipal councils of Quito and Guayaquil were reconstituted by decree. After some *pro forma* hesitation, the junta decreed all of the promotions that had been blocked by the 1962 Congress, including their own. Private capital returned and, aided by an improvement in exports, the free market value of the sucre again approached the official rate, though the overall GNP growth rate was slightly less than it had been in the previous year.[4] The suppression of suspected communists was completed with the expulsion of leftist students and professors from Central University and the University of Guayaquil. Both universities were reorganized under a new Education Law that eliminated student participation in administrative elections and banned student political organizations such as the FEUE.

Having achieved the major goals of the July coup through the ouster of Arosemena and the decrees that outlawed communism and restructured the universities, the junta turned to the more difficult task of fulfilling the aspirations of those who saw in the military government an opportunity for implementing a variety of reforms that the Velasco and Arosemena governments had promised but had not delivered. In the words of Colonel Gándara, "The revolution of July 11 was not merely a product of immediate or circumstantial causes. A long series of defects and errors obliged the armed forces to judge the national reality and, consequently, to assume not only the responsibility to end the chaos and rectify mistaken paths, but also the responsibility to promote a new socioeconomic structure that would permit the State to comply with its function of serving the common interests of its citizens, thus laying the foundation for a true democracy."[5] In September of 1963, a modus vivendi with the United States on a de facto fishing limit of twelve miles quickly unclogged international aid channels, and the military government began announcing a series of development projects financed by foreign loans. In October the junta officially adopted the ten-year General Development Plan drawn up by the National Planning Board and brought that agency under the authority of the president, giving it responsibility for coordinating and planning economic policy.[6] With the assistance of the planning board and the United States Agency for International Development (AID) advisors, the government began to draw up a reform program, incorporating several measures proposed but never implemented by the previous government. In February the corporate income tax established by Arosemena was supplemented by a decree establishing a personal income tax and tightening other tax collection procedures.

In July, to celebrate its first anniversary, the junta issued the long-awaited Agrarian Reform Law. The immediate aim of the decree was the abolition of the semifeudal *huasipungo* system, in which a peasant received a small plot of land for his house and family garden in exchange for four or five days' labor on the landowner's fields. The decree also set maximum limits on the size of landholdings, established an agricultural minimum wage at more than twice the prevalent sierra rate, and provided for the gradual elimination of all land tenure forms except free wage labor and individual ownership.[7] Compensation was to be in the form of fifteen- to thirty-year bonds, bearing from 4 to 6 percent interest, depending on the conditions of expropriation. Landowner reaction (especially in the sierra) was predictably hostile,[8] but the liberal press and the urban middle-class public overwhelmingly approved.

Despite squabbles with political leaders over the lack of a concrete plan for returning to constitutional government and the necessity of obtaining prior approval for political gatherings, the junta's first year in office was clearly a popular success. Nevertheless, in a first-anniversary meeting of the junta, the high command, and the general staff, Generals Cabrera and Gándara expressed their belief that the junta should stick to its initial promise to limit itself to a maximum of two years in power. Buoyed by the public's favorable reaction to the improving economy and to the progressive, technocratic orientation of the government, all but two of the forty-odd officers disagreed. Most argued that the junta should remain until its reforms were firmly established, even if this required another four to six years in office.[9]

Shortly thereafter, when it announced its intention to decree a new constitution (which included a prohibition against presidential re-election), the junta began to encounter its first real political resistance. Despite support for the no re-election thesis from the Liberal and Conservative parties, *velasquistas* and the followers of Ponce Enríquez expressed their resentment by strongly attacking the government's subsequent decree, which, as part of its continuing tax reform program, gave financial control of several Guayaquil autonomous agencies to the government.[10] The Guayaquil economic elite, unhappy over the new income tax laws, joined with the various functionaries of the agencies involved to attack the "all-absorbing centralism" and *serrano* bias of the government. When a committee of economic notables came to announce to the junta members assembled in Guayaquil their rejection of a compromise settlement that had been worked out between the agencies and the government, the first impulse of the outraged junta was to arrest the whole *Comité de Fuerzas Vivas* and send them to the Galápagos Islands. However, the junta changed its mind before the prisoners actually arrived in the Galápagos, and all were subsequently released.[11] The Galápagos incident was the first case of what became a characteristic vacillation by the junta between its adherence to reformist principles and its desire to be an accepted and "democratic" dictatorship—a vacillation that later came to cost the junta dearly in both popular and military support.

Meanwhile the plural executive proved to be an encumbrance. Having already replaced General Naranjo as minister of defense because he was excessively close to the conservatives, the junta also began to have problems with Colonel Freile, who displayed a troublesome penchant for acting without consultation and who, on three occasions, provoked the resignation of cabinet officers by criticizing them in public speeches. The government's façade of unity and somber dignity was further shaken by petty squabbles over equal protocol privileges for all four members, which led to rejection of an invitation to visit the United States and a ludicrous episode in which the junta returned to the French government the decorations presented to its members during President De-Gaulle's trip to South America.[12]

Still, the junta could point with pride to a 1964 gross national product increase of nearly 8 percent (due, for the most part, to a record year for banana exports),[13] and on 1 January 1965, Rear Admiral Castro announced a complicated eight-stage plan for the return to constitutional government. Reflecting the bureaucratic mentality of its authors, the plan called for reform of the constitution by executive decree, municipal and provincial elections followed by presidential elections in June 1967, and, three months later, transmission of power to the new president. Political opposition from all sides to the proposed plan was so intense that two months later the junta announced a revised version, which called for a plebescite on the reformed constitution concurrently with presidential elections in November 1966.[14] Not placated, the political sector began to solidify around the demand for immediate installation of a civilian to convoke a Constituent Assembly, which would elect an interim president and write a new constitution. The junta, on the other hand, was dead set against an assembly that might become a forum for its political enemies and insisted on maintaining control over the constitution writing in order to force inclusion of a clause prohibiting re-election of ex-Presidents Velasco, Arosemena, or Ponce.[15]

In April 1965, faced with a rapidly growing budget—already swollen by public works projects and an expanding bureaucracy—the junta announced plans for a general rise in import tariffs, which, despite the various tax reforms, still accounted for nearly half of the central government's revenues. The announcement drew sharp protests from Quito and Guayaquil merchants through their respective Chambers of Commerce. Pointing to the generous tax and tariff privileges granted industrialists under the January Industrial Development Law, the merchants also flatly rejected a revised version offered by the government and organized a general strike in Guayaquil, closing down the city and provoking a cabinet crisis.[16] Despite offers from the Concentration of Popular Forces and organizations from lower-class *barrios* to provide shock troops for a confrontation with the merchants, members of the junta refused to even consider the idea of radicalizing the conflict.[17] After naming a new cabinet, the junta dispatched the four ministers from Guayaquil to try new negotiations with the Guayaquil Chamber. Following the failure of a negotiated solution and renewal of the strike, the junta and the merchants finally reached an accord on the basis of wholesale concessions by the government.

As if to defy the increasingly popular joke that this was not a dictatorship (*dictadura*), but a powder puff government (*dictablanda*), Colonel Freile launched a vitriolic attack on the critics of the regime and challenged the opposition parties to produce an antigovernment demonstration on its second anniversary. Several hundred protestors turned out to meet Freile's dare despite the ban on demonstrations. The list of those arrested included most of the nation's political leaders, who managed during their involuntary togetherness in the Penal García Moreno to merge the competing opposition factions into a single, loosely knit *Junta Constitucionalista.*[18] The temporary deportation to Paraguay of fifteen of their number led to new protests and the closing of the Quito daily *El Tiempo* for "systematically distorting the truth and making slanderous and deliberately deceptive accusations injurious to the dignity and authority of the government."[19] In August 1965, the major parties jointly advanced a plan calling on the junta to name a civilian as interim president in September who, with an all-party cabinet, would preside over Constituent Assembly elections. Despite the accompanying pledge to exclude the extreme left, protect the armed forces, and maintain the reform programs and General Development Plan, the proposal was rejected by the junta.[20]

At this point, while the younger officers in the provincial garrisons argued for a tougher line against the economic oligarchy, the feeling began to grow within the higher ranks that the time had come for the junta to step down. Three of the five general staff department heads—including the chief of intelligence for the armed forces, Colonel Jaime García Naranjo—began collaborating with the political opposition. Working with ex-President Camilo Ponce, García began sounding out other officers who might be in favor of an early return to civilian government. In November 1965, the junta was forced to meet a more immediate challenge from within, and, finally, moved to depose Colonel Freile, who had become increasingly active in his efforts to become its one-man successor. An attempt by Freile to organize air force support for the ouster of the air force commander without consultation with the military junta led to his immediate removal and arrest.[21] Slipping out of house arrest to hold a press conference, Freile counterattacked by attributing his arrest to his opposition to secret junta plans to maintain itself in power for two more years.[22] Even as the junta reaffirmed its commitment to step down the following September, economic bad news competed with renewed student disorders for public attention. At the end of the year, economic growth was estimated at only 3 percent, leaving per capita income virtually unchanged. Following suppression of an antigovernment demonstration on the anniversary of the Rio Protocol, student strikes and clashes with police became an almost daily occurrence and resulted in several deaths. In a February joint meeting of the general staff and the high command, Chief of Staff General Antonio Rivas—the highest-ranking officer outside of the junta—unexpectedly delivered a blistering analysis of the political situation, emphasizing his belief that the increasing unpopularity of the military regime was endangering the institutional prestige of the entire armed forces. Despite backing from members of the general staff who were working with the opposition, Rivas failed to convince the air force or naval commanders, or the head of army intelligence, who countered with a strong defense of the junta's performance and of its popular support.[23] Rivas was immediately forced into retirement and was replaced by General Telmo Vargas, who had recently returned from a diplomatic assignment abroad.

Buoyed by the signs of disunity within military ranks, the opposition parties finally reached a compromise agreement, designating a political independent, Guayaquil economist Clemente Yerovi, as their candidate to replace the junta until an elected assembly could choose the next president. Constitutionalist fronts were then established in all major cities to coordinate the political campaign with the efforts of its economic, student, and military supporters.[24] Simultaneously, the tariff war with the Guayaquil merchants was resumed when the government announced new export and import taxes and other import restrictions in order to protect dwindling foreign reserves and to provide revenue to reduce the growing budget deficit. After negotiations failed (amid angry charges that the junta was reneging on the accords of the previous year), the Guayaquil Chamber of Commerce, seconded by the coastal Chambers of Agriculture and Industry and supported by labor and student groups, began another general strike, which effectively halted all economic activity in the port city.[25] Four days later the strike became nationwide with the participation of the Commerce Chambers of Quito and Cuenca.

The same day, in the accompanying student disorders, Central University students seized and burned an American Army truck on loan to the military geographic institute, which was carrying several months' worth of aerial photo-mapping films. Indignant, General Vargas and Army Commander Aguinaga asked permission for a punitive attack on the university residence hall, which was alleged, in intelligence reports being circulated by Colonel García, to be the site of a terrorist arsenal.[26] With the pressure mounting, the government began to lose control. Despite the objections of General Cabrera and the minister of defense, Gándara and Castro signed the attack order. Instead of being carried out as planned—at noon when only the dormitories would normally be occupied—the troops, which included raw conscripts, arrived to launch a frontal assault just at 5:00, as students were coming to evening classes. What was supposed to be a surgical strike quickly degenerated into a confused melee in which one student and one soldier were killed. Several more were wounded (including the daughter of an army lieutenant colonel), while mass arrests of students and professors netted at least one high-ranking government official. News of the attack sparked a general public protest, redoubled student rioting across the country, and evoked sharp criticism from even progovernment newspapers. *El Comercio,* which had steadfastly defended the junta's return program, concluded that the Central University attack made the resignation of the junta "the only solution capable of easing the terrible unrest and leading to a return to constitutionality."[27]

Military supporters of the junta were completely demoralized by the heavy toll of dead and wounded in the disorders.[28] In a meeting with the service commanders and general staff that was devoted to sharp criticism of the junta, Castro, Cabrera, and Gándara announced their decision to accept the opposition demands and turn power over to a civilian interim president within eight to ten days rather than be the cause of further bloodshed.[29] Delegations composed of members of the three services were then sent to Guayaquil and to the southern garrisons to explain the junta's decision. Meanwhile, General Coba tried to organize support for his argument that the interim government should be headed by a military man to prevent political retaliations against the armed forces,[30] but an atmosphere of mutual suspicion completely undermined interpersonal trust within the higher ranks.[31] At dawn the next morning, the junta found itself faced, not only with the merchants' strike and student protests, but with a nationwide transportation strike as well. When General Aguinaga reported that military units stationed in Quito were refusing to go into the streets to oppose the students and strikers, General Gándara hastily wrote a resignation proclamation for the junta, turning power over to General Staff Chief Vargas.[32] Vargas communicated the decision to the rest of the military and to the press, and announced that the next day there would be an assembly of economic, cultural, and political leaders to select a new president. In a carefully orchestrated gathering, the opposition parties, in accordance with their prior agreement, backed Dr. Yerovi, who was duly nominated by ex-Presidents Plaza and Ponce and elected by acclamation. Speaking for the military, General Vargas accepted the decision of the assembly without reservation, leaving a carte blanche for the new government, which was officially inaugurated the next day.[33] Shortly thereafter, the members of the junta, minister of defense, chief of staff, commanding generals, and officers who had held civilian positions were officially retired, bringing to an end Ecuador's longest experiment in military rule in fifty years.[34]

The majority of the principal military participants in the crisis leading to the fall of the military junta argued, basically, that the junta had tried to stay in power too long, and had dealt poorly with the socioeconomic crisis; that public disillusionment with the junta and increasingly serious public disorders had resulted in a sharp loss of prestige for the entire armed forces. Defenders and

Table 6.1  Factors Entering into
Military Decisions: 1966

| Explanations | Cited | Most stressed |
|---|---|---|
| Weak reform effort—*la dictablanda* | 12 (54%) | 7 (32%) |
| Damage to military prestige | 13 (59%) | 5 (23%) |
| Adverse public opinion | 13 (59%) | 4 (18%) |
| Opposition of oligarchy, politicians, and military dissenters | 11 (50%) | 4 (18%) |
| Public disorders—Central University attack | 11 (50%) | 0 |
| Personal ties/antipathies to the junta | 8 (36%) | 2 ( 9%) |
| Antidictatorship, proconstitution | 3 (14%) | 0 |
| | N = 22 | |

some opponents of the junta also pointed to the efforts of the Guayaquil economic elite and the professional politicians as an explanation of the junta's demise. Again, personal ties played a role, generally in favor of the junta.

In terms of the coup-provoking outcomes postulated in the initial hypotheses, the 1966 crisis most closely resembles the overthrow of Velasco in 1961, in that the most important factors were those related to the institutional consequences—specifically the damage done to military prestige—of supporting the government in the face of a high level of civilian opposition. Using the index for measuring public disorders developed in chapter 4, the antigovernment riots and protests of 1966 exceeded the 1961 disorders in frequency and intensity by a considerable margin, despite the smaller number of deaths that occurred in 1966. On the other hand, the opposition to the junta came primarily from university students and elite groups, rather than from urban labor as it had in 1961. Even the principal civilian opposition leader has privately affirmed that this "was not a popularly based movement."[35] As measured in *El Universo* editorial opinion, the Guayaquil elite's opposition to the junta was even stronger than its opposition to Arosemena. In the month prior to the coup, the junta received negative ratings in a total of thirty-three editorials dealing with its performance and its policies, as opposed to only fourteen negative editorials published about the Arosemena government the month before the 1963 coup. On the other hand, the junta received favorable ratings in thirteen of thirty-four *El Comercio* editorials in the six weeks prior to the coup. Thus it appears that sierra middle-class opinion was not extremely hostile to the junta—or at least not until the attack on Central University. The communist threat played no role in the 1966 coup. And, despite the junta's desire to promote fresh political leadership by banning presidential re-election, the electoral factor was not cited as a reason for supporting or opposing the coup.

Nevertheless, while these chapters illustrate the complex and multifaceted nature of the coup d'état process, these first attempts to test the initial hypotheses raise more questions than they answer. How do these events relate to the decisions of individual officers to support or oppose the overthrow of the government? Given the same set of events, why are some officers willing to support the government and others not? Why do military officers care about these political outcomes and not about others? How have military attitudes toward their political role changed in response to these events? How have these changing attitudes altered the way political events are judged? How is this pattern of crises related to larger trends in the economic and political context of civil-military interaction? Having established the necessary historical base, each of these questions may now be confronted directly.

# part three

# Decision Criteria for Military Coups in Ecuador

# chapter seven

# Individual Decisions to Support or Oppose a Coup d'Etat

As indicated earlier, in the discussion of the coup d'état as a political process, it is analytically useful to conceive of the military as monitoring the domestic political scene to determine whether or not the overall situation of the government has reached a "crisis point" requiring military intervention. The initial hypotheses suggested that Latin American military officers respond primarily to the following situational criteria in making that decision:

1. Public opinion hostile to the government.
2. Large-scale public disorders.
3. The officer's private political opinions, as indicated by those of the group or class with which he identifies.
4. Government attentiveness to institutional interests.
5. The level of perceived communist threat.
6. The proximity of a threatening election.

The object of the present chapter is to test, directly and systematically, this set of working hypotheses—a test based on the experience of military officers participating in each of the coups described in the previous chapters.

In order to test the accuracy and completeness of this list of coup decision criteria, ninety-four interviews were conducted with seventy-two military officers, all of whom were retired at the time of the interview.[1] The sample of officers interviewed was selective rather than random,[2] with priority given to the key officers favoring and opposing the coup, to higher-ranking officers, and to the army rather than to the other services. The number of officers interviewed probably represents 70 to 80 percent of those who played key roles in each crisis and 20 to 25 percent of all officers with the rank of lieutenant colonel or above

Table 7.1  Characteristics of the Interview Sample

| Branch of service | | Rank at time of coup* | | Participants per crisis* | |
|---|---|---|---|---|---|
| Army | 58 | General | 14 | 1954 | 19 |
| Navy | 7 | Colonel | 54 | 1961 | 25 |
| Air force | 7 | Lieutenant colonel | 26 | 1963 | 35 |
| | | Major | 7 | 1966 | 23 |
| | | Captain | 1 | | |

*Including multiple interviews with same respondent.

who were in the country at the time of the coup. While for the purposes of statistical analysis a larger, random sample and a more rigid questionnaire[3] would have been desirable, this is to date the largest systematically interviewed research sample of military officers in any Third World country.

The first check on the initial hypotheses is derived from the responses of the participants in each crisis to an open probe, which asked what factors affected their decision to take a position for or against the government. Considering the responses for all four crises, the data clearly indicate that there is no single criterion, but rather a multiplicity of decision criteria used in coup decisions. Only "personal ties and antagonisms" appears as a relatively constant item in all four cases, although public opinion was consistently mentioned in the three successful coups. As hypothesized, public disorders were cited by a large proportion of the sample on two occasions, while concern for the institutional

Table 7.2  Factors Entering Coup Decisions of Individual Officers
(Uncued, open-ended explanations of four civil-military crises)

| Factors | 1954 | 1961 | 1963 | 1966 |
|---|---|---|---|---|
| Constitutionality of government | 68% (47%) | 92% (52%) | 40% ( 0%) | 14% ( 0%) |
| Public disorders | 0% ( 0%) | 56% (16%) | 9% ( 0%) | 49% ( 0%) |
| Public hostility to government | 0% ( 0%) | 48% ( 0%) | 40% ( 0%) | 59% (18%) |
| Threat of communism | 0% ( 0%) | 0% ( 0%) | 86% (34%) | 0% ( 0%) |
| Institutional interests | 42% (11%) | 8% ( 4%) | 11% ( 0%) | 59% (23%) |
| President's personal behavior | 5% ( 0%) | 4% ( 0%) | 94% (51%) | 0% ( 0%) |
| Socioeconomic problems | 5% ( 0%) | 16% ( 0%) | 20% ( 9%) | 54% (32%) |
| Personal ties/antagonisms | 68% (42%) | 40% (12%) | 20% ( 3%) | 36% ( 9%) |
| Unfounded opposition | 89% ( 0%) | 36% (16%) | 9% ( 3%) | 49% (18%) |
| Miscellaneous | 0% ( 0%) | 8% ( 0%) | 11% ( 0%) | 9% ( 0%) |
| | N = 19 | N = 25 | N = 35 | N = 22 |

NOTE: Figures indicate the percentage of each sample citing that factor, with multiple responses permitted. The figures in parentheses indicate the percentage of each sample stressing that factor as the most important element in that coup.

interests of the military figured prominently in the explanations of two of the four crises. Concern with the threat of communism was significant in only one crisis, although it was cited by nearly all of the 1963 respondents. Without any major distortion, the "unfounded opposition" category—citing such factors as the efforts of the political opposition or "evil oligarchs" to overthrow the government—can be interpreted as a progovernment judgment, implicitly denying the existence of valid substantive complaints about government performance.

Given this interpretation, a comparison of the list of decision categories drawn from the previous literature and those revealed in these interviews discloses a number of inconsistencies. Neither the emphasis on personal ties nor the question of constitutionality was foreseen in the initial hypotheses. Likewise, the hypotheses do not account for the complaints against the president's personal behavior in 1963 or against the socioeconomic policies of the *dictablanda*. Conversely, in the self-explanations of coup decisions, there is no mention of either threatening elections or of officers' personal political opinions. These responses suggest that the initial hypotheses be revised to incorporate the personal interest and constitutionality criteria. Nevertheless, the self-explanations by themselves do not constitute a compelling argument for the validity of those hypotheses. It remains to be demonstrated that there is, in fact, a relationship between the progovernment or procoup attitudes of individual officers and the appraisal by each officer of government performance in terms of these decision criteria.

If the list of decision criteria posited in the revised hypotheses is to be accepted as being reasonably complete and accurate, then those officers who rated the government negatively on these criteria would be expected to have taken significantly different positions in the coup situation from those officers who considered that the situation was, on balance, satisfactory in these areas. In other words, if the affective components of military attitudes toward the government (that is, what the military officer cares about), have been correctly identified, then knowing the cognitive components of those attitudes should enable one to predict which officers supported and which officers opposed the coup. Accordingly, each officer was specifically asked about his perceptions of the state of public opinion, of public disorders, of government attentiveness to institutional interests of the armed forces, and of the government's handling of the communist threat. The responses were coded on a three-position scale as being positive, neutral, or negative ratings on each criterion. Consulting the open-ended section of the questionnaire for information on how each respondent rated the constitutionality of the government's behavior and on his personal loyalties or antipathies toward the government, an index of perceived government performance can be constructed, based on the sum of the six individual performance scores.[4] This index is, in effect, a summary measure of individual perceptions of the government's success or failure in avoiding those political outcomes that are hypothesized to contribute to perceptions of "a national crisis."

Using the summary index of perceived government performance, there are significant differences in the proportions of pro- and antigovernment officers across the various performance categories in all four of the coup samples. In each case, officers who rated government performance negatively on these six issues favored the coup, while those who rated government performance positively opposed the coup, with only a small overlap among those whose ratings of the government were, on balance, mixed, or only slightly negative. According to the

Table 7.3 Coup Attitudes and
Summary Ratings of Government Performance

| | Performance category | | Performance ratings | |
|---|---|---|---|---|
| Position on coup | $\leqslant -1$ | $\geqslant 0$ | Range | Mean |
| 1954 Unsuccessful coup, N = 17 | | | | |
| Procoup | 5 | 0 | −3, −1 | −1.8 |
| Progovernment | 0 | 12 | 0, +4 | +2.4 |
| | | p = .0002 | | |
| 1961 Successful coup, N = 18 | | | | |
| Procoup | 12 | 0 | −5, −1 | −2.8 |
| Progovernment | 2 | 4 | −2, +1 | −0.2 |
| | | p = .005 | | |
| 1963 Successful coup, N = 28 | | | | |
| Procoup | 23 | 1 | −4, +1 | −3.0 |
| Progovernment | 1 | 3 | −2, +3 | +0.5 |
| | | p = .005 | | |
| 1966 Successful coup, N = 19 | | | | |
| Procoup | 12 | 0 | −4, −1 | −3.1 |
| Progovernment | 2 | 5 | −2, +3 | +0.3 |
| | | p = .002 | | |

NOTE: Officers retired at the time of the crisis are excluded here and in all subsequent tables.

Fisher Exact Test, it is unlikely that the observed differences could have occurred by chance.[5] Looking at the same data from a slightly different perspective, the mean ratings of government performance in the four cases analyzed ranges from -1.8 to -3.1 among those who favored the overthrow of the government, as opposed to mean ratings ranging from -0.2 to +2.4 among those who opposed the coups.

Rating each officer's attitude toward the coup, at the moment he chose sides, on a five-point scale ranging from strongly supportive to strongly opposed,[6] it can also be shown that, in each of the coups, there is a strong relationship between how negatively or positively each officer appraised government performance and the position he took in that coup. All four cases conform to the prediction that those officers who were most critical or favorable in their perceptions of government performance on these six issues also took the most ardent stances for or against the coup in question. With the exception of four respondents in the 1961 sample, the distribution of cases also confirms the expectation that less strongly critical or less strongly positive summary evaluations of the government will be associated with less extreme positions in the coup. Using Kendall's Tau as a measure of rank order correlation, the results

Table 7.4 Officers' Attitudes toward the Coup (Five Position Scale)
and Summary Ratings of Government Performance on
Public Opinion, Public Disorders, Military Institutional Interests,
Communist Threat, Constitutionality, and Personal Interests

| Interview Group | Number of officers | Kendall's Tau | Significance level | Pearson r | Pearson $r^2$ |
|---|---|---|---|---|---|
| 1954 | 18 | .79 | .001 | .91 | 83% |
| 1961 | 20 | .57 | .001 | .73 | 53% |
| 1963 | 29 | .83 | .001 | .85 | 73% |
| 1966 | 19 | .86 | .001 | .92 | 85% |

show a consistent pattern of strong association. Using the Pearson correlation coefficient for interval scale data[7] again results in high positive correlations. The attractive feature of the latter measure is that the square of the correlation coefficient can be interpreted as the percentage of the total variance in one variable, which is accounted for by the variations in the other. Thus, except for the 1961 sample, between 70 and 85 percent of the variance in positions taken by the respondents for or against the government can be explained by the variations in the responses of these officers to the government performance questions comprising the summary index.

The results of the analysis thus far constitute strong evidence in support of the revised set of decision criteria hypotheses. Regardless of the type of test utilized, the consistently strong correlations suggest that public opinion toward the government, public disorders, the communist threat, and the military's institutional interests, as well as the constitutionality of the government and their personal ties to it, are in fact issues that matter to most officers when they decide to support or oppose the government in a coup d'état. Knowing how individual officers perceived the performance of the government in terms of these six issues enables a reasonable prediction to be made of the attitudes of these officers toward the coup d'état. The unexplained variance in coup attitudes, which reaches 47 percent in the 1961 coup, can be attributed either to faulty measurement of these variables (in particular, the equal weighting of each issue in the index), or to the omission of other, significant, coup decision criteria.

Before proceeding to the question of the relative salience of these issues, it must be determined whether further revisions are needed in the list of decision criteria. The logic of the test is relatively straightforward. If significant variables have been omitted, then these should explain part of the residual variance in coup positions not accounted for by the six-issue index of government performance. To be considered significant elements of the coup decision, the additional variables should produce increased accuracy in the prediction of coup attitudes.[8]

In the initial hypotheses, it was postulated that military officers are subject to more or less the same determinants of political attitudes as are civilians, and that the prevailing political orientation of the officer corps would influence its decision to support or overthrow a given government. In considering the personal political orientations of individual officers as an additional determinant of their behavior in the various coups, the first point to be noted is that, except for the condemnation of the president's personal behavior in 1963, nothing readily interpretable as "personal political views" appeared in the self-explanations of coup decisions discussed at the beginning of this chapter. Still, this might only indicate a reluctance to reveal partisan motives, so, as a check, each officer was asked—as part of a series of background questions—if he had any personal preferences among the various parties and political groups. Somewhat unexpectedly since all of the respondents were legally free to participate in partisan politics, over 85 percent replied "No," and many did so rather emphatically. The remaining 15 percent were distributed fairly evenly among the Liberal, Conservative, and several minor parties. Approximately one quarter of the sample, while declining to name any particular party, did offer a general characterization of their political views, generally along left-right lines. These officers were then classified with the party identifiers as partisans of the left, center-left, center-right, or right,[9] and this crude measure of political orientation was tested as a possible explanation of the residual variance in coup attitudes among those officers for whom such information was available. Although the simple correlation is relatively high in one of the four coups,[10] the number of observations for that case is insignificant. Personal political

Table 7.5 Personal Political Orientation
and Attitudes toward the Overthrow of the Government

|  | 1954 | 1961 | 1963 | 1966 |
|---|---|---|---|---|
| Pearson correlation | +.175 | +.612 | −.260 | −.172 |
| Variance explained ($r^2$) | 3.1% | 37.2% | 6.8% | 3.0% |
| Increase in multiple $r^2$ over perceived performance index alone | .7% | 18.6% | 1.1% | 3.0% |
| Number of officers | 10 | 4 | 9 | 6 |

orientation, then, seems not to be a separate coup decision criterion, although the possibility remains to be explored that there were systematic biases in the way liberals, leftists, conservatives, or moderates rated the government's performance in the other six areas, or in the way they weighted these criteria in their coup decisions.

Another possible omission was suggested by the criticism of the Arosemena government in 1963 and the military junta in 1966 for having failed to take strong action to reform the country's archaic and unjust social and economic structures. Again, in only one of the coups does the evaluation of the government's reform policies seem to have had a significant impact on coup attitudes and, even in the 1966 case, the additional variance explained is small relative to

Table 7.6 Ratings of Government Performance on
Socioeconomic Reforms and Attitudes toward the Overthrow of the Government

|  | 1954 | 1961 | 1963 | 1966 |
|---|---|---|---|---|
| Pearson correlation | +.425 | −.079 | +.123 | −.243 |
| Variance explained ($r^2$) | 18.1% | 0.6% | 1.5% | 5.9% |
| Increase in multiple $r^2$ over perceived performance index alone | 1.0% | 0.0% | 0.4% | 3.4% |
| Number of officers | 17 | 18 | 28 | 18 |

the number of negative ratings of the *dictablanda*. This would seem to indicate either a specious complaint by opponents of the junta, or some intervening variable that prevented a negative evaluation of its reform policies from affecting the position of its supporters. As a check on the latter possibility, the "lack of reform" criterion was retained for the 1966 coup.[11]

The preceding analysis established that the six decision criteria comprising the summary index constitute a reasonably accurate and complete list of the situational factors that entered into the decision of these Ecuadorian officers to support or oppose a coup. Although allowances must be made for the deficiencies of the data, it is now possible to use standard multiple regression techniques to determine the relative significance of these factors in each of the four coups.[12]

As seen in part A of table 7.7, in the unsuccessful attempt to overthrow President Velasco in 1954, the perceived constitutionality of the government is by far the best single predictor of positions taken in the coup and, as indicated by the regression coefficients, also the most important factor in determining the outcome of individual coup decisions. Personal ties or antagonisms toward Velasco and his minister of defense also had a significant impact, in part by biasing attitudes toward the constitutional legitimacy of the Velasco government.[13] The quantitative evaluation of the relative significance of these two

Table 7.7  Multiple Regression of Coup Positions on
Ratings of Government Performance on Individual Decision Criteria

| Independent variables | Simple r | Increase in multiple r² | Regression coefficient |
|---|---|---|---|
| A. Dependent variable: Attitudes toward unsuccessful 1954 coup | | | |
| Constitutional issue rating | .916 | .840 | 1.625 |
| Public opinion rating | .699 | .025 | ..497 |
| Personal ties rating | .785 | .039 | .585 |
| N = 18 | Total | 90.4% (89.1%)* | |
| B. Dependent variable: Attitudes toward 1961 coup | | | |
| Constitutional issue rating | .849 | .721 | 1.996 |
| Public disorder rating | −.094 | .074 | −1.381 |
| Communist threat rating | −.219 | .044 | −1.150 |
| N = 18 | Total | 83.9% (81.7%)* | |
| C. Dependent variable: Attitudes toward 1963 coup | | | |
| Personal ties rating | .742 | .551 | .845 |
| Constitutional issue rating | .723 | .121 | .669 |
| Communist threat rating | .535 | .060 | .870 |
| Public opinion rating | .599 | .055 | 1.015 |
| N = 28 | Total | 78.7% (76.0%)* | |
| D. Dependent variable: Attitudes toward 1966 coup | | | |
| Institutional interest rating | .688 | .474 | .674 |
| Personal interests rating | .695 | .270 | .849 |
| Public opinion rating | .694 | .061 | .856 |
| Socioeconomic reform rating | .243 | .040 | −.777 |
| Communist threat rating | .504 | .043 | .755 |
| N = 18 | Total | 88.7% (85.2%)* | |

*Multiple r² corrected for sample size and number of variables.

influences is supported by the experience of several young officers in Quito who resolved the conflict between their ties to Varea and their belief in the constitutionality of the government by denying that the Quito movement, which they supported, was ever intended to overthrow the president.[14] Interestingly enough, while public opinion was not mentioned in the open-ended self-explanations, perceptions that public opinion was favorable or hostile to Velasco emerge as the third significant determinant of individual coup decisions.

In 1961, ratings of the constitutionality of the government's behavior were, again, by far the most important factor determining the positions taken by individual officers in the overthrow of Velasco. This suggests that the other decision criteria were not, in fact, independent determinants of coup positions, but, rather, that their impact was mediated through the differing appraisals of the constitutionality of the Velasco government after the vice-president's arrest. A glance at the partial correlations indicates that this is the case. Personal ties to the government or, in a few cases, to the vice-president, played a definite role in biasing interpretations of the constitutional question, as did the positive

Table 7.8 Simple and Partial Correlations
among Decision Criteria Ratings: 1961

| Variable pair | Simple $r^2$ | Partial $r^2$ controlling for: | |
|---|---|---|---|
| A. Constitutionality and coup position | .72 | Personal ties | .55 |
| | | Personal ties and institutional interests | .49 |
| B. Personal ties and coup position | .45 | Constitutionality | .11 |
| | | All other criteria | .00 |
| C. Institutional interests and constitutionality | .16 | Personal ties | .14 |
| D. Institutional interests and coup positions | .14 | Constitutionality | .00 |

responses of some officers to the salary increases and other institutional benefits supported by Velasco. The negative signs of the regression coefficients for the remaining two variables—public disorders and policy toward the communist threat—should not be construed as indicating that negative ratings on these criteria increased support for the government. Rather, those officers whose support exceeded that predicted by their rating of the constitutionality of Velasco's government were more negative than most in their ratings of government performance on these two criteria.

Even though in the self-explanations of the 1963 coup approximately the same number of officers stressed the threat of communism and President Arosemena's personal behavior (reflected here in perceptions of negative public opinion), the regression analysis indicates that the latter had a somewhat greater impact. Personal ties also played an important role in exp'aining the positions of the few officers who remained loyal to the government. The relatively small regression coefficient for the constitutional issue in 1963 reflects the anticonstitutional positions taken by nearly all of the officers subjected to cross-pressures by their belief in the constitutionality of Arosemena's government and their negative ratings of the president on one or more of the other criteria.

In the fall of the military junta, differing perceptions of public opinion played a crucial role, reflecting the opposition charges that "popular" hostility to the junta and the increasingly violent public disorders were seriously endangering the institutional prestige and security of the entire armed forces. With the military in power, personal factors played an increased role, as various officers cited personal loyalties to their fellow officers or expressed personal resentments over their treatment by the junta. The generally satisfactory ratings given to the junta's handling of the communists competed with the general disappointment over the lack of responsiveness to the "institutional needs" of the military as secondary determinants of military attitudes. Again, the negative sign for the socioeconomic reform criterion indicates that those officers whose support for the junta exceeded that predicted by their appraisal of its performance in other areas tended to be critical of the *dictablanda's* weak reform efforts.

While the simple regression coefficients add an interesting and important dimension to the explanation of the individual coups, from a theoretical perspective, the most important question is the relative salience of these criteria across the four cases—in particular, the stability or instability of their relative impact through time.[15] As indicated in table 7.9, where the situational factors identified by the various decision criteria were actually present, their impact on coup decisions was neither constant nor, in most cases, unstable. With the

Table 7.9 Standardized Regression Coefficients: Individual Coup Decision Criteria (Dependent Variable: Pro- or Antigovernment Position in Coup)

| | Beta | | | |
|---|---|---|---|---|
| Independent variables | 1954 | 1961 | 1963 | 1966 |
| Personal ties rating | .322 | – | .384 | .423 |
| Constitutional issue rating | .489 | .905 | .277 | – |
| Public opinion rating | .291 | – | .270 | .381 |
| Institutional interests rating | – | – | – | .403 |
| Communist threat rating | – | −.211 | .262 | .226 |
| Public disorders rating | – | −.254 | – | – |
| Socioeconomic reform rating | – | – | – | −.259 |
| | N=18 | N=18 | N=28 | N=18 |

exception of the three negative coefficients,[16] most of the shifts in the standardized coefficients seem closely related to the changing salience of the constitutional norm, which, after more than a decade of constitutional rule, came to be the all-inclusive issue in 1961, only to disappear as a salient issue by 1966. With the decline of constitutional guidelines for military intervention, public opinion toward the government and the institutional interests of the military became increasingly important in the coups that followed. Not unexpectedly, the increasing politicization of the military through 1966 appears to have been accompanied by a gradual rise in the influence of personal interests in the decisions of individual officers to support or oppose the overthrow of the government. Ignoring the change in sign, beginning in the early sixties, concern over the threat of communism emerges as the most stable military concern.

Keeping in mind that the salience of the various decision criteria is, in fact, changing somewhat over time, the four coup samples can be combined to derive an empirical estimate of the relative impact of each of the decision criteria for the 1948–1966 period as a whole. Given the political circumstances encountered by the Ecuadorian military during these years, the most salient factors in the decision of Ecuadorian officers to defend or oppose the government in these four crises have been their perceptions of the constitutional legitimacy of

Table 7.10  Multiple Regression of Attitudes Toward Coup on
Decision Criteria: Combined Sample (N = 84)
(Dependent Variable: Coup Position of Ecuadorian
Military Officers in 1954, 1961, 1963, and 1966)

| Independent variables:<br>Ratings of government performance | Standardized regression coefficient |
|---|---|
| Personal interests of the respondent | .370 |
| Constitutionality of government | .349 |
| Responsiveness to institutional interests | .278 |
| Public opinion toward the government | .240 |
| Suppression of the communist threat | .149 |
| Multiple $r^2$ = .81 | |

the government and the pull of their personal loyalties or antagonisms to the government or to its supporters and opponents. Perceptions of public opinion toward the government and of government responsiveness to the institutional interests of the military have also been important but secondary determinants of the coup positions of individual officers. Finally (given that the problem was of limited magnitude), government willingness to follow an actively anticommunist policy emerges as the least important factor for the period as a whole. On the other hand, the multiple regression analysis does not confirm the evidence obtained from the open-ended questionnaire items that the level of public disorders and the lack of progress toward socioeconomic reforms also entered into military coup decisions.[17]

The interpretation and significance of these findings are discussed in detail in the chapters that follow, but the evidence presented thus far clearly suggests that the decision of military officers to support or oppose a coup d'état largely reflects their appraisal of the political situation in terms of a finite set of decision criteria, no one of which is, by itself, sufficient to explain any single coup d'état. Moreover, this set of decision criteria was found to be subject, over time, to change in its internal composition and in the relative impact of its components on military behavior in political crises. In several respects these findings—based on interviews with Ecuadorian coup participants—differ significantly from those of two cross-national studies of coup antecedents, one by Mauricio Solaun and Michael Quinn, who studied 30 successful Latin American coups,[18] and the other by William R. Thompson, who analyzed 229 coups from around the globe.[19]

Whereas Solaun and Quinn's study of Latin American coups attributed little importance to the constitutionality of executive actions, the regression analysis points to the constitutional norm as a critical factor in two of the four Ecuadorian coups. Thompson's broader study simply omits this or any similar factor from his list of coup-maker grievances. If the emphasis on constitutionality in 1954 and in 1961 can be shown to be not simply a *post hoc* rationalization, then several interesting questions are raised. First, why was this norm salient to Ecuadorian officers and apparently (according to other authors) not an important element in coup decisions elsewhere? To the extent that one can adequately answer this question, to the extent that one can explain the initially high but declining salience of the constitutionality criterion, these results suggest that in certain contexts, the constitutional norm has been much more important in Latin American coups than previous studies have indicated. If so, might there be equivalent norms, perhaps favoring other types of regimes, in countries that lack a Western constitutional tradition?

Likewise, the emphasis on electoral outcomes as causes for military coups in these studies presents an obvious contrast with the Ecuadorian findings. The Argentine coup of 1962 (following Peronista electoral victories) and the 1962 Peruvian coup against the *apristas* constitute clear evidence for the existence of electoral veto coups elsewhere. Yet it is not clear whether an extension of this analysis to the Peruvian or Argentine cases would require a new decision criterion or whether perhaps these and the Ecuadorian response to the "communist threat" are special cases of a more general pattern of institutional self-defense against any group that threatens to acquire a paramilitary capability. Nevertheless, especially given the opportunities presented by Velasco's multiple presidencies, the Ecuadorian evidence does suggest that the true "veto coup" is perhaps less common in Latin America than was previously anticipated. Pending replication of this kind of study in other countries, these results do call for the exercise of considerable caution in attributing antielectoral motives to coups that fall near the end or the beginning of a presidential term.[20]

Finally, the already-noted discrepancies and the discovery that the set of decision criteria used in Ecuadorian coups did vary substantially over time raise a serious methodological question, since both of these studies base their conclusions on the average frequency of certain coup characteristics or coup-maker grievances across twenty or more countries for a twenty to twenty-five year time span. This procedure contains an implicit assumption of constant salience across countries and over time, which is at variance with the Ecuadorian data and with the contextually oriented process-approach emphasized in this study. For this study, the regression analysis poses the problem of explaining the changes in the criteria by which Ecuadorian officers made coup decisions, a subject that is explored in chapter 12.

## chapter eight

# Personal Backgrounds and Coup Decisions

Thus far the analysis has focused on explaining the coup decisions of Ecuadorian military officers in terms of their perceptions of government performance on the various decision criteria. Only in the cases where negative perceptions on one criterion (such as personal interests) spilled over to bias other perceptions have we been concerned with the question of explaining what determines how a given officer will rate the government on any of these criteria. Some disagreement has existed, however, on the major issues in each of the four crises. Since the real state of public opinion, the actual level of public disorders, the amount of military appropriations, and so on, are givens in each particular coup, it seems logical to seek explanations of variations in the way these factors are *perceived* in the personal characteristics of the perceiver. Indeed, students of Latin American politics have frequently argued that regional and class origins, political orientations, military training, and similar factors are major determinants of military behavior, although the specifics of the arguments vary widely, from liberal and Marxist debates over the influence of American training[1] to Victor Alba's distinction between *los oficiales del cuartel* and *los nuevos oficiales del laboratorio,*[2] from isolated observations such as the disproportionate recruitment of politically active Venezuelan Army officers from the Andean provinces[3] to José Nun's highly theoretical analysis of the significance of the military's class origins.[4]

Thus far, however, the only major empirical test of such arguments has been Alfred Stepan's analysis of the special career characteristics of the group of Brazilian officers that formed the nucleus of the first military government under Castello Branco in 1964.[5] Reviewing the limited progress in this area, Martin Needler has written:

The correlates of [the military's] political orientations have not yet been systematically evaluated and weighed for the Latin American military along the lines of Morris Janowitz's *The Professional Soldier.* Available evidence suggests, however, that on top of the primary set of conditioning factors such as those which the American voting studies indicate are the significant ones in determining party preferences (family tradition, social and economic level, and ethnic or other particularistic identification) is imposed a second set of factors peculiar to the military profession: rank, branch of service, occupational specialty and career pattern.[6]

For each of the four samples of Ecuadorian coup participants, data was collected on many of the variables suggested by Needler: age, region of birth, type (public or parochial) and level of nonmilitary education, family ties to the military profession, year of entry and age at entry for basic military education, military schools attended in Ecuador, training received abroad, military specialization, rank at time of coup, socioeconomic self-identification, and party preference or political orientation. The basic question is whether these are, in fact, significant determinants of military attitudes. Are these personal background characteristics related in some systematic way to the coup positions taken by these officers, to their different perceptions of government performance, or to the selection of those issues that individual officers considered most important in a given coup? The question has practical as well as theoretical implications. "Contemporary political elites, especially at the national level, are quite often inaccessible and attitudinal information is therefore difficult to obtain,"[7] especially in the case of the active duty military. To the extent that the attitudinal correlates of these background characteristics can be established, such findings would permit at least tentative inferences about the attitudinal consequences of known trends in regional or class recruitment patterns, levels of military education, foreign training, etc. Such inferences rest, however, on the assumption that social backgrounds are related to military attitudes.[8]

Looking first for direct relationships between these background variables and the decision of Ecuadorian officers to support or oppose the various coups, none of the relationships is consistently significant in all four crises. The closest approximation to a consistent relationship is between coup positions and age or rank at the time of the coup, which, in three of the four cases, shows the younger, less senior officers more likely to take an antigovernment stand.[9] Even here the less-than-surprising conclusion is that governments that select their senior officers on the basis of personal loyalty or political reliability are often overthrown in coups led by less senior officers.[10]

Personal background characteristics also failed to correlate in any consistent fashion with the officers' perceptions of government performance on the different decision criteria.[11] In two of the four coups—1954 and 1963—those officers from military families rated the government more favorably on the constitutionality issue. However, lack of a similar finding for 1961 suggests that, at least in 1963, the relationship is a spurious one, based on the personal ties between Arosemena and a few officers whose ancestors were Liberal veterans of

Table 8.1  Coup Decisions and Rank at Time of Coup

| | 1954 | | 1961 | | 1963 | |
| | Pro-Coup | Pro-Gov | Pro-Coup | Pro-Gov | Strongly Pro-Coup | Other |
| Rank | | | | | | |
|---|---|---|---|---|---|---|
| Generals, Colonels | 0 | 5( 42%) | 4( 29%) | 6( 86%) | 5( 38%) | 10( 67%) |
| Lt. Colonel and below | 6(100%) | 7( 58%) | 10( 71%) | 1( 14%) | 8( 62%) | 5( 23%) |
| Total | 6(100%) | 12(100%) | 14(100%) | 7(100%) | 13(100%) | 15(100%) |
| | N = 18 | | N = 21 | | N = 28 | |
| | p = .09 | | p = .02 | | p = .13 | |

the civil wars at the turn of the century. None of the remaining relationships was significant in more than one case. In turn, these single-case relationships chiefly serve to identify the characteristics of the officers with whom the government had particularly good or particularly bad personal relations. Most of the 1954 Varea group had attended public primary schools, several were engineers with some university training, and none were sons of military officers. Hence all of these variables are associated with a willingness to ignore the constitution in the 1954 movement against Velasco, but more extensive interviews would be necessary to determine what, if anything, these characteristics had to do with their more aggressive views on civil-military relations, with their selection for study in Peronist Argentina, or with the formation of their personal connections with the minister of defense. In 1963 the case is somewhat easier, as coastal origins, some university education, military traditions in the family, left-of-center political orientations, and higher-than-middle-class self-identification all serve to identify the few personal friends who remained Arosemena's only supporters to the bitter end.

Likewise, there are few significant relationships between the personal characteristics of the coup participants and the issue given the highest stress in their self-explanations of the coup events and their personal role in them. Again, most of these relationships are spurious, reflecting either idiosyncratic events or the distribution of personal ties among the higher-ranking officers. For example, in the 1961 sample, the apparently strong relationships between stress on the constitutional issue (or, alternatively, stress on public disorders) and foreign training and socioeconomic identification mostly reflects the atypical education and postretirement incomes of the military engineers in the Chimborazo battalion, who revolted rather than face more riot control assignments.

Despite the general pattern of weak or spurious correlations, there was, in the 1963 sample, an interesting relationship between military family background and the issues stressed in the self-explanation of that coup. Sons of military officers tended to place greater stress on the threat of communism than on

Table 8.2  Military Family Background
and Anticommunism: 1963

| Issues | Sons of military officers | Other officers |
|---|---|---|
| Communist threat | | |
| Mentioned | 3 ( 37%) | 17 ( 77%) |
| Most stressed | 5 ( 63%) | 5 ( 23%) |
| | N = 8 (100%) | 22 (100%) |
| | p=.06 | |
| President's personal behavior | | |
| Mentioned | 5 ( 63%) | 5 ( 24%) |
| Most stressed | 3 ( 37%) | 16 ( 76%) |
| | N = 8 (100%) | 21 (100%) |
| | p=.07 | |

Arosemena's drinking habits. Inasmuch as Ecuadorian officers frequently explained their aversion to communism in terms of their fear that the communists were determined to destroy the armed forces,[12] the stronger anticommunist reaction of the sons of officers may indicate a stronger self-identification with the military institution. Further support for this conclusion may be drawn from the 1966 coup sample, in which sons of military officers were more likely to have criticized the weak dictatorship of the military junta—*la dictablanda*—and to have given the junta negative ratings on its responsiveness to the institutional needs of the armed forces. (In his study of the Brazilian military, Stepan reports a similar finding, where sons of officers were much more likely to have favored the overthrow of Goulart in 1964.)[13] If sons of military officers are, in fact, more strongly identified with the military

Table 8.3  Military Family Background and
Attitudes toward the Military Junta: 1966

| | Sons of military officers | Other officers |
|---|---|---|
| Open Probe | | |
| Criticized *la dictablanda* | 4 ( 80%) | 5 ( 38%) |
| No mention | 1 ( 20%) | 8 ( 62%) |
| | 5 (100%) | 13 (100%) |
| | p=.15 | |
| Rating of junta's responsiveness to military's institutional needs | | |
| Negative | 4 ( 80%) | 5 ( 38%) |
| Positive or ambivalent | 1 ( 20%) | 8 ( 62%) |
| | 5 (100%) | 13 (100%) |
| | p=.15 | |

institution, as these findings seem to suggest, then it may be less than coincidental that institutional military regimes have emerged in precisely those countries where the trend toward internal recruitment of military officers seems to be most advanced.[14] Still, given the demonstrated problems of spurious correlation in this type of attribute correlation analysis, the existence of a relationship between military family background and institutional self-identification must be more directly confirmed before postulating any connection with the aggregate political behavior of the armed forces.

Pooling the four groups of coup participants into a single sample reveals a few statistically significant, but nevertheless substantively weak, relationships. Younger officers were again more likely to be against the government. Those officers who were born in the sierra, those who had attended a Catholic primary school, and those who considered themselves political conservatives were somewhat more likely to have favored a coup against these governments. As expected, the latter three variables are closely related. Those officers who attended Catholic primary schools tended to be more conservative in their political orientation, which probably reflects a more conservative family background as

Table 8.4  Region of Birth, Primary Schooling,
and Political Orientation

|  | Party Preference or Political Orientation | | |
|  | Left and Center-left | Right and Center-right | No expressed party preference |
| --- | --- | --- | --- |
| Primary Education |  |  |  |
| Religious | 7 ( 41%) | 6 ( 67%) | 16 ( 47%) |
| Public | 10 ( 59%) | 9 ( 33%) | 18 ( 53%) |
|  | 17 (100%) | 9 (100%) | 34 (100%) |

|  | Region of Birth | | | |
|  | Pichincha (Quito) | Central sierra | North/south sierra | Coast |
| --- | --- | --- | --- | --- |
| Religious | 10 ( 43%) | 12 ( 55%) | 7 ( 87%) | 0 |
| Public | 13 ( 57%) | 10 ( 45%) | 1 ( 13%) | 7 (100%) |
|  | 23 (100%) | 22 (100%) | 8 (100%) | 7 (100%) |
| Party preference or political orientation |  |  |  |  |
| Left, Center-left | 9 ( 82%) | 7 ( 70%) | 1 ( 33%) | 0 |
| Right, Center-right | 2 ( 18%) | 3 ( 30%) | 2 ( 66%) | 2*(100%) |
|  | 11 (100%) | 10 (100%) | 3 (100%) | 2 (100%) |
| (No expressed preference) | (12) | (12) | (5) | (5) |

*Both Partido Liberal.

well as the impact of conservative Catholic doctrines in their early socialization experiences. In turn, about 55 percent of the officers born in the sierra attended a Catholic grade school, whereas all seven of the officers from the coast had attended public schools.

These data also suggest that Catholic schooling may have a greater impact on military attitudes than urbanization. Even though almost all of the officers born in Pichincha province were from the capital city of Quito (which, in 1950, had a population of more than 200,000), the proportion of conservative officers from Pichincha is only slightly lower than that of the central sierra provinces, where, in 1950, the two largest cities both had populations of less than 35,000 inhabitants. Despite the much more rural, small-town, provincial backgrounds of those from the central sierra, the differences in political orientation are relatively minor. Moreover, these differences are easily explained by the slightly higher proportion of officers from the central sierra who attended Catholic, rather than public schools, suggesting that parochial education, not rural origins, is the primary determinant of conservative political orientations among the Ecuadorian military.[15] Nevertheless, as indicated earlier, differences in political orientation are, at best, only weakly related to differences in behavior in coup situations.

Another way of testing the influence of personal background characteristics on the attitudes of military officers in a coup situation is to compare the coup attitudes of Ecuadorian army and air force officers, who differ not only in their branch of service, but in a large number of background variables as well.[16] (Given the drastic underrepresentation of air force officers in the sample, the four coup groups have to be combined and some analytical categories collapsed to make the analysis possible.)[17] In two respects, the backgrounds of army and air force officers are almost identical. A great majority of officers in both services are recruited from the sierra and both services are split evenly between those officers who attended a parochial elementary school and those who attended public schools. In most other respects the backgrounds of army officers differ substantially from those of their air force counterparts. Less than half as many air force officers come from military families, as would be expected in the more recently created institution. One third of the army group—mostly the engineers—had had some university education, while none of the air force officers had attended a university. The air force officers were substantially younger, reflecting, in part, their more rapid ascension and retirement. The air force sample consisted mostly of higher-ranking officers; the army sample was more evenly divided. All of the air force officers had had some training in the United States. Only half the army officers had attended United States schools, and 25 percent had had no foreign training at all. As a result of their higher military pay and pensions, as well as of their substantially higher postretirement earnings, air force officers on the whole enjoyed a higher standard of living and were more likely to identify themselves as part of the upper-middle class rather than of the middle class. Finally, the air force officers were much less willing to identify either a party preference or a basic political orientation. In general, then, there are substantial differences in the background characteristics of Ecuadorian army and air force officers.[18] Given that each service is operated almost entirely independently—subject only to the common authority of the minister of defense and the president—the comparison that follows can be considered a "controlled" quasi-experiment. Here there are two military institutions with different specializations, different skill structures, and a host of differences in the personal characteristics of their members, yet in this experiment, both are located within the same country and within the same social and economic context, and both are analyzing the same political situations. How do the two groups—army officers and air force officers—react to these political crises?

In terms of which issues were cited and which received the most stress in the open-ended self-explanations of individual coup positions, there were slightly higher proportions of the air force officers stressing constitutional issues and the threat of communism, and, not surprisingly, slightly fewer were concerned with public disorders. The lesser emphasis on public disorders probably derives from the fact that the air force is not involved in riot control, and the other differences could, plausibly, be linked to differences in personal backgrounds, but only the differential stress on the constitutional issue even approaches statistical significance.[19] Likewise, there is a striking degree of similarity among air force and army officers in the ratings of government performance on the six different decision criteria. In their assessment of public opinion toward the government, air force and army officers gave virtually identical ratings. Even on public disorders, there are only slight differences. Air force officers gave slightly higher proportions of negative ratings on protection of their institutional interests and constitutionality, but these differences were, again, far from being statistically significant.[20]

In terms of the actual positions taken by these officers in four military coups, almost identical proportions of army and air force officers supported and opposed the government. Despite the significant differences in the personal backgrounds of the army and air force officers, this "experiment" suggests that

Table 8.5 Branch of Service
and Military Coup Decisions

|  | Supported coup | Supported government |
| --- | --- | --- |
| Army | 71% (47) | 29% (19) |
| Air force | 75% ( 6) | 25% ( 2) |

NOTE: The probability that the observed or greater differences could have occurred by chance is greater than .80 using a two-tailed Chi-square test or .59 using a single-tailed Fisher Exact Test.

these different backgrounds had very little impact on the decisions of these officers to join in or oppose a military coup d'état.

With the exception, then, of military family background, the age-rank conflict, and the influence of foreign training on abstract role definition (discussed in chapter 12), the personal background characteristics of Ecuadorian military officers seem to offer little assistance in explaining the differences in the attitudes and behavior of these officers in political crises. In turn, this finding lends itself to two rather different interpretations. First, it could be argued that coup attitudes among Latin American officers are by nature highly volatile, depending largely upon a given officer's position among the "ins" and "outs" at a given time. According to this interpretation, coup attitudes are essentially unpredictable by social background characteristics or by any factor other than the perceived sum of personal costs and benefits in taking one side or the other.[21] The high salience of the personal ties variable in all four Ecuadorian coups suggests that this interpretation is, to a degree, applicable to the Ecuadorian armed forces. Nevertheless, the previous chapter also revealed a larger pattern of order in coup attitudes in which personal ties and antagonisms constituted only one element among several.[22]

A second, somewhat less cynical interpretation is that, where the armed forces have achieved at least a moderate degree of professionalization, military officers are relatively unaffected by their social origins and premilitary socialization experiences.[23] As indicated previously, the effect of the postwar military reforms in Ecuador—particularly the expansion of the military training system—was to increase the intensity and duration of the military socialization process. As a result (in contrast to the prewar period), premilitary identifications and experiences have come to be less significant, especially relative to the individual officer's identification with the military institution itself. By this interpretation, the significant determinants of the attitudes and behavior of military officers are primarily situational, reflecting in a complex and multi-faceted way the indulgences and deprivations of both the institution and the individual in a given political context. Given the substantial variations in political contexts across countries and over time, one would not expect these attitudes to exhibit stable correlations with personal background variables.

In the present case, to the extent that military perceptions of the political situation were influenced by such factors,[24] the most important personal characteristics seem to be those which are the most widely shared among Ecuadorian officers (specifically their common origins in the middle class and the sierra) and which are, therefore, the least useful in explaining differences among them. Even these characteristics, however, seem to be less important than the one personal characteristic that all of the respondents have in common—that of being a military officer.

*part four*

# The Military and the Political System: The Individual Components of the Coup Decision

In the preceding chapters evidence has been presented that shows a clear relationship between military officers' perceptions of the state of the larger political system in terms of certain specified decision criteria, and their willingness to support or oppose the overthrow of the government in a military coup d'état. This analysis is crucial in that it identifies the primary linkage points between the military coup and the rest of the political system; yet it is not in itself sufficient. These correlations between the officers' perceptions of political events and coup decisions are of limited significance without further specification of these relationships. The relationship between military perceptions of the political environment and political reality must be determined for each decision criterion. How, for example, does the military define and measure the state of "public opinion" toward the government? Under what conditions will the military perceive that the constitution has been violated? Important questions also remain about the nature of the relationship between, for example, the level of public disorders and coup attitudes. Intervening or conditioning variables, such as the identity of the protesting groups, must also be specified.

In the chapters that follow, each of the individual components of the coup decision is examined in terms of the way that component operated in the four Ecuadorian coups described earlier. This analysis provides answers to the remaining questions posed by the larger theoretical framework. Why these decision criteria? Why these political events and not others? And finally, why have the decision criteria used by Ecuadorian officers changed over time?

# chapter nine

# The Armed Forces and the Constitution

The salience of the Ecuadorian military's concern for constitutional issues was strikingly clear in both the 1954 and the 1961 crises. In the former case, 68 percent of the participants interviewed mentioned the constitutional status of the Velasco government as a factor in their decision to support or oppose the government, with 47 percent citing this as the basic issue. In 1961, when President Velasco found himself on the other side of the issue, allusions to the constitutionality question were even more prevalent (95 percent), with a majority giving most weight to constitutional considerations. Contrary to initial expectations, the constitutionality of the government's position—as perceived by the coup participants—provides the best single predictor of the outcomes of their

Table 9.1  Correlations of Constitutionality
Ratings and Coup Positions

| Year | (N) | Pearson correlation | Partial correlation (controlling for personal interests) |
|------|-----|---------------------|----------------------------------------------------------|
| 1954 | 18  | +.92                | +.79                                                     |
| 1961 | 20  | +.85                | +.74                                                     |

decision to support or oppose the government in these two coups. Even when the tendency of personal interests and personal loyalties to bias perceptions of constitutionality is taken into account, there remains a strong relationship between belief in the constitutionality of the government and the willingness of individual officers to defend that government. In both cases, proponents of the constitutionalist cause pointed to Article 153 of the constitution, which entrusted the defense of that constitution to the armed forces. "For the defense of the Republic and the maintenance of constitutional order, there shall be military armed forces."[1]

This designation of the armed forces as defenders of the constitution was hardly novel, having appeared as far back as 1830, in the Gran Colombian Constitution.[2] The presence of more or less identical provisions in previous Ecuadorian constitutions and in the constitutions of other Latin American countries[3] raises the question of whether this emphasis on the legality of the government's behavior was merely a *post hoc* rationalization. The repeated warnings given Velasco by loyalist officers that Arosemena's arrest would cause a military revolt prove that this is not the case.[4] Still, why did these Ecuadorian military officers take seriously constitutional injunctions that historically had been honored more in the breach than in practice? Here the extremely bitter experience of this generation of officers in the 1941 war with Peru must be recalled and re-emphasized. Half the officers interviewed for this study entered military service in either 1936 or in 1937, and thus were serving their first tour of duty when the Peruvian invasion began. Many were stationed in isolated, undermanned frontier posts; others were in units withheld from combat by the Arroyo government. The humiliation of the 1941 defeat and of the Rio Protocol provoked a deep reaction against the old tradition of civilian and military interference in each other's affairs and against the aggravated political instability of the 1930s, both of which were singled out as the primary causes for Ecuador's military weakness in 1941. In the words of one officer, "The political instability (of the 30s) was the fundamental reason that the country suffered this dismemberment of its territory. Unfortunately the country was known for its coup d'états rather than as a country respectful of the constitution and the laws. If we had been better organized—had we lived the constitution—it would have been a different situation."[5] This generation of officers adopted the slogan "Respect the laws and the popular will [as expressed in free elections]" in hopes of establishing clearer boundaries between the civilian and the military spheres.[6] After the overthrow of the Arroyo government, the new attitude manifested itself in the unsuccessful resistence by a nucleus of young officers to President Velasco's assumption of dictatorial powers in 1946, and in the successful counter-coup also led by junior officers, which forced a return to constitutional government after Colonel Mancheno's attempt to replace Velasco as dictator in 1947.

The doctrine of the "constitutionalist" military was further strengthened by its incorporation into various stages of the military socialization process. The constitutional definition of the military role—external defense, internal order, and maintenance of the constitution—was drilled into new cadets in the military academy (which eventually became the exclusive source of officer recruitment). In the graduation ceremony each cadet knelt, individually, before the flag, and pledged his life to defend the flag and the constitution. That the oath was not purely ceremonial is reflected in later references to the commitment of an officer's military honor to defend the constitution.[7] The middle-level *cursos de capacitación* also served to unite the younger generation of officers around the constitutionalist norm. One officer recalls an infantry course, attended by sixty army captains, that ended with a group oath "to maintain the constitutional government, whatever its political stripe may be, because this was and is the only formula by which the country can mature."[8] In like manner, it was reported that a training course for tank officers had been used to disseminate and reaffirm the constitutionalist doctrine.[9] In 1948 a course in constitutional law was added to the war academy curriculum and, after the 1956 reopening of the academy, it became a permanent part of the program.[10]

Another important, perhaps critical, source of support for the constitutional norm was the prestige of the liberal-democratic political model among hemispheric reference groups—particularly the military officers of other Latin American countries encountered through military attaché duty or through schooling abroad.[11] A retired general recalls that he was chided by Colombian officers who asked "What government is in power in Ecuador today? " "I replied, 'If the government is doing its job, it is the same one as yesterday,' but it was shameful; it made me feel inferior. I promised myself that when I had the chance to make my voice heard, I would make it my personal labor to see that the armed forces stayed out of politics."[12]

A former army commanding general reports that a similar incident took place in Argentina shortly after the famous year of four presidents (1947), when he was asked by friends, "What is going on in Ecuador? The armed forces overthrow their governments, overthrow their generals, even overthrow their colonels! "[13] The association of the low international prestige of the country with the lack of political stability was, therefore, another powerful underpinning of the constitutionalist doctrine.[14]

Ironically, despite the public and press acclaim for the military's "noble and patriotic" defense of the constitution in 1961,[15] this was to be the last of the four crises in which the constitutionalist norm figured very prominently. By 1966, even though the coup was directed against a military dictatorship, criticism within the military was aimed almost entirely at that dictatorship and its policies. In a few cases junta opponents argued against military governments

Table 9.2 Open-ended Responses
Mentioning/Stressing Constitutional Norm

|  | 1954 | 1961 | 1963 | 1966 |
|---|---|---|---|---|
| Mentioned | 68.5% | 95.7% | 37.5% | 9.6% |
| Most stressed | 47.4% | 52.2% | 0 | 0 |
|  | N = 19 | N = 23 | N = 32 | N = 21 |

in general, but not in terms of a desire for a return to constitutional government as a value in itself.

These same data suggest that most of the decline in the salience of the constitutionalist norm took place between 1961 and 1963, when many of the officers who had supported Arosemena's succession in 1961 reported only minor qualms about deposing him two years later. To begin with, both the officers primarily concerned with the "communist threat" and those concerned with the president's personal behavior claimed, with some justification, that the constitutional avenues for terminating an "intolerable" situation had been exhausted. Military protests within channels, the petition/ultimatum of the Cuenca garrison, impeachment proceedings in Congress, and congressional elections had all failed to produce any "significant" results. Secondly, the "communist threat" charge against Arosemena posed a clear dilemma of choosing between defending the constitutionally designated president or defending fundamental democratic institutions against the "subversive elements." As alternative means of dealing with Arosemena were tried without result, more officers began to adopt the notion that the military was obliged to protect "the national interest," even at the expense of a legally constituted government. Thus the way was paved to install a military dictatorship in order to "save democracy."

At the same time, the rising level of social concern, particularly among the younger officers, further eroded support for the constitutionalist norm. The ineffectiveness of civilian governments in delivering on electoral promises of social reforms led to an increasing lack of trust in both "demogogic" politicians and in "archiac, obstructionist" institutions like Congress.[16] One of the last of the traditional legalists lamented upon retiring in 1970, "Since the laws have been designed for the benefit of privileged minorities, the younger officers place their faith not in the constitution, but rather in a Peruvian style government." [17] Thus, at the same time that the armed forces committed itself to deeper involvement in political affairs by breaking a fifteen-year tradition of constitutional successions, new attitudes were forming among the younger officers that also militated against a return to the pure constitutionalist norm.

In addition to external defense and defense of the constitution itself, the constitutions of Ecuador have traditionally assigned to the armed forces the responsibility for maintenance of public order. The Constitution of 1946 additionally entrusted them with responsibility for guaranteeing the purity of the electoral process, but omitted the maintenance of public order, leaving that responsibility, by default, to the national police.[18] Perhaps because all the higher ranking officers had received their basic orientations under earlier constitutions, this omission in no way affected actual practice during the next two decades. (The traditional joint responsibility of the *Fuerzas Públicas,* police and armed forces, for public order was re-established in the Constitution of 1967.)

In both 1961 and in 1966, public disorders figured prominently in many officers' explanations of their decision to support the overthrow of the government. The month-long wave of riots and demonstrations preceding Velasco's overthrow was mentioned by nearly 40 percent of the respondents, and 17 percent placed greater emphasis on this issue than on the constitutionality of the vice-president's arrest. Particularly in army units that had been

Table 9.3 Open-ended Responses
Mentioning/Stressing Public Disorders

|  | 1954 | 1961 | 1963 | 1966 |
|---|---|---|---|---|
| Mentioned | 0 | 39.1% | 9.4% | 52.4% |
| Most stressed | 0 | 17.4% | 0 | 0 |
|  | N = 19 | N = 23 | N = 32 | N = 21 |

repeatedly used during this period to break up opposition demonstrations, there was a deep feeling that the country was approaching civil war, with the people on one side and the armed forces on the other,[19] a feeling that played a key role in the decision of the war academy to ask the president to resign "in order to restore peace to the country, since the presence of Velasco was the cause of all the disorders."[20]

Likewise, over half the 1966 respondents cited the constant opposition demonstrations, mostly by antigovernment students, in explaining their attitudes toward the military junta. Nearly all agreed that the punitive military raid against Central University was the key event in the fall of the junta. Whereas a month before the raid the junta had successfully overcome a challenge to its authority from the chief of the general staff, after the attack on Central University supporters of the junta were divided and demoralized by the deaths that occurred and the even more massive protests that these deaths sparked across the country. As one of the loyalists sadly remarked, "There are times when military force is impotent. When the popular forces fill the streets, it would be senseless to oppose them."[21] Two members of the junta itself expressed a similar feeling in identical terms: "We know we could have maintained the government, but only at the price of many deaths. We preferred to leave power to the civilians."[22]

Paradoxically, whereas the armed forces' responsibility for maintaining public order is overwhelmingly accepted by Ecuadorian officers as part of their military mission,[23] in both 1961 and in 1966, large numbers of officers withdrew their support from governments that called upon them to fulfill that responsibility. As one officer explained in a report on his unit's role in 1961,

The Chimborazo Battalion has always been disciplined and removed from any political problem, but it could not agree with the increasingly difficult police missions to which we were assigned. If in reality the specific mission of the armed forces is to guarantee Law and Order, then this police activity was displacing strictly military activities with great danger for the external security of the country. . . The general popular discontent also reached the armed forces and every day this discontent grew, since it was evident that employing the army as a police force was transforming the citizenry into a force antagonistic to the military.[24]

Another officer, recalling his reluctance to use violence against a student demonstration in 1956, explained that "a soldier's first duty is to his country as a citizen, but his second duty is to safeguard the prestige of the military institution."[25] Defending an unpopular government against manifestations of public hostility exposes the army to the danger that antigovernment attitudes will become antimilitary attitudes as well. In the absence of a compelling reason for supporting the government, military officers will likely respond to public outcries over the deaths of demonstrators and bystanders by deciding that the only way to restore public order is to remove the object of popular hostility.

Unfortunately the correlations between the positions taken by Ecuadorian officers in the various coups and their perceptions of public disorders in the months preceding the coups are not especially high. In both 1954, where there were no prior disorders, and in 1961, where there were extreme problems, the correlations are insignificant. (This was true in 1961 because both supporters and opponents of the coup were unanimous in their negative ratings.)[26] As a result,

Table 9.4  Correlations of Ratings on
Public Disorders and Attitudes toward Coup

| 1954 | 1961 | 1963 | 1966 |
|------|------|------|------|
| −.17 | −.09 | +.41 | +.38 |
| N = 18 | N = 20 | N = 29 | N = 19 |

in the statistical evaluation of the relative importance of various decision criteria, public disorders appeared to be rather insignificant. Even though quantitative evidence is lacking, the qualitative data from the interviews caution against disregard for public disorders as a coup decision criterion. As one officer replied when asked about public disorders in 1954, "There were the normal problems with students and workers, but no strong tension between the government and the people. No great problems. . . . Had there been, we surely would have supported the minister of defense and accepted the dictatorship."[27]

In order to provide a check against the arbitrariness of any procedure used to summarize individual acts of public protest in an overall measure of public disorders, the data used in earlier chapters to measure trends in public disorders prior to each coup were recoded in accordance with a system designed by James Payne "to produce a score which reflects the incidence of collective action hostile to the government."[28] Despite some differences in the scoring procedures, the trends using the Payne system are essentially the same as those that were reported earlier. In both 1961 and in 1966 high and rapidly rising levels of public disorders immediately preceded each coup. In both cases, a substantial number of officers mentioned public disorders in the self-explanations of the positions they took in the coup, and almost all the officers gave the government negative ratings when the question was put to them directly.

The 1963 coup does present something of an anomaly, since neither the raw scores nor the cumulated totals seem very high compared to those of 1961 or 1966. This fits the low percentage of open-ended responses mentioning public disorders, but not the substantial number of negative ratings on the direct questions, nor the moderate correlation between the public disorder ratings and the coup decisions taken against the Arosemena government. However, when we apply statistical controls for the perception of a communist threat, perceptions of public disorders lose most of their explanatory power. There is still a

Table 9.5  Public Disorders, Communist Threat, and Coup Attitudes: 1963

|  | r | r² |
|---|---|---|
| Simple correlation of public disorder ratings with coup attitudes | .41 | 16.8% |
| Partial correlation controlling for personal interests | .48 | 23.0% |
| Partial correlation controlling for communist threat | .27 | 7.3% |
|  | N = 29 | |

relationship between negative ratings on public disorders and negative ratings on the level of "communist threat," and this provides an indirect path for disorder perceptions to influence coup decisions. This connection and various allusions to "acts of sabotage and of terrorism,"[29] in answering that questionnaire item, suggest that the public disorder issue (to the extent that it existed in 1963), was only superficially similar to the issue posed by the widespread riots and demonstrations of 1961 and 1966. Whereas in the latter two coups the military reacted against being used to suppress disorders for which the government was held responsible, in 1963 the complaint was against the failure of the government to take repressive action.[30]

This ambivalent attitude toward compliance with its mission to maintain public order suggests the general proposition that the military response to public

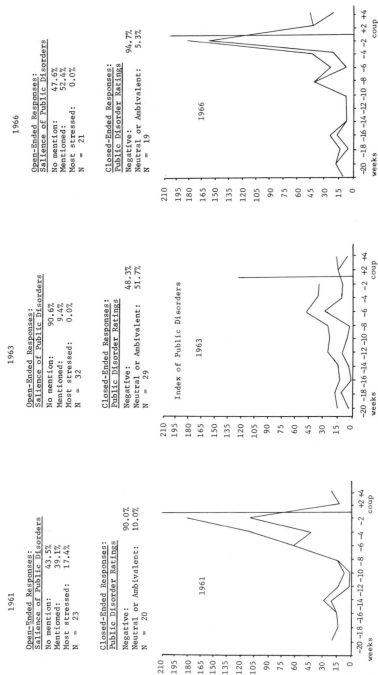

Figure 9.1. Perceptions of Public Disorders

disorders will vary according to whether or not the government is taking strong action and to whether or not the protests being suppressed are compatible with the attitudes and values of military officers. While the typical officer might be reluctant to take action against workers protesting for higher wages or against students demonstrating for "democracy" in opposition to a personalist military dictatorship, the same officer might be quite willing to suppress demonstrations of pro-Castro students or political strikes by leftist-oriented unions. Thus in

Table 9.6 Military Responses to Public Disorders

| Response of government | Groups Involved in Disorders: | |
| --- | --- | --- |
| | Neutral or sympathetic | Antimilitary |
| Action | Strongly negative reaction against police role; repression threatening institutional prestige. (1961, 1966) | Positive reaction for support in suppressing threat to the institution. (1970) |
| Inaction | Mildly negative reaction. Disorders as an indication of public opinion. | Strongly negative reaction. Disorders as an indicator of a communist threat. (1963) |

1955 the chief of the general staff refused to accept a presidential directive that he employ army troops against students on strike at a Quito high school—a move that cost him his job. Yet four years later, no one questioned the massive use of military forces to suppress the Guayaquil riots, which most officers saw as an anarchist or communist uprising linked to the mob murder of an army officer in Manabí.[31] In similar fashion, while the army rebelled against the high command in 1961 rather than face public demonstrations against Velasco's violation of the constitution, in 1970 the military's support for the civilian dictatorship proposed by Dr. Velasco appears to have been achieved through an agreement that the first act of the new dictatorship would be the closure of Central University, where daily antigovernment demonstrations had taken on such an antimilitary tone that officers were beginning to worry about wearing their uniforms on the streets adjacent to the University.[32]

In general, then, the response of the Ecuadorian military to its constitutionally defined functions has been more complex and variable than a simple reading of the constitutional prescriptions would suggest. The constitutionality of the government in power (which was the major issue in the abortive coup of 1954 and in the overthrow of Velasco in 1961) has largely ceased to be a salient factor in military coup decisions. On the other hand, maintenance of public order has been a less salient but more constant military concern. As the nature of the opposition forces participating in public disorders has changed, however, the traditional opposition to police missions has had to compete with the newer perception of public disorders as part of the internal security, counterinsurgency problem requiring repressive action.

# *chapter ten*

# T he Influence of Public Opinion

According to the stereotyped view held by most Americans—especially American liberals—of Latin American military coups, most coups are arbitrary military decisions imposed by armed force against popularly supported democratic governments. Hence, it is interesting to note that "the pressure of public opinion" was one of the factors most consistently advanced by Ecuadorian officers to explain their decision to support or oppose a coup attempt. In the open-ended questionnaire items, public opinion against the government and/or for military intervention was mentioned by about 50 percent of the sample of participants in each of the three successful coups. In the unsuccessful coup attempt of 1954, public pressures were not mentioned even once.

Table 10.1  Open-ended Responses
Mentioning/Stressing Public Opinion

|  | 1954 | 1961 | 1963 | 1966 |
|---|---|---|---|---|
| Mentioned | 0 | 47.8% | 46.9% | 61.9% |
| Most stressed | 0 | 0 | 0 | 19.0% |
|  | N = 19 | N = 23 | N = 32 | N = 21 |

In each case, the participants offered a variety of recollections emphasizing the importance of civilian opinion: "There was a clamor in the streets for change";[1] "The armed forces intervened only because it was demanded by the people",[2] "The civilians were asking 'How much longer?' "[3] Another officer recalls with some bitterness that his attempts to defend constitutional principles in 1963 found little support, as "Politicians of both the left and the right came knocking at the barracks door."[4] The importance of public opinion is again demonstrated in the high correlation between an officer's final decision and his perception of the state of public opinion at the time of the coup. On the other hand, Ecuadorian officers rarely cited public opinion as the most important factor influencing their position in the coup.

That perceived public opinion is highly correlated with coup decisions, but is not a strongly stressed uncued explanation of these decisions, suggests that

Table 10.2 Correlations of Coup Attitudes
with Ratings of Public Opinion

|  | 1954 | 1961 | 1963 | 1966 |
|---|---|---|---|---|
| r | .70 | .11* | .60 | .69 |
| r² | 49% | 1% | 36% | 48% |
| Partial r controlling for personal ties | .77 | .18* | .50 | .54 |
|  | N = 18 | N = 20 | N = 29 | N = 19 |

*Perceptions of public opinion were so uniformly negative that the coding scheme left little variance on which any correlation could be based.

these officers simply adjusted their perceptions of popular opinion retroactively in order to rationalize a decision taken for other reasons. The "rationalization" interpretation is strongly contradicted by a variety of instances in the interviews where the respondent was clearly not engaged in *post hoc* rationalization. One of Velasco's strongest supporters in 1961 warned the president a month before his overthrow, "The high command cannot guarantee the loyalty of the armed forces indefinitely, since the armed forces are subject to the influence of public opinion."[5] Another Velasco loyalist reported that the public disorders and general opposition to the government "divided the armed forces, which always reflect the feelings of the majority."[6] Likewise, one key officer in 1954 characterized that coup attempt as irresponsible, since "there was no pressure of public opinion to induce military intervention. On other occasions, yes, but not in 1954."[7] Finally, perhaps the most convincing argument against the rationalization hypothesis comes from the logic employed by an army colonel when he was confronted with the task of recalling, sixteen years later, the state of public opinion in 1954. Although he personally supported the constitutionalists, he reasoned that "Velasco had lost the support of his partisans. *Lógico*, if not, they [the pro-Varea group] would not have attempted a coup."[8] In each of these cases the officer in question implicitly recognized an empirical relationship between public hostility toward the government and the loss of military support. Despite the tendency (documented earlier) for personal ties to bias perceptions of public opinion, the relationship with coup attitudes is not entirely spurious.

The notion of public opinion "inducing" military intervention suggests an alternative to the pure rationalization hypothesis—that is, that public opinion strongly hostile toward the government serves as an invoking and legitimating mechanism for that majority of officers who would prefer to remain "nonpolitical." While a few officers advocated military role definitions implying that the military ought to act as an instrument of the public will,[9] this view was held by only a very small minority. On the other hand, among those officers not advocating a strict constitutionalist definition of the mission of the armed forces, almost all agreed that there could be circumstances in which the military might have a duty to overthrow the government in power. Almost invariably, however, these same officers could not specify, except in the vaguest terms, what those circumstances might be.

> The armed forces should change the government or take power in case of a dangerous international situation [as in 1941] or when the country is headed for an *abyss,* a *disaster* that it might not survive.[10]

> Any nation that is headed toward *chaos, disintegration,* or its *disappearance* has to seek among its institutions the one that can save it from this situation. If the popular voice trusts the armed forces for this mission, then the military, out of patriotism, self-defense, and to justify its existence, has a duty to replace the government in order to end the crisis.[11]

As the second statement suggests, public opinion hostile to the government invokes and legitimates military intervention to end a vaguely defined crisis with which the military is concerned for other reasons (patriotism, self-defense, etc.). If the formal role definition specified in more concrete terms what would constitute a national crisis, there would be no need for an invoking mechanism. In the absence of a formally articulated set of conditions legitimating military intervention, the nonconstitutionalist officers require some way of knowing whether the country is close enough to "chaos" or "disintegration" to allow them, in good conscience, to take the extreme step of overthrowing the government. Public hostility to the government fulfills this need by reassuring the military officers that military intervention will be met with applause. Consequently, popular discontent is generally a prerequisite for the achievement of a general military consensus in favor of intervention, even though the military's reasons for wanting to replace the government may be only marginally related to popular discontent or to the causes of that unrest.[12] This conception of public opinion as an invoking mechanism is congruent with both the high correlation of perceived public opinion with coup decisions and the lack of stress on public opinion in the uncued explanations for those decisions.[13]

Given that military perceptions of public opinion play an important role in coup decisions, the relationship between military perceptions and the actual state of public attitudes becomes a critical question. How then do military officers know what public opinion is? When queried about their sources of information, Ecuadorian officers most commonly cited civilian friends and relatives,[14] the press,[15] political leaders,[16] and public demonstrations.[17] Yet the procedures involved were far from systematic. Several officers cited chance encounters with civilians, while one recalled being impressed by the poor turnout at a military concert in honor of the president.[18]

To the extent that military officers rely on their friends and relatives for information about public opinion, they are, in fact, tapping only a narrow sector of the public—the sierra middle class. Approximately 84 percent of the officers interviewed were born in the sierra and of the seventy-nine officers originally selected as interview targets, 84 percent were living in Quito. Similarly (as indicated previously) the Ecuadorian officer corps is overwhelmingly middle class in terms of living standards, self-identification and social origins. The friends and relatives with whom these officers are likely to be in contact are almost certainly also part of the sierra middle class. Needless to say there is no reason to believe that the attitudes of this social sector toward the government would be representative of "public opinion" or of "the popular will."

Ironically, in Ecuador, the Quito press generally reinforces this sierra, middle-class bias in perceptions of public opinion. Whereas the major newspapers of Guayaquil tend to closely reflect the views of the economic elites centered in that city, *El Comercio,* the major daily of Quito that is read widely throughout the sierra, has historically been associated with the Plaza faction of the Liberal party, and throughout the period in question consistently espoused a mildly progressive "Alliance for Progress" view on economic and social affairs, including a strong advocacy of agrarian and tax reforms bitterly opposed by the landed elites of the sierra.[19]

In contrast to the military's ready access to several indicators of middle-class sentiments, the major access point for upper-class attitudes to enter into the military's conception of public opinion would appear to be through contacts with political leaders, although here again the rank and file political activists likely to get involved in civil-military conspiracies are, probably, largely from the middle class. Lower-class attitudes toward the government are unlikely to be communicated to the military except by way of public demonstrations, but here also there is wide latitude for individual interpretation as to whether a given demonstration (or opposition leader) really represents popular discontent with the government, or is only the work of a few outside agitators and the usual political ambitions. Neither demonstrators nor the political opposition are likely to be accorded great credibility, unless the information given about public opinion is congruent with that encountered through friends and relatives.[20] In general, there would seem to be little opportunity for that 50 percent of the population living on the coast or for the 35 percent of the population composed of Indians to enter even marginally into the military's definition of public opinion.

Given this rather extreme bias in the military's perception of what "public opinion" really is, the military does seem to reflect fairly accurately the opinion of that social sector to which it is most closely attuned. The lack of systematic public opinion surveys does not permit us to test this proposition directly, but some evidence for this conclusion can be gathered from a simple content analysis of the pro- or anti-government sentiments of editorials appearing in *El Comercio* and *El Universo* before and after each coup.[21]

Table 10.3 Editorial Opinions and
Military Perceptions of Public Opinion

| | | Net editorial opinion score | | | | Public opinion toward government | | |
|---|---|---|---|---|---|---|---|---|
| Q = *El Comercio*, G = *El Universo* | | | | | | Military perceptions | | |
| | *t–2* * | *t–1* | *Coup* | *t+1* | *Hostile* | *Neutral* | *Favorable* | *N* |
| 1954 Q | +5 | +5 | +5 | | 28% | 17% | 55% | 18 |
| G | –15 | +1 | +4 | | | | | |
| 1961 Q | –7 | –9 | –20 | +25 | 90% | 10% | 0% | 20 |
| G | | –8 | –18 | +12 | | | | |
| 1963 Q | –19 | –1 | –24 | +24 | 90% | 10% | 0% | 29 |
| G | | –30 | –27 | +10 | | | | |
| 1966 Q | –8 | –14 | –4 | +3 | 74% | 16% | 10% | 19 |
| G | | –35 | –53 | +22 | | | | |

*Each time period consists of four weeks.

Regardless of whether we consider the editorial opinion of *El Comercio* to be shaping or paralleling Quito middle-class public opinion—or both—there is generally a close fit between this editorial opinion at the time of each coup and the military's perception of "public opinion." For all three successful coups, editorial concern with the government increased sharply during the two months prior to the coup and, particularly in 1961 and 1963, the net balance of editorial appraisal was consistently negative over the whole period and sharply critical in the four weeks immediately preceding the fall of the government. In each of these cases almost all the officers interviewed reported that "public opinion" was strongly hostile to the government.[22]

In the 1966 coup, however, the balance of editorial appraisal of the junta's performance was, up until its last two weeks, at worst a mixed review, even though the junta was strongly condemned after the military attack on Central University. Still, nearly three-fourths of the officers interviewed reported public opinion as being hostile to the government. Interestingly enough, five of the fourteen officers reporting a negative opinion were members of the general staff. These officers appear to have been influenced in part by "so much opposition from the students and workers"[23] and in part by the reports of the general staff intelligence department, whose chief was working with the political opposition, which included, incidentally, the chief editorial writer for *El Universo*. Several of these general staff officers later arrived at the conclusion that the military junta had not been as unpopular as they had originally believed.[24] This would suggest that the conflicting reports of the general staff and army intelligence units contributed to a collective perception of "public opinion" as being more hostile than it really was, even in the social stratum to which the military is normally attuned.[25]

Finally, the limited analysis of editorial opinion in the unsuccessful 1954 coup attempt would seem to indicate that it is not solely the editorial position of the major newspapers that determines the direction of the "public opinion" the military is perceiving, since the revolt broke out in Quito, where *El Comercio* had been rather favorable, and the government was saved by the garrison in Guayaquil, where *El Universo* had been relatively more critical. Still, both papers strongly supported the government against the coup attempt, which is congruent with the perception of the majority of officers who thought that public opinion was still favorable to the government. Thus even though none of the officers involved cited public opinion as a factor in the open-ended explanation of their personal decisions in 1954, the absence of this complaint against the Velasco government remains an important part of the explanation of why the bulk of the armed forces failed to support the coup attempt.

In conclusion, then, it may be stated that public opinion does seem to play an important role in the coup d'état process—not because military officers see themselves as agents of the popular will, but because public opinion adverse to the government performs an important function for those officers who believe that the military has an obligation to change the government, if need be, in a situation of "national crisis." In the absence of a specific definition of what would constitute such a crisis, hostile public opinion invokes and legitimates military intervention by serving as a surrogate for the guidelines available under a constitutionalist type of role definition, and by reassuring the normally apolitical officers that the personal and institutional risks of taking military action are minimized. Finally, it should be repeated that the military's perception of "public opinion" is heavily influenced by the strong regional and class biases in the average Ecuadorian officer's network of informal civilian contacts through friendships and family. The civilian sector attitudes being tapped by the military are thus obviously not necessarily representative of even the politically participant public, much less the nation as a whole.

# chapter eleven

# Anticommunism and Institutional Interests

Statistical evidence clearly suggests that Ecuadorian officers share the Latin American military's obsession with the threat of communism—though the issue was raised in only one of the four Ecuadorian coups. In fact, the quantitative analysis of the importance of the 1963 "soft on communism" charges against President Arosemena probably understates the salience of the military's concern with that issue. A more impressionistic, but perhaps more accurate test of salience might be the degree of latitude military officers were willing to allow for minor transgressions of their standards for acceptable government behavior. On other issues the military demonstrated a certain margin of tolerance, even for minor violations of the constitution, but not for lax government policies toward communism. The emergence of a communist regime in Cuba and the widespread belief that similar revolutionary movements would soon engulf Latin America[1] severely restricted the range of policies considered acceptable by the military. President Arosemena's attempt to improve his international bargaining position by maintaining diplomatic relations with communist regimes was, in the words of one sympathetic officer, "simply incomprehensible" to most of his military colleagues.[2] This low tolerance for neutralist policies was matched by an extreme sensitivity to any indication of increasing communist activity or any communist infiltration in the government, which in turn rendered the armed forces vulnerable to partisan attempts to exaggerate the magnitude of the actual threat. A number of minor "terrorist" bombings of the residences of public figures—including that of the Archbishop of Quito—were staged by members of ARNE as part of the U.S. Central Intelligence Agency's campaign to manipulate military perceptions of the political situation.[3] Only one of the more than thirty 1963 participants interviewed voiced any doubts about the authenticity of such incidents. On the contrary, many officers felt that a communist takeover was quite possible—if not probable.[4]

Along with the CIA propaganda campaign,[5] the openly anticommunist and anti-Arosemena sentiments of American military personnel undoubtedly affected Ecuadorian officers with whom they were in fairly frequent contact. In spite of disagreements with some U.S. policies, Ecuadorian officers generally have a positive image of the United States, and especially of the American armed forces, which serve for many as a model of the modern military institution. Even apart from the activities of the American military attaché (which were unanimously interpreted as an invitation to overthrow the government), the scarcely concealed antipathies of American officers toward the president could not help but provide cues to their Ecuadorian counterparts that a communist threat did exist, that the president—if not a communist—was at least susceptible to communist influence.[6] American influence should not be overstated, however. If American influence were to be considered a decisive factor, reference group theory would suggest that receptivity to that influence and sensitivity to the communist "threat" would be enhanced by training received in the United States. As indicated in table 11.1, American-trained officers were somewhat less likely to support the coup against Arosemena, and were also less

Table 11.1  American Military Training
and Attitudes toward 1963 Coup

|  | Attended American military schools | No experience in U.S. schools |
|---|---|---|
| Attitudes toward coup |  |  |
| Neutral or Progovernment | 4 ( 20%) | 2 ( 15%) |
| Favor | 7 ( 35%) | 4 ( 31%) |
| Strongly favor | 9 ( 45%) | 7 ( 54%) |
| Total | 20 (100%) | 13 (100%) |
| Stress on communist issue as factor in personal decision |  |  |
| No mention | 4 ( 21%) | 1 ( 8%) |
| Mentioned | 9 ( 47%) | 8 ( 61%) |
| Most stressed | 6 ( 32%) | 4 ( 31%) |
| Total | 19 (100%) | 13 (100%) |

likely to stress communism rather than the other issues as the major factor in that coup. To the extent that a cue-taking process was operative, it seems logical that its greatest effect would be to influence the perceptions of reality on those issues to which the Ecuadorians were already sensitive. Thus, U.S. attachés and CIA agents were probably more successful in creating a belief that the communist threat in Ecuador was real than they were in creating a concern with that threat. In any event, both the stricter limits on acceptable government performance and the clear distortion in military perceptions of actual conditions suggest that the anticommunist norm was, in fact, highly salient in 1963, even though it was only one of several factors affecting individual decisions to support the 1963 coup.

In addition to contributing to the overthrow of Arosemena, military fears of communism also contributed significantly to the decline of the constitutionalist norm after 1961. As legal means for exerting pressure on the Arosemena government to take a hard line against international and domestic communism failed to produce the desired results, the idea spread that the military's responsibility to preserve the fundamental democratic traditions and institutions of the country was more important than was its obligation to support a government whose only claim on the loyalty of the armed forces was that government's constitutionality.[7] Military officers were far from alone, however, in arguing that the constitution in no way limited military action in fulfillment of their "duty" to combat the communist menace. In a lead editorial two weeks before the coup, the Quito daily, *El Comercio,* reacted to the latest "terrorist" incident with the warning, "If the office of criminal investigation is not sufficient, then the armed forces are constitutionally obliged to intervene in order to preserve the laws, peace, and liberty in the Republic. If the aggressive campaign of red imperialism has begun, the state and its citizens must combine defenses and protect the country."[8] Writing in the 1962 edition of the *Revista del Colegio Militar,* a prominent political columnist concluded, "Since the fundamental democratic institutions of the country are entrusted by the constitution to the armed forces, the military, in order to defend those institutions, must declare itself anticommunist."[9] Partially as a result of such appeals to military fears, the rise in the perceived threat of communism in Ecuador was accompanied by a corresponding decline in the military's willingness to abide by the constitutionally defined limits on its political role.

Somewhat ironically perhaps, the "democratic institution" whose preservation most concerned the military was, clearly, *la Institución Armada.*[10] Reasoning from the Cuban example, Ecuadorian officers repeatedly made statements such as the following, depicting communism as a threat to the military itself:

The declared goal of the communists is to do away with the armed forces since, where the armed forces still exist, there cannot be communism.[11]

Where military men have been thoughtful and appreciative of liberty, the armed forces have always been against communism. However, in recent years, anticommunism has become an obligation of every military officer, as a result of direct communist attacks on the armed forces.[12]

The objective of communism everywhere is to destroy the armed forces and replace them with militias, without instruction, imbued only with their anarchic opposition to all organized institutions, especially of a democratic nature.[13]

Systematic attacks, open and concealed, on the armed forces are only part of the tactics of international communism . . . [but] we shall comply with our duty as soldiers to combat the campaign . . . to discredit and destroy the armed forces.[14]

As part of their responses to other questions, a number of the Ecuadorian coup participants made comments suggesting several rationales for their hostility toward communism. A simple classification and tabulation of these comments reveals the primacy of the perception of communism as a threat to the institutional survival of the armed forces. Seventy percent of the officers offering such comments cited the institutional threat and, more specifically,

Table 11.2  Uncued Rationales for Military Anticommunism
(N = 20, Multiple responses permitted)

| | |
|---|---|
| Communists will destroy armed forces | 14 (70%) |
| Reject as antidemocratic | 8 (40%) |
| Reject as a foreign ideology | 3 (15%) |
| Reject economic system | 2 (10%) |
| Other reasons | 3 |

their concern over possible displacement by Cuban-style militias and their fear of pro-Castro proselytizing and infiltration among the younger officers and soldiers. Another 40 percent opposed communism on the grounds that it was an avowed enemy of democracy and of the democratic institutions of the country,[15] while a smaller number specifically emphasized that they rejected communism because it was a foreign doctrine, and as such, was inappropriate to the solution of Ecuadorian problems. Two other officers implied rejection of communism as an economic system, while only one linked his rejection to the struggle of world communism against Ecuador's great power ally, the United States. The most outspoken anticommunist among the respondents argued that the very existence of Ecuador was at stake, since a communist takeover would inevitably lead to civil war and to invasions by Peru and Colombia aided by the CIA.[16] The overwhelming majority of Ecuadorian officers would, under direct questioning, defend with conviction their rejection of communism for most, and perhaps all, of the reasons cited above. In that sense, the anticommunist orientation of the Ecuadorian military is overdetermined by the perception of communism as being antithetical to all of the institutions and ideas with which military officers identify positively. It is the conviction that communism is antimilitary *and* antidemocratic, foreign *and* atheistic, etc., that accounts for the high salience in military coup decisions of government policy for dealing with the communist threat. The uncued comments cited above, however, offer more convincing evidence than could be obtained through direct inquiry that the military's primary concern is with the threat posed by communism to the institutional survival of the armed forces.

If the Ecuadorian military's demand for tough government policies against communism was, indirectly, a demand for protection of its institutional interests, then the same concern was expressed in a more direct fashion through the inclusion of government responsiveness to the institutional needs of the armed forces as an important factor in the decision of individual officers to support or oppose the government in times of crisis. In each crisis we find a consistently positive relationship: those officers who rated a government positively on its willingness to provide the armed forces with the tangible and intangible resources and rewards they considered their proper due were more likely to favor the government in a crisis situation; officers who felt that a government was unresponsive or unsympathetic in its dealings with the military were more likely to favor the forcible overthrow of that government.

Table 11.3 Correlations of Attitudes toward the Coup and
Ratings of Government Responsiveness to the Military's Institutional Interests

|          | 1954   | 1961   | 1963   | 1966   |
| -------- | ------ | ------ | ------ | ------ |
| $r$      | .431   | .377   | .516   | .688   |
| $r^2$    | 18.6%  | 14.2%  | 26.6%  | 47.4%  |
|          | N = 18 | N = 20 | N = 29 | N = 19 |

Thus it was not purely coincidental that the only full four-year term in office completed by Dr. Velasco Ibarra in his five presidencies was also an era of unparalleled government concern for the modernization and material progress of the armed forces. Major purchases of new equipment, generous pay raises, and a significant increase in military manpower more than doubled military expenditures, sending the military's share of the central government budget over 25 percent for the first and only time in contemporary Ecuadorian history.[17] Nor was Velasco's generosity limited to budgetary matters. He also supported the reorganization of the army and of the general staff[18] and the reopening of the army war academy, which had been closed by the preceding administration. To critics of the armed forces Velasco replied, "To speak of the armed forces as an unproductive force is treason."[19]

The armed forces demonstrated their gratitude for Velasco's efforts on behalf of the institution. A high-ranking naval officer recounted the material and

Table 11.4  Average Annual Increase in
Defense, Education, and Public Works Budgets
(In current sucres)

| Government | Years | Ministry of defense | Ministry of education | Ministry of public works | Total Budget |
|---|---|---|---|---|---|
| Plaza | 1950–1952 | +6.8% | −0.8% | −4.6% | −1.2% |
| Velasco | 1954–1956 | +36.1% | +5.5% | +45.4% | +22.3% |
| Ponce | 1958–1960 | −0.2% | +40.4% | +13.0% | +13.4% |
| Velasco | 1962 | +13.6% | +37.3% | −27.8% | +64.5% |
| Arosemena | 1963 | 0.0% | +9.7% | −29.8% | −3.7% |
| Military junta | 1964–1966 | +19.9% | +17.9% | +67.9% | +16.5% |

NOTE: The total central government budget and the ministerial totals were obtained by combining the regular operating budget and the supplementary capital investment budget in order to generate a uniform series. The only data available on actual expenditures (Junta Nacional de Planificación, *Indicadores Económicos* 1, no. 3 (Quito, Ecuador: July 1967): H4) cover only the former and are thereby subject to some discontinuities, although the average annual changes for the Ministry of Defense parallel those of the budget series with a somewhat smaller variation. Since the budgets are approved in the fall for the following calendar year, the first year's budget of any new government is largely the product of its predecessor. Therefore, these transitional budgets are not included in these calculations.

professional advances of the navy under Velasco, contrasting them to "the total neglect of the armed forces by the Plaza government . . . which was the reason Velasco had support in 1954 [when he needed it]."[20] When asked how Velasco had treated the military, an army colonel replied, "The armed forces never had it so good. . . . The [abortive] Varea coup could not be justified on military grounds. One had to recognize the contribution of the president to the armed forces."[21] Despite Velasco's equally unprecedented disregard for military seniority rules in naming a newly promoted lieutenant colonel to the Ministry of Defense over a number of outraged senior officers, and despite the number of officers who felt that Varea, not Velasco, deserved the credit for the military's progress, a majority of the participants in the 1954 coup attempt gave Velasco a positive rating on his government's military policies. Replying to praise for having rejected the last conspiracy that might have kept Velasco from finishing his first full term, a young army major expressed the military's general feeling of contentment. "Dr. Velasco, during his four years as president, has done a great deal to give the armed forces the prestige and opportunities that enabled them to achieve the place of honor which they now enjoy."[22]

By contrast, most of the participants in the 1963 coup were exceedingly critical of President Arosemena's treatment of the armed forces. The military budget was held constant as part of the government's austerity program, and so declined slightly in terms of real purchasing power. General staff expositions of Ecuador's military inferiority vis-à-vis Peru and petitions for more modern

Table 11.5  Ratings of Government Responsiveness
to the Institutional Needs of the Armed Forces

|  | Velasco 1954 | Velasco 1961 | Arosemena 1963 | Military junta 1966 |
|---|---|---|---|---|
| Negative | 22.2% | 10.0% | 65.5% | 52.6% |
| Ambivalent or neutral | 22.2% | 25.0% | 27.6% | 15.8% |
| Positive | 55.6% | 65.0% | 6.9% | 31.6% |
|  | N = 19 | N = 20 | N = 29 | N = 19 |

equipment were coolly received by the president,[23] whose more immediate concern was to smooth the public scandal and the congressional furor over the acquisition of some totally useless equipment by the previous government. [24] Yet the symbolic side of Arosemena's relations with the armed forces was an equally, if not more, important source of institutional discontent. The failure of the government to rescue the annual military promotions bill from partisan bickering in Congress,[25] the government's handling of the *chatarra* scandal, [26] the presence of friends and appointees of the president in a student demonstration demanding cuts in military spending,[27] and other, similar, incidents encouraged the conclusion that by his actions the president had shown himself to be unsympathetic, if not hostile, to the armed forces.[28] Whereas Velasco seldom missed an opportunity to speak before a military audience and never lacked generous words of praise and respect for the "noble mission," "exalted patriotism," and "dedication" of the armed forces,[29] Arosemena failed to provide equivalent symbolic reassurances of his respect and affection for the armed forces at a time when military insecurities had been heightened by the emergence of the "communist threat." The lack of symbolic payoffs in turn contributed to complaints that Arosemena was unresponsive to the institutional interests of the armed forces.

Somewhat surprisingly, a majority of the 1966 sample of coup participants also gave negative ratings to the military junta on its treatment of the armed forces. Since with one exception[30] the symbolic dimensions of the government's relations with the armed forces do not seem to have been grounds for complaint, the military junta's poor rating provides several important clues as to the standards by which military officers judge the adequacy of the material resources allocated to them by the government. The fact that by the government's own figures the Ministry of Defense budget climbed over 70 percent during the junta's three years in power suggests, in the first place, that the armed forces expected considerably higher levels of budgetary largess from a military government than it was accustomed to receiving from civilians. Thus even an average annual increase of 20 percent fell short of the 36 percent increases implemented during Velasco's third term.[31]

Table 11.6  Average Distribution of Central
Government Budget: 1950–1966

| Government | Years | Ministry of Defense | Ministry of Education | Ministry of Public Works |
|---|---|---|---|---|
| Plaza | 1950–1952 | 17.2% | 16.5% | 17.7% |
| Velasco | 1954–1956 | 25.1% | 13.6% | 18.0% |
| Ponce | 1958–1960 | 21.1% | 13.4% | 19.6% |
| Velasco | 1962 | 11.2% | 13.1% | 9.0% |
| Arosemena | 1963 | 11.7% | 14.9% | 6.6% |
| Military junta | 1964–1966 | 12.8% | 15.1% | 15.6% |

SOURCE: *Presupuesto general del Gobierno Nacional de la República,* annual series (Quito, Ecuador: Talleres Gráficos Nacionales).

Nevertheless, the primary standard of judgment seems to have been how much the armed forces received relative to the resources allocated to other purposes.[32] By that standard, the junta could indeed be termed wanting in generosity, since the increase in the military budget was only slightly more than the increase in the educational budget and less than one-fourth as large as the increase in the public works budget. Moreover, given the substantial increase in total spending, even with a 70 percent budget hike the Ministry of Defense share of the central government budget was only one percentage point higher than it had been under Arosemena and only half of what it had been at its high point in 1955. Any hopes held by the military of returning to that level of military expenditure must have been sorely disappointed. In fact, the military junta was the first government since World War II to devote more money to both education and public works than to the Ministry of Defense. If the negative reaction to the junta's military policies was based on disappointed expectations of substantial increases in the military share of available resources, then the Ecuadorian experience raises a serious question about the stability of reformist military governments. While the record of the military junta challenges the facile assumption that military governments invariably divert government resources away from socially and economically productive investments into military spending,[33] the Ecuadorian experience also suggests that the price of giving equal or higher priority to nonmilitary expenditures is an erosion of military support through the perception of the government as being unresponsive to the institutional needs of the armed forces. According to the preceding analysis, this erosion by itself is probably not sufficient cause for the overthrow of a reformist military government. Nevertheless, when opposition arises from entrenched elites or from popular sectors disillusioned with weak reform policies, the lack of institutional payoffs may become an important argument for a return to the barracks.

Thus far in this chapter the emphasis has been on the military's concern with protection of its institutional interests. This concern raises the question of the extent to which the political role of the Ecuadorian military can be explained in institutional terms or, alternatively, as José Nun has proposed, in terms of the special relationship between the military and the middle class in Latin American societies.[34] According to Nun's analysis, the key to understanding the political role of the armed forces lies in the "early" professionalization of the armed forces in societies where the middle class—despite its increasing numerical significance—lacks both internal cohesion and a clear vision of its own class values and interests as distinct from those of the traditional elites. Given the fragmentation and ideological dependence of the middle class,

> this early professionalization produced two main consequences: Army careers were opened to the middle class through the creation of military academies; and the military, in contrast to the organizationally weak middle class, emerged as a group possessing an unusual degree of institutional coherence and articulation. . . .[35] [In Latin American societies, with] a middle class fragmented by the particularism of its orientations and formed in a context of negotiation and compromise . . . it is the military that tends to fill the role of a protective stratum for that middle class. It was with the support of the military that the middle class achieved, in the first decades of this century, political recognition by the oligarchy; it was with their protection that it later consolidated itself in the government, and it is now with their intervention that it intends to guard against the threat posed to it by the popular sectors, which it is unable to lead.[36]

Thus, according to Nun's analysis, the political role of the Latin American military has been to represent the interests of the politically weak Latin American middle class from which it is recruited and to compensate for the inability of that class to assert itself as a hegemonic class capable of sustained stable political leadership in the face of opposition from both the traditional elites and the politically active sectors of the working class.[37]

While other scholars have questioned the logic and the empirical validity of the premises of Nun's analysis[38] as well as the historical interpretations cited as evidence for his argument,[39] the interviews with Ecuadorian military officers offer an opportunity for an empirical evaluation of the theoretical core of Nun's thesis, the proposition that "it is the association of the military with the interests and values of the middle class that explicates most [military] interventions."[40] On the surface, the political behavior of the Ecuadorian military is not inconsistent with Nun's hypothesis. It has already been demonstrated that the majority of the members of the Ecuadorian military are and have been recruited from the middle strata of Ecuadorian society. On the basis of the social and economic status of their profession, these officers are characterized by themselves and by others as members of a middle class that has, historically, exhibited the political weaknesses predicted by Nun's thesis.[41] Moreover, the decision criteria used by Ecuadorian military officers in coup decisions are such that a successful coup d'état probably will have the support of most of the Ecuadorian middle class. As indicated previously, military officers' perceptions of public opinion toward the government are heavily biased by their reliance on their friends and relatives among the sierra middle class as sources of information on public opinion. Like military personnel, most members of the Ecuadorian middle class seem to be strongly anticommunist, and middle-class attitudes toward public disorders probably parallel those of the military. During the 1950s the middle class was also a proponent of constitutional democracy, although there is no evidence to suggest that the middle class has favored greater government attention to the institutional needs of the armed forces.[42]

Nevertheless, the crux of Nun's argument is not the compatibility of the interests and values of the military and the middle class but the assertion that military interventions can be explained by the middle-class interests and values of military officers. Since many of the military coup decision criteria—public disorders, public opinion toward the government, and opposition to communism—could just as easily be construed as being in the interests of the propertied classes, the crucial empirical question is why Ecuadorian military officers should be concerned with these particular factors in deciding to support or to overthrow a particular government. Is it a concern for protecting middle-class interests or values that leads military officers to withdraw their support from governments whose performance is unsatisfactory in terms of these decision criteria?

In the case of the Ecuadorian armed forces, the answer is clearly "no." The key underlying concern for the Ecuadorian military has been the protection of the institutional interests of the armed forces. This concern is voiced directly in the "institutional interests" decision criterion, and also seems to underlie military fears of communism. In contrast to the large number of officers who saw communism as a threat to the institutional survival of the armed forces, not a single officer related his anticommunist beliefs to his membership in or concern for the middle class.[43]

Likewise in 1966, with a military government in power, the connection between public hostility to the government and a concern for the effects of that hostility on the military's institutional prestige was readily apparent. In the words of the military junta's most dedicated opponent, "The laboring forces, students, and public opinion in general joined with the political parties in an antimilitaristic front. In order to avoid a civil-military confrontation, to save military honor, and to save the military institution, an immediate transfer of power to civilian elements was the only advisable course."[44] While the junta's claim to be the "government of the armed forces" generated a special concern that continued support for the junta would lead to further loss of institutional prestige, that same concern was present in lesser degree when the armed forces exhibited a reluctance to continue maintaining unpopular civilian governments. By a similar logic, the military's traditional opposition to being used as a police force to suppress public disorders is based in large part on fears that suppressing expressions of popular discontent would lead to an erosion of public good will toward the armed forces. The exception to this rule only confirms the argument, as this resistance to a repressive role generally disappears if the protesting groups are perceived to be broadly antimilitary. Even the military's concern for the constitutionalist norm, while largely unrelated (in military thinking) to institutional interests, grew out of the military's efforts after the war with Peru to prevent the kind of political instability and civilian interference in military affairs that led to military defeat in 1941. Likewise, the limited shift toward the constitutionalist norm that occurred after 1966 was largely based on the object lesson provided by the aftermath of the military junta "that the armed forces suffer—more than any other national organization—the morally, economically, and professionally destructive consequences of military dictatorships,"[45] that "always in the end lead to purges of the officer corps and a general loss of prestige."[46] In terms of our analytic framework, it is the officers' strong, corporate self-identification with the military institution, rather than their peripheral identification as members of the middle class, that provides the underlying rationale for the decision criteria employed in Ecuadorian coups.

As indicated earlier, in the description of the military socialization process, this concern for the institutional interests of the armed forces is legitimated through the reification of the "Military Institution" and its association with a series of higher values and, ultimately, with the very survival of the country as a sovereign entity.

> We united forces and worked hard to nurse the institution back to life, profoundly conscious of our responsibility to the profession and to the *patria* [fatherland], which is, for military officers like ourselves, like the altar of a religion. . . . The individual member of the armed forces is one thing—a man—subject to the vicissitudes of the human condition; not so the institution. The institution is sacred, with its own principles, regulations, and laws.[47]

> The armed forces are the ultimate safeguard of the life of any country. Thus, if the armed forces disappear or become politicized or lose their authority or their prestige, there is no hope that the country can survive.[48]

> The libelist embodies negativism and thus it is not surprising that, upon choosing the army as one of his themes, he merely insinuates that it ought to disappear. While saying this, he doesn't bother to mention that he is attacking the entire nation or that he is predisposing the public to boycott

any hope held by the armed forces for self-improvement and strengthening. He has written an invitation to national suicide.[49]

Defense of the institutional interests of the armed forces is, therefore, defense of the national interest, and hence it is the patriotic duty of the military officer. As one officer said (perhaps unintentionally) of the 1963 coup, "There was no disagreement within the armed forces—it was for the defense of the institution in the name of the fatherland."[50] Given the subtle but pervasive impact of his institutional environment, it is difficult for a military officer to believe that the armed forces would not serve the national interest or that the national interest could be protected without the armed forces. As one officer put it, "There are some things [about the military] that were so much easier to understand before I retired. On active duty you only see the institutional perspective."[51]

This is not to say that *only* a concern for the military's institutional interests underlies the criteria employed in military coup decisions, nor to deny that these norms for government performance may become institutionalized patterns of military behavior that are more or less autonomous from their initial relationship to the institutional interests of the armed forces. In the latter process, the support of other groups in society—including the middle class—and of external reference groups obviously plays a critical role.[52] Yet by postulating that military interests and values are essentially middle-class in nature and in origin, Nun's analysis obscures the extent to which the institutional interests of the military may also be quite compatible with regimes not dominated by the middle class. The end of military support for the Liberal oligarchy in the July Revolution of 1925 had less to do with the middle-class origins of the rebel officers than with the consequences of the economic crisis of 1922 and the failure of Liberal leaders to understand the changes in the nature of institutional demands brought about by their own attempts to professionalize the army.[53] Likewise, the decline of the constitutionalist norm was facilitated by the support of extramilitary groups, but nonmiddle-class groups appear to have been both quicker to abandon democratic principles and more organized and vocal in their support for a corresponding change in military role definitions.[54] If, in general, protection of the institutional interests of the armed forces has been compatible with the interests of the middle class in Latin American societies, then the explanation of that compatibility has to be sought in the similarities of the insecurities of the two groups in changing societies and in the nature of their common political environment, rather than in the middle-class origins of military officers.[55]

## chapter twelve

# The Changing Role of the Ecuadorian Armed Forces

The argument thus far has been that the outcome of a military officer's decision to support or oppose the government in a coup d'état depends primarily on his perceptions of the political scene at a given time. Yet that outcome is also partly determined by the individual officer's beliefs about the political role of the armed forces in his society. In discussing their conceptions of the mission of the armed forces and the circumstances under which the military might be obligated to intervene, Ecuadorian military officers generally subscribed to one of four distinct types of formal role definitions: the classic professionalist, the constitutionalist, the arbiter, and the developmentalist. Each of these formal role definitions embodies an implicit doctrine of civil-military relations, stipulating the object of an officer's ultimate allegiance and the extent and form of legitimate military participation in political questions.

Table 12.1 Definitions of the Role of the
Armed Forces among Ecuadorian Officers

| Type | Allegiance to | Degree of politicization |
|------|---------------|--------------------------|
| Professionalist | Constituted order | Totally "apolitical" |
| Constitutionalist | Constitution | Fixed, limited scope |
| Arbiter | National interest | Variable, expanding in national crisis |
| Developmentalist | National security | Total politicization |

According to the classic professionalist definition of the role of the military, the armed forces are an instrument of the state, created primarily for the external defense of the country and secondarily for the maintenance of internal order. The allegiance of the military officer is to the constituted order *(el orden constituido)*—the government in power—regardless of what kind of government it might be or what it might be doing—provided that its policies are not inconsistent with military professionalism.[1] Matters unrelated to the arts of war are irrelevant to the military officer and are outside his sphere of competence. Needless to say, this was the least common type of role definition among Ecuadorian officers and even among its proponents it was often overlaid with constitutionalist doctrines. Yet invariably, those officers who spoke in terms of loyalty to the constituted order exhibited some of the attitudes of classic professionalism:

> On Monday, 6 August, the military garrison of Portoviejo revolted against the constituted order. It is well known that this senseless act of disloyalty and indiscipline was inspired by ambitious politicians who tried to lead the armed forces into fratricidal conflict without any consideration of the terrible consequences this would have for the fatherland.... It must be remembered that the air force achieved its enviable position in the hearts of the public through its total separation from these [political] conflicts and through its complete dedication to our professional and technical progress.[2]

In addition to diverting the armed forces from their responsibilities for external defense, military intervention in a coup d'état would be an attack against the state, a violation of the principles of discipline and loyalty that are the essence of the military profession.

Whereas the proponents of the professionalist model derived their definitions of the political role of the military from their conception of the nature of the military profession, a much larger group of officers accepted as legitimate and definitive the missions assigned to the armed forces by the constitution. These officers defined the role of the military in the following terms:

> Our mission is to maintain order, to observe faithfully the constitution and the laws, and to defend the territorial integrity of the Ecuadorian state. [Could there be circumstances in which the armed forces might have a duty to replace the government?] Such actions are not authorized by the constitution. The armed forces are not an arbiter in political or administrative affairs, but a force that has to comply with the mission stipulated in the laws. It would be inconceivable that the armed forces should throw out and impose presidents. It is not possible to change governments from one day to the next.[3]

> The principal functions of the armed forces are to defend our national sovereignty and to cooperate in maintaining order, the laws, and the constitution of the Republic.... Our mission is not to change governments, but to defend the constitution.[4]

While a strict interpretation of traditional professionalism would require that the military be totally apolitical, according to constitutionalist doctrine, overtly political action by the armed forces is considered both legitimate and desirable—within the limits specified by the constitution. That is, military intervention is acceptable only when it is necessary in order to oppose unconstitutional acts by either the government or the political opposition.

In contrast to the fixed, relatively well-defined limits placed on military intervention by the constitutionalist doctrine, the arbiter type of role definition is characterized by the absence of any clear guidelines specifying when the armed forces may legitimately depart from their normally apolitical tasks. When asked if there could be circumstances in which a military coup might be justified, officers subscribing to this type of role definition typically replied, "It depends on the situation."[5] As one member of the military junta put it, "My feeling has always been that the armed forces should stay out of politics and defend the constitution, but that is so, so easy to say and so difficult to apply when a crisis arises. There are moments and circumstances in the political life of the nation when you begin to fear that the country would be endangered if the military failed to take action."[6] The armed forces, therefore, have a natural responsibility to be the ultimate guardian of the "national interests" in times of "national crisis." "Someone has to have final responsibility."[7] "I have never believed that the armed forces should take it upon themselves to change governments just because they have the force to do so. Nevertheless, when the country is threatened with chaos or anarchy, those who have the force must act, must intervene temporarily to give the people the government they want."[8] As indicated previously, in the absence of clear guidelines indicating when this responsibility should be exercised, public hostility toward the government becomes an important mechanism for invoking and legitimating military intervention. "When government actions are contrary to the welfare of the people, public opinion becomes a strong pressure forcing the armed forces to take power to make the changes necessary for a return to democracy."[9] As all of these quotations suggest, there is a strong presumption in the arbiter model that military intervention will be limited in duration, that once the crisis has been resolved (generally by the removal of the president) the military can return to its essentially military functions.

The developmentalist type of role definition is distinguished from the arbiter type by an emphasis on the more or less permanent need for political involvement by the armed forces.

> The armed forces cannot be indifferent to the socioeconomic development of the country and must participate in a direct way in the life and development of Ecuador. . . . In addition, the armed forces should be prepared and disposed to take over political-administrative responsibility when the circumstances require it. If the government does not pursue

policies that guarantee the stability and progress of the Republic, if there exists an inclination to permit a penetration by communism or by the extreme left, then the obligation of the armed institution is to intervene to resolve the problem in an opportune way.... In all the branches of the armed forces and among a majority of the Ecuadorian people there exists a feeling that Ecuador will require a long period of de facto government headed by the armed forces to do away with the old politicians who have been responsible for the backwardness and underdevelopment of the country.[10]

Like the first type of role definition, developmentalist doctrines are derived internally, from a consideration of the nature of the military profession, but post-World War II changes in the military's concept of warfare resulted in a military role definition that is the antithesis of classic professionalism. Since the obligation of the armed forces is to maximize national security, the armed forces have a legitimate concern, not just with traditional problems of military preparedness, but also with any economic, political, or diplomatic policies that affect the ability of the country to deal with a potential security threat.[11] Since the primary security problem facing the country is the threat of internal insurgency, the armed forces must insist that the socioeconomic conditions upon which revolutionary movements thrive be eliminated. If civilian leadership proves to be incapable of effecting a pre-emptive program of structural transformations, then the armed forces must take over directly to plan and oversee the implementation of such reforms.[12]

The distinctions between these types of role definition were less sharply drawn in the minds of the Ecuadorian officers who espoused them. Nevertheless, these different conceptions of the proper role of the armed forces significantly influenced their behavior in a political crisis. In 1961, for example, the advocates of classic professionalism reacted to the conflict between Vice-President Arosemena and President Velasco in an entirely different manner from that of the constitutionalists. Whereas the latter reacted strongly against the government in the face of the rising tide of opposition demonstrations, one of the old professionalists described the riots in Cuenca as "an insurrection against the state. The armed forces were obligated to maintain the authority and stability of the state against such attacks."[13] The constitutional issue in 1961 was also given a different interpretation by the proponents of the professionalist model: "The openly declared opposition of Dr. Arosemena finally reached the point where President Velasco was forced to order the arrest of the vice-president. Afterwards it was said that the constitution had been broken, ... but the president always has the right to defend the peace of the Republic, to defend the constituted order."[14] Allied with the old professionalists in defense of the Velasco government were a few officers on the general staff who had begun to articulate developmentalist doctrines, and who were likewise only marginally concerned with the constitutionality of the government as a decision criterion. The professionalists were concerned with maintaining order and the developmentalists with stopping the infiltration of communist propaganda. Hence negative ratings on these two criteria were found to be associated with support for the government in the regression analysis of the 1961 coup. Despite their widely divergent beliefs about the extent of legitimate military intervention, both groups could agree on supporting Velasco[15] because neither was very concerned about the constitutionality of the vice-president's arrest.

Table 12.2 Abstract Role Definition and
Attitudes toward the 1961, 1963, and 1966 Coups

| 1961 | Classic professionalist | Constitutionalist and arbiter* | Developmentalist |
|---|---|---|---|
| Strongly favor | 0 | 10 ( 67%) | 0 |
| Favor | 0 | 3 ( 20%) | 0 |
| Strongly oppose, oppose, or ambivalent | 3 (100%) | 2 ( 13%) | 3 (100%) |
| Total, N = 21 | 3 (100%) | 15 (100%) | 3 (100%) |
| 1963 | Constitutionalist | Arbiter | Developmentalist |
| Strongly favor | 1 ( 17%) | 8 ( 53%) | 7 ( 70%) |
| Favor | 3 ( 50%) | 5 ( 33%) | 3 ( 30%) |
| Strongly oppose, oppose, or ambivalent | 2 ( 33%) | 2 ( 13%) | 0 |
| Total, N = 31 | 6 (100%) | 15 ( 99%) | 10 (100%) |
| 1966 | Constitutionalist | Arbiter | Developmentalist |
| Strongly favor | 3 (100%) | 4 ( 29%) | 2 ( 40%) |
| Favor | 0 | 4 ( 29%) | 0 |
| Ambivalent | 0 | 2 ( 14%) | 0 |
| Oppose | 0 | 3 ( 21%) | 1 ( 20%) |
| Strongly oppose | 0 | 1 ( 7%) | 2 ( 40%) |
| Total, N = 22 | 3 (100%) | 14 (100%) | 5 (100%) |

*Because many of the earlier participants subsequently shifted from a constitutionalist to an arbiter position, there are some problems in distinguishing between these two categories, especially in the 1954 sample.

In 1963, on the other hand, we find the expected positive relationship between belief in military intervention and attitudes toward the coup against President Arosemena. Seven of the ten developmentalist hardliners strongly favored Arosemena's overthrow and joined or led conspiracies for that purpose, while the percentage of officers strongly opposed to the government was reversed among the constitutionalists. Both the hardliners and the constitutionalist officers placed a greater stress on the government's lack of firm anticommunist policies than did the proponents of the arbiter model, but for adherents to the constitutionalist position and for some advocates of the arbiter role, the constitutionality of Arosemena's government acted as a partially offsetting factor. In 1966, the differences in coup behavior are, again, somewhat obscured by the shifts in role definitions that occurred in the aftermath of the military junta. The position of those who went back to a constitutionalist role definition was clearly in favor of an immediate return of power to the civilians. Among those officers espousing an arbiter role the issue was less clearly drawn. Some argued that the junta had overextended its stay in power, considering its original promise of a brief transitional military government. Others argued that the opposition to the junta was, in fact, superficial. In the absence of any real "national crisis," no military action was necessary. The government could be terminated according to the timetable for a return to civilian rule already announced by the junta. The developmentalists split more sharply over the failure of the junta to execute a strong program of socioeconomic reforms. Here the question was not the legitimacy of a military regime, but what course to take in light of the junta's reluctance to take a strong stand behind its reformist rhetoric.

In addition to shaping the way in which the issues were perceived in each crisis, the role definitions espoused by individual officers also affected the weighting of the different criteria by which they decided to support or oppose a coup. If we disaggregate the combined sample according to formal role definitions, the relative magnitude of the correlation coefficients between decision criteria ratings and coup positions provides a crude measure of these differences in the relative salience of the different criteria. Knowing how the respondent rated the constitutionality of the government, for example, is a powerful variable for explaining differences in coup behavior among constitutionalists, but useless in explaining differences among officers espousing developmentalist doctrines. On the other hand, different ratings of government performance in dealing with the communists and in serving the interests of the armed forces were most important among the developmentalists, and least so among the constitutionalists. Controlling for other factors biasing perceptions of public opinion, differences in ratings of public opinion toward the government were most important among the advocates of an arbiter role. Ratings on public disorders against the government were weakly correlated with coup decisions among constitutionalists, but not among proponents of other role definitions, where there was no agreement as to whether these were "subversive" or "popular" demonstrations.

A look at the role definitions espoused by the participants in each of the four coups reveals several major shifts in the way Ecuadorian officers conceive of the political role of the armed forces. The proportion of officers subscribing

Table 12.3 Correlations of Decision Criteria Ratings
and Coup Positions among Proponents of the Same Role Definition

| | Formal Role Definition | | |
| --- | --- | --- | --- |
| Issue | Constitutionalist | Arbiter | Developmentalist |
| Constitutionality rating | .781 | .332 | — |
| Public opinion rating | .662 | .500 | .580 |
| Controlling for other ratings | .378 | .544 | — |
| Institutional interests rating | .351 | .591 | .687 |
| Communist threat rating | .275 | .413 | .482 |
| Public disorders rating | .373 | — | — |
| Socioeconomic policy rating | .288 | — | — |
| Personal ties rating | .674 | .420 | .770 |
| | N = 31 | N = 30 | N = 15 |

NOTE: While a regression analysis to determine relative BETA weights would be preferable, the greater homogeneity in the salience attached to particular criteria and in interpreting government performance within each role definition group creates a much higher degree of multicollinearity than is present in any of the individual coup samples or in the combined sample.

to a constitutionalist role definition (the overwhelming majority in 1954) declined sharply after 1961, while classic professionalist doctrines disappeared entirely. Even the remaining constitutionalists shifted to a position closer to that of the arbiter. In 1954 and in 1961, about half of the constitutionalists had argued that the armed force's only political responsibility was to uphold the decisions of Congress as to the constitutionality of government actions. By 1963, with the disappearance of professionalist and strict constitutionalist attitudes, there were no respondents who felt that there could not be some circumstances that would justify a military decision to overthrow the government. The percentage of hardline advocates of strong military participation in the socioeconomic and political affairs of the country rose substantially throughout this period, only to decline somewhat among the participants in the 1966 crisis. The notion that the armed forces have a legitimate responsibility to act as political arbiters in times of national crisis (which was advocated by less than 15 percent of the 1954 participants) had, by 1966, replaced constitutionalist doctrines as the predominant conception of the political responsibilities of the Ecuadorian armed forces. The steady military role expansion during the postwar period can also be seen in the proportion of officers subscribing to the more interventionist arbiter and developmentalist doctrines, which rose from 21 percent in 1954 to 86 percent by 1966.

As indicated in previous chapters, these changes in role definition are in part a reflection of the changes in the political environment in the early 1960s, but they also reflect the cumulative impact of the interaction of civilian and military leaders during the whole 1948 to 1966 period and changes in the military itself. The critical mediating variable and motive force behind these shifts in role definition was the changing balance of military perceptions of the relative capabilities of military officers and civilian political leaders to deal with the problems of state.[16] The set pattern of military beliefs in civilian/military political capabilities associated with each of the four types of military role definition is the logical and empirical precondition for the credibility of doctrines advocating that pattern of civil-military relations. When the military's perceptions of these relative capabilities undergo substantial change, the formal definitions of the role of the armed forces must also change. The existing pattern of civil-military relations has been undermined.

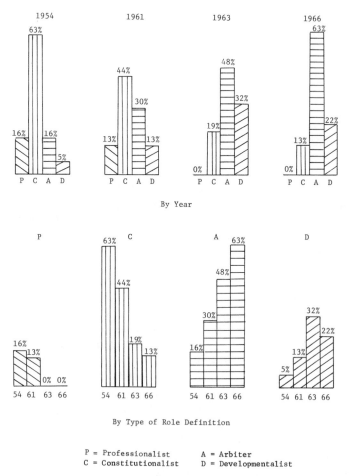

P = Professionalist  A = Arbiter
C = Constitutionalist  D = Developmentalist

Figure 12.1.  Trends in Role Definition among Ecuadorian Officers 1954–1966

Table 12.4  Formal Role Definitions and
Perceptions of Civilian/Military Capability to Govern

| Balance of perceived political capabilities | Formal role definition |
| --- | --- |
| Civilians high/Military low | Classic Professionalist |
| Civilians moderate/Military low | Constitutionalist |
| Civilians mixed or moderate/Military moderate | Arbiter |
| Civilians low/Military high | Developmentalist |

Belief in classic professionalist doctrines, for example, is difficult to reconcile with low esteem for the capabilities of the civilian political leadership. Unquestioning obedience to the highest civilian authorities, which is a necessary consequence of the classic professionalist's emphasis on discipline, assumes a certain faith in the wisdom of the authorities who control the destiny of the military institution. With the onset of the depression and the collapse of the military-backed reform government of Dr. Isidro Ayora, the Ecuadorian military withdrew to a position of almost total institutional subordination to civilian control approximately equivalent to the Prussian model to which the officer corps had secondhand exposure through the German-trained Chilean and the Italian military missions. In contrast to the situation in Chile or Argentina at roughly the same time,[17] in Ecuador, this subordination was based less on strong professionalist convictions within the armed forces than on the substantial gap in social status that existed between socially marginal military officers and the predominantly aristocratic, university-educated civilian political elite. The Ecuadorian defeat in the Peruvian invasion of 1941 did not improve the military's perceptions of its own capabilities, since most of the initial public recrimination fell on the army. Nevertheless, especially for those young officers who faced Peruvian divisions without troops, equipment, or supplies, and for all those withheld from combat for political reasons, the claim of civilian authorities to absolute military loyalty was no longer credible. For the military generation of 1941, the formula for avoiding any future recurrence of the 1941 disaster was constitutionalism[18] —a military guarantee of free elections to avoid the kind of electoral fraud that brought the Arroyo government to power in 1940, complete military abstention from partisan conflicts, devotion to raising the professional level of the armed forces, and a guarantee of military support to constitutional governments to make political interference in military affairs unnecessary for political survival.

Despite the substantial improvement in the public prestige of the armed forces resulting from its role in the constitutional interlude of 1947–1961, military support for constitutionalist doctrines began to weaken in the early 1960s. The importance of the emergence of the communist threat in bringing about this change has already been sufficiently stressed. If the constitutional government was incapable or unwilling to take strong action to control the spread of communism, then the military could not be constrained by the constitutional limits on its political actions. Other factors also contributed to a declining faith in the capabilities of the civilian political elite and to an improved self-image among military officers. The military had promoted political stability by consistently suppressing conspiracies and barracks revolts— "The politicians always try to overthrow governments, but the armed forces made them respect the constitution,"[19] —but many officers felt that the governments protected in this way were not reciprocating by assisting the professional progress of the armed forces. Of the five governments in power between 1948 and 1963, only Velasco's demonstrated a concern for the general modernization of the armed forces—a concern that was, however, tied to a 1930s-style assault on the professional autonomy of the military in its internal affairs. Their persistent failure to recognize the professional aspirations of the armed forces contributed little to the image of the civilian political leaders as true statesmen. In addition, whatever sense of political decorum and dignity remained in the 1950s was soon lost in the 1960s. The rising level of mass participation, the slackening of economic growth, and the emergence of *velasquismo* as a full-blown populist movement led to sharply higher levels of partisan conflict. The corruption scandals of the fourth Velasco administration, the increasing use of the army against political demonstrations, and the decline of Congress into a public forum for rancorous and rowdy debate, all contributed to a perception of "politician" and "statesman" as mutually exclusive categories.[20] Thus President Arosemena's personal conduct and lack of strong action against the communists merely capped the growing disrespect for "a garrulous political class excessively chained to its private interests."[21]

At the same time, there was some cause in the early 1960s for military officers to enjoy a moderate rise in self-esteem. Included in this particular generation of officers were a number of engineers who had had university training before entering military service, and twenty or thirty who had studied international law at Central University while they were stationed in Quito.[22] Ironically, the closure of the war academy by the Plaza government to stifle complaints about Ecuador's military preparedness seems to have promoted this psychic mobility. Fifty-five percent of the officers interviewed were forced to go abroad, to countries where the military profession was generally held in higher esteem, for their general staff school. Even for those who remained in Ecuador, the revised curriculum after the war academy reopened in 1956 offered several courses in geopolitics and law, and some opportunities to discuss national problems.[23]

The weakening of the constitutionalist role definition by the changing balance of capability perceptions was already evident in a speech by the director of the engineering school to the graduating class, given less than a month after the successful defense of constitutional principles in the 1961 coup.

> It has been said [Article 153 of the constitution] that the military officer is
> not deliberative, but only obedient. The principle of nondeliberation is
> questionable from every point of view. How can the high command be only
> obedient and not deliberate when dealing with important national interests?
> How can it arrive at a decision if, before, it has not discussed the pros and
> cons in order to be able to decide? The military officer has to make deci-
> sions and he has to discuss problems of the *patria*, problems that he must
> study and prepare himself to understand in order to define his personality as
> a true servant of the Ecuadorian nation.[24]

From questioning the nondeliberation clause it was not a large step to
entertaining the idea that the good qualities of military officers could be
substituted, at least temporarily, for the disreputable qualities of the politicians.

> The lack of quality, quantity, and organization of the political class had to
> be substituted by an authoritarian, dynamic, and renovative action that
> only the armed institution was in a position to provide. For this temporary
> and exceptional task, the military officer is in a position to provide, better
> than anyone else, his special qualities; in addition to the disinterest and
> sobriety that are necessary to his daily life, the officer normally has the
> virtues deriving from discipline; he knows the reality of the Ecuadorian
> people, by having lived in the most diverse corners of the country; he
> knows better than the civilian, for having seen it, the geography of the
> *patria;* his studies in the general staff have given him a complete vision of
> the principal problems; and so on. But above all, the military officer
> belongs entirely to the nation, to the whole more than to any part or party
> and, still less, to the interests of the great plutocratic enterprises, national
> or foreign. Therefore he is prepared morally and intellectually to confront
> moments of crisis, restoring order and giving impulse *from without* to the
> renovation of a political system that has not been able to correct and
> regenerate itself, and that had not been, in practice, a true democracy.[25]

Only when the crisis finally arrived, in July 1963, did the full extent of the
erosion of constitutionalist doctrines become clear. As opposed to the situation
in 1961, when the alternative of a military successor to Velasco was briefly
raised and unanimously rejected, in the official deliberations to discuss the fate
of Arosemena's government, the alternative of a civilian replacement was never
even considered, nor does the question seem to have occurred to many of the
participants.[26]

While these changes in perceptions of capabilities were widespread—as
indicated in the abandonment of the constitutionalist doctrine by at least 80
percent of the 1963 respondents—they were also, for most of these officers,
limited in scope. Many (including at least three key members of the military

government) shared the anxieties of one officer who said of his new assignment as civil-military governor of a southern province, "I didn't want to go to such a difficult post. I did not feel prepared for a position of political power."[27] The optimism that filled the early days of the military junta was based more on belief in the superior moral qualities of military leaders than on any real technical preparation or training for dealing with complex policy problems. "We wanted to make certain important structural changes, but down deep we knew this had to be done by capable civilians, so we sought civilian advisors to draw up the laws."[28] Still, despite the lingering doubts about military preparedness, the failures of civilian leadership were increasingly well-known, whereas the potentialities of military government had not been tested for a quarter of a century.

For a smaller group of officers, the transformation in attitudes toward military participation in the political process was more profound. The diffusion of new doctrines of warfare after the Second World War changed both the definition of the professional responsibilities of the armed forces and military attitudes toward civilian leaders. The result was a movement toward adoption of the developmentalist role, especially among those officers who had been exposed to these new doctrines through advanced training abroad. Those officers who attended general staff school in Argentina, Brazil, Spain, or Italy, and those who had attended a superior war college were much more likely to

Table 12.5  Foreign Training and Formal Role Definition

| Formal role definition | General Staff School Attended | | | | |
|---|---|---|---|---|---|
| | Ecuador | Chile | U.S. | Subtotal* | Spain, Italy, Brazil, Argentina |
| Constitutionalist | 12 (44%) | 5 ( 56%) | 3 (27%) | 20 ( 43%) | 2 ( 15%) |
| Arbiter | 9 (33%) | 3 ( 33%) | 5 (45%) | 17 ( 36%) | 7 ( 54%) |
| Developmentalist | 6 (22%) | 1 ( 11%) | 3 (27%) | 10 ( 21%) | 4 ( 31%) |
| Total | 27 (99%) | 9 (100%) | 11 (99%) | 47 (100%) | 13 (100%) |
| | Attended Superior War College | | | | |
| | No | | Yes | | |
| Constitutionalist | 24 ( 40%) | | 1 (14%) | | |
| Arbiter | 27 ( 45%) | | 1 (14%) | | |
| Developmentalist | 9 ( 15%) | | 5 (71%) | | |
| Total | 60 (100%) | | 7 (99%) | | |

*The influence of the Americans and Chileans who were advisors to the Ecuadorian war academy after it reopened in 1956 may account for the lack of major differences in role definitions among those with American, Chilean, or Ecuadorian general staff school experience.

espouse the developmentalist definition of the role of the armed forces. In spite of the role of the U.S. military in developing these new doctrines,[29] training in the more advanced Latin countries seems to have been more effective in disseminating these ideas than was training in the United States. The enormous differences in the economic and political systems of the United States and Ecuador seem to have blunted the impact of doctrines that were seen as transferable when encountered in the Argentine or Brazilian context. Most of the developmentalists who had not received advanced training abroad were the personal protégés of those officers who had.

The first stage in this diffusion process occurred in the late 1950s as Ecuadorian officers became aware of the revisions being made in military doctrine based on the Second World War and the Cold War. The former demonstrated that victory in modern warfare depended less on the preparedness of military forces in existence at the onset of the conflict than on the total capacity of the nation to mobilize its resources for all-out war. The Cold War suggested that, in the contemporary world, military success was not just a matter of battles won or lost in some future confrontation, but should be measured in terms of national security, i.e., the ability to guarantee the survival of the country and the protection of its vital interests at any time. Since the degree of national security achieved is dependent upon all the elements of national power, an elaborate conceptual framework was developed for the planning of national security policy that coordinated the efforts of the "military, diplomatic, economic, and internal fronts."[30]

The primary effect of the new national security doctrines was to legitimate military interest in all the nonmilitary policies of the government and to decrease military respect for civilian leadership. If the political leaders of the country generally failed to comprehend the old definition of military professionalism, they were even less successful in comprehending the new professionalism. Two of the officers interviewed specifically denounced the failure of civilians to do their part for national security.

> With a false concept of professionalism, the government has put a wall between military matters and political, social, and economic problems. The high command needs to understand the problems of Ecuador. Moreover, the problem of national defense is not just a problem for military officers but for the civilians as well.[31]

> The problem is that the civilians are not aware of *their* role in national defense. Economists, industrialists, agriculturalists, and government officials all have to take part in formulating and executing the national strategic plan.[32]

Although in 1960 the Velasco government requested and received passage of a National Security Law, the National Security Council that it created rarely, if ever, met. The post of secretary-general was used for the next decade as a convenient means of occupying a series of senior officers by having them write and then rewrite proposals for the creation of an institute of higher military studies—proposals that were not accepted by civilian leaders who were rightfully wary of the political implications of the institute's announced objective of training civilian and military leaders in their new responsibilities.[33] If the old political leaders were incapable of understanding the problem of national security, then the necessity for new leadership was the obvious remedy.

> Some ingenuous, ignorant, or ill-intentioned individuals persist in calling 1941 a military defeat. If it was a defeat, it was one born in the spirit and mentality of the political leaders of that dark period. . . . The errors and defects of the past persist, aggravated by new circumstances and internal contradictions. . . . It follows that the renovation of national leadership [los cuadros dirigentes], in respect to its physiognomy and social composition, its formation and perfection, its ideas, concepts, and goals, is a question of vital importance, indispensable to the formation of a new national conscience with eyes to the true development, progress, and fortification of the people as a factor in the greatness and power of the Ecuadorian state.[34]

According to the developmentalists, the old politicians must be replaced with statesmen: military officers and civilians socialized to the military's new vision of effective government.

The second stage in the shift in definition of military responsibilities came with the introduction of counter-insurgency doctrines stressing that revolutionary guerrilla warfare was the primary threat to national security. In turn, the focus on internal security gave rise to a concern for eliminating the conditions that could provide the basis for insurgency movements.[35]

> The armed institution saw with alarm that the unity of the internal front was declining every day because of the increasing divisions between Ecuador's social classes.[36]

> To the panorama of problems resulting from the exhaustion of a political system inadequate for new times, an unjust social structure, and an economic system of accentuated colonial dependence on the exterior, was superimposed the violent agitation of Castroism, then at its height. Its dynamic action had to find fertile ground in the desires of the dispossessed classes.[37]

> The traditional definition of the mission of the armed forces has in fact converted the military into an instrument of support for a tiny privileged economic minority, combating demonstrations of popular discontent without inquiring as to its origins. When demands for change are simply obstructed by force, eventually the guerrilla problem arises, dividing the

armed forces from those seeking change. For their survival, to maintain the institution, the regular forces will have to fight. A new position is necessary, to open the way to groups seeking a better way of life rather than constituting a barrier to them, as in the past.[38]

This critical view of the country's socioeconomic structure was accompanied by an even more negative attack on Ecuador's "superficial" democracy. The announced goal of the developmentalists was a "governing democracy, not a democracy governed by the pressure groups of the oligarchy."[39] "Nominal power had passed alternatively from a small group in conservative dress to another small group in liberal dress, and lately to a popular caudillo, . . . while real power and its principal benefits remained, invariably, in the hands of those who managed the great economic forces of the country, dominated the press and other media, and financed the election campaigns of all the possible winners."[40] Exposure to counterinsurgency doctrines was, therefore, an additional impetus toward adoption of the developmentalist role definition. In turn, developmentalist doctrines positing the necessity of true socioeconomic development in order to achieve national security formed the basis for military demands for major socioeconomic reforms.[41]

Another major shift in military role definitions occurred in the aftermath of the military junta, which was widely faulted for having failed to meet the demands of the developmentalists for a thorough socioeconomic transformation. The junta's moderate agrarian and tax reform decrees and its attempts to establish a career civil service virtually exhausted its reform program, most of which was inherited from the previous administration. Despite the positive public reception of these measures, in the critical confrontation with the economic elite of Guayaquil over control of autonomous agencies and tariff rates, the junta consistently refused to take a strong stand behind its policies and, rather than radicalize the conflict, made repeated concessions to the Guayaquil merchants.[42] The junta's attempt to be a "democratic dictatorship"[43] directly conflicted with the desires of many officers for "a government vindicating the claims of the socioeconomic majorities."[44] The junta's vacillations led to widespread complaints against *"la dictablanda."* As one disgruntled officer put it, "It is not a dictatorship when those who deserve a firm hand are treated with such consideration."[45]

As indicated in chapter 7, however, these complaints do not have the expected simple relationship to attitudes toward the overthrow of the junta. In large part this seems to derive from the extreme ambiguity of developmentalist doctrines for purposes other than criticizing the status quo. Depending, perhaps, on whether they emphasized the national power or pre-emptive revolution rationales for linking national security and development, some of those criticizing the *dictablanda* seem to have had in mind a tough, but economically and politically conservative regime à la Brazil, while others envisioned a more nationalistic, antioligarchical program, along Peruvian lines.[46] There is some evidence that the former supported the overthrow of the junta, while the latter's discontent over the junta's weakness was offset by their even stronger antipathies toward the opposition alliance of old politicians, oligarchs, and antimilitary students.[47]

The immediate impact on military role definitions of the experiment in military government was a diminished faith in the ability of the military to govern the country effectively. The increased awareness of the limited opportunities available to Ecuadorian officers for acquiring nonmilitary expertise reversed the trend toward adoption of developmentalist doctrines and reinforced the position of those who argued that the armed forces should limit their involvement in political questions to temporary intervention in time of national crisis. "The military junta came to power unexpectedly. They were not really prepared to govern the country, . . . [and] their mistakes fell on the armed forces."[48] Several officers even made it clear that their obvious sympathies for the Peruvian military regime were not transferrable to the Ecuadorian context. "Our officers are basically trained only in the techniques of war. The Peruvian military has been preparing [for this government] for years."[49]

If the military's perceptions of their own capabilities changed as a result of the military government, the same experience radicalized attitudes toward the civilian elites, especially among those who had previously advocated or shifted now toward an arbiter role definition. Since the junta's reform efforts were generally seen as well-intentioned (even when unsuccessful), the intransigent opposition of the entrenched economic interests embittered military officers toward "the oligarchy, especially the merchants, who have always benefited themselves and exploited the people."[50] The attacks of the parties in the constitutionalist front were even more difficult to stomach, since the same politicians who had urged and applauded the overthrow of Arosemena now proclaimed themselves to be the defenders of democracy against the military dictatorship they had helped bring to power. The alacrity with which these leaders lined up to seek government patronage and then changed their stance to opposition when it was refused them led even politically moderate officers to the conclusion that "Politics in Ecuador is nothing more than fighting to get a good post in the government and getting as much out of it as one can in the least time possible."[51]

Any lingering support for civilian leadership quickly vanished when the fall of the junta ushered in a period of harsh recrimination against the military government and against the armed forces in general. Led by ex-President Arosemena, the opponents of the junta opportunely took advantage of the weak interim governments that followed to get their revenge. In a televised interview, Arosemena blamed his overthrow on "a corrupt high command . . . that the last Congress refused to promote, deeming them incompetent or dishonest, [on] civilians who forgot that officers incapable of directing a barracks or fighting a heroic war even in a losing cause could hardly be expected to guide the destiny of the country, [and on] a handful of officers who dreamed of assaulting the customs houses and monopolies of the country in order to illegally enrich themselves."[52] In an official resolution of the 1967 Constituent Assembly that denounced the modus vivendi with the United States in the dispute over fishing limits, the military junta was attacked in the harshest possible terms—"Liberty was shackled, political power [was] prostituted, and the nation [was] scorned and reviled by the most incompetent of her sons: . . . the military dictators."[53] Taking advantage of the military's weakened political position, Congress subsequently passed a stiff new Personnel Law governing promotion and retirement that included an unprecedented provision forcing the twenty officers of highest rank in the three services to present, at the end of each year, their resignations to the president for his consideration.[54] While teaching the bitter lesson that the armed forces will suffer the consequences of military dictatorships, these attacks on the armed forces also undermined the efforts of the high command to return the armed forces to a constitutionalist position by demonstrating the total inability of democratic governments to restrain the antimilitary campaign.[55]

In doing so, the recriminations against the armed forces made it extremely unlikely that the reduced political role of the military could be institutionalized. Even the arbiter role presupposes some recognition of civilian capabilities for effectively governing the country. The arbiter model is not stable when the political system is seen to be in a state of permanent, rather than temporary, crisis. Only the immediacy of the junta's failure and the military's inability to believe in military government as a viable alternative prevented the re-emergence of developmentalist doctrines. Four years later, in a most perceptive insight, one former opponent of the junta disagreed with most of his colleagues: "The lesson of the military junta has not yet been written, but is being written at this very moment. Now we are recognizing, through comparison to the present civilian dictatorship, the constructive achievements of the military junta."[56]

A year and a half later—in 1972—the armed forces again seized power, declaring that

> the constant failures of [civilian] governments, the absence of the people from the centers of decision-making, the administrative inefficiency and immorality, the incapacity and insincerity of the political parties, and, fundamentally, the economic structure, have contributed to the existence of an unjust and backward society . . . [that] has dangerously weakened national security. . . . Faced with this situation, the armed forces, in accordance with their responsibility for the survival of the Ecuadorian state, have assumed power, without leaders or caudillos, but as an institution, to implant a new national political doctrine, which will make possible the execution of the substantial transformations of the socioeconomic and legal order that the present chaotic state of the Republic demands.[57]

*part five*

# The Coup d'Etat as a Political Process

# chapter thirteen

# The Variable Political Environment

From 1948 to 1966, six different governments occupied the Ecuadorian presidential palace; three were overthrown in military coups. As indicated earlier, at one level the differing fates of these governments—the survival of some, the demise of others—can be explained in terms of the variations over time in the level of political crisis. More specifically, their varying fates reflect variations in the extent to which the political situation was unacceptable according to the decision criteria of Ecuadorian officers. But, this level of explanation is not in itself sufficient. A comprehensive analysis of the coup d'état as a political process must also link the political outcomes entering into coup decisions with the larger social, economic, and political processes at work in a given society. While much more research will be required in order to refine our understanding of these processes, the primary concern of this chapter is to identify the larger forces shaping the political environment with which the Ecuadorian military interacts.

The 1948–1966 period in Ecuadorian history presents a curious contrast in terms of military coups. The first twelve years of this period were characterized by relatively low levels of political conflict and no irregular changes of government. This period of calm was, however, followed by three successive coups. After experiencing, during the 1930s and 1940s, one of the highest rates of government turnover in Latin America (averaging one government each year), Ecuador emerged in the 1950s as one of the region's more stable constitutional regimes. For the first time in the history of the Republic, freely elected presidents completed their full four-year terms of office—an accomplishment made all the more impressive by the fact that each of these governments represented different political parties. On the basis of this record, both Ecuadorian and American observers made confident predictions that "Ecuador had overcome the stage of coup d'états and military intervention in politics"[1] – predictions that were belied by the events of the next six years.

In retrospect it seems clear that these predictions were not merely overly optimistic, but were based on the false premise that Ecuador had achieved a degree of political "maturity" or political development superior to that of the 1930s and 1940s. A more accurate explanation for the contrast between this twelve year period of relative political peace and the renewed instability that followed can be found in the varying degrees of support for the government generated by Ecuador's export-dependent economy. Given the continuing debility of the country's political institutions in the face of rising levels of participation and the general absence of elite or mass belief in the legitimacy of the political system, the stability of that system varied according to the vagaries of the international market for primary products.

Following the classic pattern of outward-oriented development, in the late 1940s the Velasco and Plaza governments encouraged the use of fallow coastal lands for production of exports in order to take advantage of favorable circumstances in the world market. After World War II, having already returned to pre-Depression levels, the dollar value of Ecuadorian exports increased more than 150 percent from 1948 to 1954, generating a 25 percent increase in national income in the 1950–1954 period alone.[2] Domestic agricultural production was also strongly stimulated by the rising demand.[3] The new economic prosperity promoted a substantial lessening of tensions between the coastal oligarchy, the traditional landowning aristocracy of the sierra, and the increasingly numerous members of the urban middle class. With the increased opportunities for elite mobility outside of the political system and the rapid increase in the number of middle class bureaucratic positions resulting from the doubling of public expenditures,[4] control over the government ceased to be such a highly salient issue.[5] While Plaza's attempt to unite the "progressive" elements of the traditional elites in a political alliance with the middle class perhaps best exemplified the lessening of social and political tensions, this more relaxed climate was also apparent in the general disappearance of most meaningful distinctions among the traditional parties, culminating in the Liberal party's participation in the Ponce administration.

Thus despite the various attempts to launch military revolts, with the possible exception of 1953, "public opinion" toward the government was never hostile enough to support a coup d'état. With each of these governments pursuing an accommodationist political strategy, none was ever so embattled as to feel any necessity for grossly violating the constitution to maintain itself in power. Given the minimal levels of political mobilization, public disorders were relatively rare occurrences. The only political group that was antagonistic to the military—the Communist party—amounted to little more than a minor intellectual debate club.[6] Finally, while each of these three governments adopted different policies toward the professional and budgetary aspirations of the armed forces, the combined payoff was sufficient to avoid serious military unrest.

In the mid-1950s, however, the economic boom tapered off sharply, as the terms of trade began to turn against Ecuador and other producers of primary products.[7] The rate of growth in exports slowed almost as sharply as it had risen during the previous fifteen years. With the additional burden of Ponce's conservative monetary and fiscal policies, the economy stagnated. In real per capita terms, the amount of goods and services available for consumption, which had increased by more than 12 percent between 1950 and 1954, grew by less than 2 percent between 1954 and 1959.

Table 13.1  Rate of Growth of Exports

| Time period | Average annual increment | Average annual rate of increase |
|---|---|---|
| 1940–1948 | $ 5.5 million dollars | 51.8% |
| 1948–1954 | $11.8 million dollars | 21.4% |
| 1954–1963 | $ 3.2 million dollars | 2.8% |
| 1963–1968 | $11.9 million dollars | 7.9% |

SOURCE: Central Bank data reproduced in Clarence Zuvekas, "Ecuador: Selected Economic Data" (Mimeographed. Quito, Ecuador: USAID, 1970), p. 94, and Charles R. Gibson, "The Role of Foreign Trade in Ecuadorian Economic Development" (Ph.D. dissertation, University of Pennsylvania, 1968), p. 406.

The political consequences of the changing economic trends were, however, not immediately apparent, partly because the military's internal conflicts erupted at the very high point of the economic boom—in 1954—rather than amid the recession and political conflicts of 1953. Lacking any public support or external justifications, the Quito revolt failed, giving the government the opportunity to remove the most politically aggressive segment of the armed forces. The 1956 elections (in which the populist vote was divided between two candidates who had only regional support) and the opportunities for social mobility through migration provided temporary outlets for the growing economic discontents of the lower classes, but the miniature *bogatazo* in Guayaquil in 1959 and the bitter election campaign of 1960 made it clear that the brief era of prosperity had brought only a temporary respite from the political instability of the previous decades.

The end to the political truce of the 1950s was, however, not to be simply a reversion to the intraelite instability of the status quo ante. At the same time that economic growth was promoting harmony among the traditional political elites, it was also swelling the ranks of the marginal sectors of the urban working class and thereby laying the foundations for the emergence of populism as a new political force. Since the fruits of the new prosperity were overwhelmingly concentrated in the urban areas, the export boom sparked a two-pronged wave of migration to the cities and to the coast in search of higher wages and employment opportunities. The absence of a significant industrial sector, the lag between job creation and population growth,[8] and these migratory movements

Table 13.2 Changes in the Geographic
Distribution of Population: 1938–1962

Percentage of total population living on the coast

| 1938:* 32.0% | 1950: 40.5% | 1962: 46.1% |

Percentage of total population living in cities with more than 20,000 inhabitants

| 1938:* 12.1% | 1950: 17.5% | 1962: 26.7% |

*Non-census estimate.

SOURCE: Pedro Merlo, "Crecimiento de la población del Ecuador," *Indicadores Econó-micos* 1, no. 3 (July 1967):35, 46; Dirección Nacional de Estadística, *Ecuador en cifras 1938–1942* (Quito, Ecuador: Imprenta de Ministerio de Hacienda, 1944), pp. 55, 60. Merlo's work is a National Planning Board summary of the 1950 and 1962 censuses.

swelled the mass of unemployed or underemployed day laborers, porters, and itinerate businessmen in the burgeoning *barrios suburbanos* of Quito and in various "new towns" on the coast. In Guayaquil the rural-urban and sierra-costa streams converged to double the population between 1950 and 1962.[9] With the export-financed diffusion of education removing the legal barrier to political participation, the marginal "subproletariat became the base for a personalist, messianic, and clientelistic populism, which presented itself as the voice of the 'popular will.' "[10] While appealing to the concrete and immediate needs—jobs and elementary public services—of their followers, the *velasquista* movement, the Concentration of Popular Forces, and, to a lesser extent, ARNE, expressed the social frustrations of the marginal lower class in a fashion consistent with the Catholic, ruralized, political culture of the *barrios suburbanos*. As political participation ceased to be exclusively the prerogative of the upper and middle classes, the strength of populist movements increased correspondingly, culminating in Velasco's smashing defeat of the traditional parties in the 1960 elections.

As a result of the socioeconomic changes and the increased political participation of the previous decade, the Ecuadorian governments of the 1960s faced a rising volume of demands for an improved standard of living, which the economy was no longer generating independently, as it had been during the late forties and early fifties. In different ways, each of the next three governments revealed the inability of the existing political institutions to generate support without the aid of favorable economic circumstances.

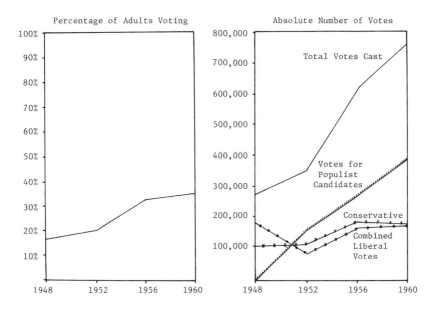

Figure 13.1. Modernization, Participation, and Populism

SOURCES: Pedro Merlo, "Crecimiento de la población del Ecuador," *Indicadores Económicos* 1, no. 3 (July 1967), 35, 46; Idem, *Ecuador: Evaluación y ajuste de la población total del año 1960 al año 2000,* Centro Latinoamericano de Demografía, Series C, no. 113 (June 1969), 21; Dirección Nacional de Estadística, *Ecuador en cifras 1938-1942* (Quito, Ecuador: Imprenta del Ministerio de Hacienda, 1944), pp. 55, 60; Georg Maier, *The Ecuadorian Presidential Election of June 2, 1968: An Analysis* (Washington, D.C.: Institute for the Comparative Study of Political Systems, 1969), pp. 74–78.

NOTE: Between 50 and 80 thousand of Velasco's votes in 1952 should be attributed to the faction of the Liberal Party, which supported his "independent Liberal" candidacy. The populist total for 1952 is therefore somewhat inflated. The populist vote is understated in 1960, as the CFP which supported the splinter left candidacy of Antonio Parra contributed perhaps 25,000 votes to the combined Liberal total.

Approximately 35 percent of the increase in the total vote can be attributed to population growth, 36 percent to increased registration, and the remaining 29 percent to increased turnout.

Despite his initially strong popular base in the marginal subproletariat, Velasco's government was perhaps the least prepared to cope with the new situation. At the start of his term, government spending characteristically rose quickly upwards, but with the sharp decline in exports in 1961, government revenues failed to keep pace. Mostly through the efforts of economic advisors tied to the Guayaquil oligarchy, the costs of the budget deficit and devaluation were shifted, through inflation and indirect taxes, to the very groups that had supported Velasco in the election. When the expectations created by the electoral campaign and the economic upswing of 1960 were so rudely dashed, Velasco's support evaporated and the country was rocked by an unprecedented nationwide wave of strikes and violent disorders. Velasco's violation of constitutional norms probably only hastened a change of government that would otherwise have occurred through impeachment by the opposition majority in Congress.

Both Carlos Julio Arosemena and the military junta rejected Velasco's populism as demagogy without substance and both proposed to resolve the problem of rising demands through the moderate reforms endorsed by the Alliance for Progress. These reforms would, theoretically, permit some of the new demands to be satisfied through a minor redistribution of the existing wealth, while increased public investment and more efficient use of existing resources would revitalize the economy. In fact, however, neither government was capable of generating sufficient support to counter the determined opposition of the established economic elites, who preferred to maintain the status quo, even though the proposed reforms were mostly intended to prevent more radical forms of change.

President Arosemena sought to mobilize support through a formal alliance with the traditional parties of the "center-left"—the Liberals and Socialists—while trying, simultaneously, to secure the backing of more radically inclined groups like the Central Labor Federation and URJE through his personal friendship with many of the leaders of the intellectual left. While the first alliance provided relatively competent cabinet ministers and a tenuous majority in Congress, neither of these parties shared Arosemena's neutralist position on foreign policy questions, and the Liberal party in particular could not be depended on to support any serious domestic reforms.[11] In any case, this alliance provided only a limited base of support from a small cadre of party activists. It did not provide any organization possessing, or capable of mobilizing mass support.[12] The more radical groups came closer to sharing President Arosemena's own views, but these, too, were rather small groups of activists with relatively weak organizational links to their constituencies, which, at the maximum, consisted of some 35,000 industrial workers and 11,000 students.[13] Given the political passivity of most workers and students and the ideological diversity of the rest, a respectable minority of either group might have been mobilized around some specific grievance (as in the 1961 campaign against the economic policies and repressive tactics of the Velasco government), but a sustained campaign of support for measures like agrarian reform, which were not directly relevant to them, was beyond their capabilities.

The military junta's approach to the problem of securing political support was more straightforward, but no more successful. Recognizing the weaknesses of the existing political parties and hoping that the nonpartisan image of the armed forces could be carried over into the government, the junta chose to simply dispense with any formal political alliances. According to General Gándara, "the adoption of any political tint was excluded, because the armed forces, as an eminently national institution, could not and should not be identified with any party or political tendency."[14] Instead, the junta preferred to recruit relatively unknown independents and technocrats to run the government.[15] According to the military's somewhat simplistic view of politics, "good government"—that is to say, decision-making without the "distortions" caused by partisan politics—would automatically generate public support for the government.

The organizational weaknesses of the existing political groups that made it difficult for the military junta and President Arosemena to mobilize political support for a reform government were not the only obstacles to the mobilization of support from the groups these reforms were supposed to benefit. In the first place, the limited nature of the reforms and the inadequacy of the administrative machinery available to implement them meant that there was little or no immediate impact in the daily lives of the alleged beneficiaries to signal that these two governments were any different from their predecessors.[16] Except for the Agrarian Reform Law (the short term effects of which were, apparently, often negative),[17] other reforms, such as the various tax reforms, were all but invisible to the average lower-class Ecuadorian. Secondly, the most likely target group—the marginal urban subproletariat—was by its very nature much more suited to spontaneous mobilization in a populist electoral campaign than to organization as a permanent political force supporting either radical or moderate reforms. "How does one convince a street vendor of the advantages of socialization of the means of production? Or make a porter understand the benefits of agrarian reform? .... How can one organize those whose work disperses them rather than concentrates them? If they are to be organized around the neighborhood as the only 'visible' bond among them, how does one keep socialism from coming to mean nothing more concrete than putting in a street, a school, or a dispensary?"[18]

Nevertheless, the most serious impediment to the organization of new sources of political support was the attitude of the armed forces toward political conflict. On the one hand, the military was not willing to permit civilians to mobilize mass support. Any attempt by President Arosemena to mobilize the marginal subproletariat would have merely heightened military fears of a "communist" takeover. On the other hand, the military was not willing to undertake any such mobilization itself, despite its immunity from soft-on-communism charges and despite its predisposition toward precisely the kind of public works and civic action projects that would have generated support in the *barrios suburbanos*. The military junta was not prepared to commit itself to the partisan task of organizing that support, even in its own defense. In the words of General Gándara, "As soldiers on active duty, we are not committed to any individual, group, or party, ... [only to] the national interest .... We believe that politics is the art of achieving the common good."[19] Even when the leaders of two migrant neighborhoods (both of which were built on speculative properties expropriated by the junta from Guayaquil millionaire Juan X. Marcos) came to offer the support of their followers in the government's conflict with the Guayaquil economic elite, their offer was refused.[20] As Huntington argues, "The problem is military opposition to politics. Military leaders can easily envision themselves in a guardian role; they can also picture themselves as the impartial promoters of social and economic reform in their societies. But, with rare exceptions, they shrink from the role of political organizer."[21] As a result, the military junta was as ill-prepared to meet the counterattack of those opposed to its policies as the government of President Arosemena was.

Against the rather weak efforts of Arosemena and the junta to defend their respective governments, the principal economic elites—the landowning aristocracy of the sierra and the commercial-financial oligarchy of Guayaquil—both mounted impressive campaigns in their own self-defense. While neither constituted a monolithic or even a cohesive group in normal times (when the interests of their members were often competitive), both were still compact and homogeneous enough to come together to protect their collective interests against any outside threat. Moreover, they possessed effective organizations for pursuing these collective interests in the Chambers of Commerce and of Agriculture for the sierra and the coast, which elected functional representatives to the Senate and were assigned permanent seats on a number of important policy-making bodies, such as the National Monetary Board. In addition, through their established ties to the Liberal and Conservative parties, the traditional elites could generally count on having their own members in the ministries that most affected them. Even in the supposedly antioligarchical government of Velasco in 1961, the Guayaquil elite was able to maintain its representation in the government through its financial backing of Velasco's electoral campaign.[22] Likewise, these elites were in a favorable position to influence public opinion through their control of most newspapers.

As the campaign against the Arosemena government clearly indicates, the power of the established elites was significantly enhanced by their ability to exploit resources and issues that were not really under their control. The most obvious ally of the status quo forces was the structure of the Ecuadorian Congress; the sierra provinces (where disenfranchisement by illiteracy was highest) elected twenty Senators; coastal districts elected only ten.[23] Although the disorganization and inefficiency of Congress might have produced the same result,[24] the overrepresentation of the sierra provinces (where the land tenure problem was the most severe) and the underrepresentation of the illiterate peasants who might benefit from land reform virtually ensured that no meaningful agrarian reform law would receive congressional approval. The established elites were also able to take advantage of the "heads-I-win, tails-you-lose" character of foreign policy issues in the early 1960s. In the elite appeals to the institutional insecurities of the church and the military, Arosemena's nationalist foreign policy could be used as evidence of his "Castroite" tendencies. On the other hand, the junta's concessions to the United

States in the modus vivendi on fishing rights could be used to mobilize nationalist opinion against the military government. Moreover, by the very nature of the basic partisan cleavage between those groups in and out of the government at any given time, no special efforts were required from the elites to mobilize the opposition parties into action.

The experience of the military junta is also revealing, since the established elites lost many of the advantages that they normally enjoy under a constitutional regime. Congress was no longer an impediment to reform legislation, nor could the junta effectively be labelled a communist threat. Even the opposition of the political parties and university students could have been avoided had the junta been willing to adopt a consistently repressive policy of banning all party activity, imposing censorship, and leaving the universities closed.[25] If the junta had followed the hard line advocated by a number of its supporters, the established elites might well have been reduced to fighting their political battle with only their own resources. It is doubtful that the sierra landowners would have been capable of offering any effective resistance. The mercantile oligarchy of Guayaquil, on the other hand, displayed an impressive amount of organizational and financial power in the merchants' strikes of 1965 and 1966, shutting down the major economic center of the country, covering the losses of the smaller merchants (who could not afford the inactivity), and, more importantly, depriving the government of a substantial portion of its normal revenues by refusing to retire any imported goods from customs.

There is evidence, however, of an even more impressive display of the political power of the economic resources concentrated in the hands of the Guayaquil elite. It is generally acknowledged that 1965, the year immediately preceding the fall of the junta, was a bad economic year. Overall per capita consumption fell slightly, and data from the manufacturing sector suggests that both wages and salaries declined in real terms.[26] Foreign reserves fell by more than 11 million dollars. The country's economic difficulties were not only frequently cited as evidence of the junta's incompetence at running the country, but they were also the immediate cause of the junta's attempt to raise import tariffs, which led to the merchants' strike. However, unlike any other swing in the economic cycle in the years 1950 to 1966, the recession and balance-of-payments crisis of 1965 cannot be traced to fluctuations in international trade.[27] The improvement in export earnings in 1965 was greater in both absolute and percentage terms than that of the previous year when wages and salaries in manufacturing and per capita consumption all increased by more than 6 percent. Examining carefully the balance-of-payments data for 1964 and 1965, it seems clear that the only significant difference between the two years is the sizeable loss of short-term private capital. Although the exact magnitude of capital flight is difficult to ascertain, such a movement of private capital was well within the capabilities of the Guayaquil economic community, since other sources indicate that privately owned Ecuadorian assets in U.S. banks alone

Table 13.3  Balance of Payments: 1964, 1965
(In million US $)

| Year | Exports | Imports | Services | Transfers | Long term capital | Short term private capital | Reserves |
|------|---------|---------|----------|-----------|-------------------|---------------------------|----------|
| 1964 | +161.9 | −140.0 | −52.5 | +11.9 | +15.1 | +7.3 | + 3.7 |
| 1965 | +180.7 | −155.2 | −53.8 | + 9.3 | +17.1 | −9.5 | −11.4 |

SOURCE: Clarence Zuvekas, "Ecuador: Selected Economic Data," (Mimeographed. Quito, Ecuador: USAID, 1970), p. 102.

NOTE: If monthly data were available for 1963, a similar pattern would, undoubtedly, emerge. Transfer payments and loan disbursements from the United States and U.S.-influenced agencies fell from 10 to 7.6 million dollars in 1963. Direct foreign investment fell from 16.2 million dollars in the 1960–1961 fiscal year to 7.0 million dollars in 1962–1963. While there was a net influx of 11.5 million dollars in short-term private capital in 1963, this undoubtedly occurred *after* the July coup against Arosemena.

totalled nearly 40 million dollars in 1965—more than the total value of the Central Bank's net foreign reserves.[28] The available evidence clearly suggests that the economic crisis of 1965 was not a "natural" recession, but a manifestation of the economic and political power of the Guayaquil elite in its struggle with the military junta.

In short, the end of the export boom exposed both the debility of Ecuadorian political institutions and the strengths of the entrenched economic elites. In the absence of political institutions that were capable of mobilizing widespread public support more than transitorily for elections, fluctuations in national economic growth (resulting mostly from changing international market conditions) tended to produce general satisfaction with or indifference to political affairs in the good years, while in the hard years, economic discontents tended to be focused on the government, regardless of its degree of responsibility for the crisis. Thus public support for the coups of 1961 and 1966 was clearly related to the sharp economic reversals in each of these years, while the lack of support for the attempted coup in 1954 is hardly surprising, given the economic prosperity of that year—which appears to have carried Velasco through the following year's economic decline. If this reasoning is correct, Ponce seems to have survived mostly by keeping expectations low and prices stable so that few politically relevant people actually experienced declining incomes; the real losers were the unemployed and unorganized members of the marginal subproletariat. The 1963 coup against Arosemena is clearly the strongest case for the influence of other factors in the determination of support levels, but the fact that the coup occurred in midyear and that disaggregated data are not available makes evaluation of the 1963 case difficult.

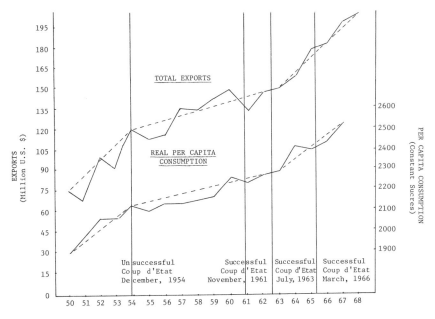

Figure 13.2.  Export Growth, Economic Welfare, and Military Coups

NOTE: Solid lines indicate actual year-to-year figures; broken lines indicate trends.

Since the economy no longer provided the government with a cushion of support, "public opinion" consistently turned against the government, aided in part by the elite's media campaign of opposition to both Arosemena and the junta. Antigovernment demonstrations and public disorders became commonplace, as student groups became radicalized and lower-class groups tried to combat the tendency toward a stagnant or declining real wage.[29]  While Velasco was, as usual, attentive to the military budget, neither Arosemena nor the military junta was willing to divert from projects they felt were more productive the increasing sums that the military felt necessary for its own operation. Both came to be viewed as threats to the institutional interests of the military. Finally, with the pall cast over the continent by the Cuban Revolution and the U.S. reaction to it, no civilian government could attempt structural changes in the system without raising the spectre of the "communist threat." Less than radical reform measures mobilized the opposition of the entrenched elites without winning the support of either the intellectual left or the groups that the reforms were supposed to benefit. When the economy slowed concurrently with rising political participation, politics again became a zero-sum game. In that political environment, none of the governments of the day could avoid political outcomes leading to military perceptions of a "national crisis requiring military intervention."

# chapter fourteen

# The Systemic Interaction

The military's response to its changing political environment can, perhaps, best be understood with the aid of a brief summary of the conclusions drawn from the preceding analysis. First, the Ecuadorian case confirms the hypothesis that the armed forces act as a monitor of the political scene, intervening to overthrow the government when, in its judgment, a "national crisis" exists. Both the quantitative and qualitative data from Ecuadorian coup participants clearly indicate that such judgments are made in terms of a finite set of decision criteria identifying those political outcomes of concern to military officers—even though the salience of those different outcomes varied over time.

> Proposition One: The level of "national crisis" perceived by a representative officer at any point in time is a weighted function of military ratings of the constitutionality of government actions, the officer's personal ties or antagonisms toward the government, public opinion toward the government, government attentiveness to the institutional needs of the armed forces, government policy toward any perceived "communist threat," the level of public disorders, and the need for socioeconomic reforms.

As indicated earlier, military perceptions of these political outcomes do not necessarily bear any resemblance to the actual state of affairs. While discrepancies in most areas were relatively minor, there were systematic distortions in perceptions of public opinion, public disorders, and the threat of communism. These findings point to manipulation of military perceptions as a key form of civilian participation in the coup d'état process.

Still, the decision to overthrow a given government is only partly a function of the external political environment. It is also strongly influenced by the officers' formal role definitions, which act as lenses through which external events are viewed and evaluated.

> Proposition Two: Military attitudes toward the overthrow of a given government are a function of the perceived level of "national crisis" and of the formal role definitions of the officers involved.

As indicated above, there have been important variations over time in the salience of different political outcomes in coup decisions. These variations reflect the changing doctrinal conceptions of the political role of the armed forces. With the shift toward adoption of "arbiter" and "developmentalist" role definitions, the constitutionality of government behavior ceased to be an important factor in the coup decision, while the salience of public opinion, institutional interests, and socioeconomic policy increased. The evidence available with regard to the weighting of these outcomes by proponents of each role definition is summarized in table 14.1.

Table 14.1  Weighting of Political Outcomes in Coup Decisions

| Decision criteria | Formal Role Definition | | | |
| | Professionalist | Constitutionalist | Arbiter | Developmentalist |
| --- | --- | --- | --- | --- |
| Personal ties | Primary | Primary | Primary | Primary |
| Constitutional norm | Nil | Primary | Secondary | Nil |
| Public opinion | Nil | Secondary | Primary | Secondary |
| Institutional interests | Secondary* | Secondary | Secondary | Primary |
| Communist threat | Primary | Secondary | Primary | Primary |
| Public disorders | Primary (–)* | Secondary | Secondary | Nil |
| Socioeconomic reforms | Nil | Nil | Nil | Primary |

*Assuming minimal real professionalization.

In addition to changing the relative importance of the various decision criteria in perceptions of national crisis, formal role definitions enter into the calculation of military responses to a given level of perceived "national crisis." Officers subscribing to a classic professionalist or constitutionalist role definition react less strongly to a given crisis or, conversely, require higher levels of perceived crisis to overcome their doctrinal inhibitions against military intervention in politics. For the classic professionalist, participation in a military coup, however well justified, is still a violation of professional norms, just as such a decision for the true military legalist is a violation of his constitutionalist principles. (This restriction obviously ceases to be operative if, as in the coup of 1961, the government makes the first unconstitutional move.) In a similar fashion, officers subscribing to a developmentalist definition of the military's political responsibilities are the most likely to decide in favor of overthrowing the government, since adoption of this role presupposes a generalized low opinion of civilian leadership.

Finally, it also seems clear that the distribution of role definitions within the officer corps is influential in determining what kind of government will be established after a coup d'état has taken place. Where the professionalists or constitutionalists are in the majority, the government will most likely be turned over to a civilian representing the opposition coalition—ideally to someone who is or can be installed in the legal line of succession. Where the "arbiter" role definition prevails, the successor to a civilian government will normally be an interim military government, and vice versa. The developmentalists, on the other hand, appear to prefer a "government of the armed forces" regardless of the type of government overthrown.

As indicated in chapter 12, the general forces behind the substantial shifts in the role definitions of Ecuadorian officers during the 1948–1966 period were the gradual but complete loss of faith in the ability of civilian political leaders to govern effectively and, simultaneously, a moderate increase in military confidence that they could provide an alternative source of national leadership in times of crisis. As the relative balance of perceived capabilities changed, professionalist and constitutionalist doctrines were abandoned in favor of arbiter and developmentalist role definitions.

> Proposition Three: The proportion of officers subscribing to professionalist, constitutionalist, arbiter, and developmentalist role definitions is a function of the balance of perceived capabilities of civilian and military leaders to govern effectively.[1]

In general, the perceived level of civilian capabilities seems to be a function of the general social status of civilian political leaders, which is subject to modification by their past record of success or failure in keeping the level of "crisis" within the limits considered acceptable by the military. However, confidence in the competence of the civilian leadership may also be directly influenced by government performance on the "institutional interest" and "communist threat" criteria as more immediate indicators of civilian capacity to provide the armed forces with a secure political environment. On the other side of the balance equation, confidence in military capabilities to govern seems to be related to the general social status of the sectors from which most officers are recruited, modified by reference to prior historical experience with military governments and by the actual level of professionalization of the armed forces. At least within Latin America, high professionalization ordinarily entails a greater variety of opportunities for military officers to acquire expertise and experience in nonmilitary problems.

Despite recent assertions to the contrary,[2] the Ecuadorian experience suggests that the level of professionalization of the armed forces does have a significant impact on the political behavior of the military. To discern that impact, however, it is necessary to avoid the common fallacy of equating the professionalist role definition with *professionalization,* which is defined as the level of technical development and complexity of the military career. Professionalization in the latter sense can quite easily be measured in terms of the number of years spent by senior officers during their careers in military educational institutions, which we know to be very high in countries like Brazil and Argentina and exceedingly low in most of the new nations of sub-Saharan Africa. The most important effect of professionalization is its impact on the relative salience of a military officer's multiple identifications as a military officer, member of the civilian social structure, inhabitant of a given region, part of a given ethnic or tribal group, and citizen of a given country. Where there is really no specialized military education (as in nineteenth-century Ecuador), the military officer is basically an armed civilian, and his political behavior is oriented accordingly. When the Ecuadorian armed forces achieved a minimal level of professionalization at the turn of the century with a separate institution for training officer recruits and a one-year war academy, military officers ceased to act as civilians, but their perceptions of relative capabilities were still derived primarily from their status as members of a highly stratified civilian social structure. This led to adoption of the professionalist role definition, even though the decision criteria thus adopted permitted gross violations of the professional autonomy of the armed forces (in contrast to the situation existing within early twentieth-century Argentine and Chilean armies, where the professionalist ethic was accompanied by somewhat higher levels of actual professionalization). The reorganization of the Ecuadorian armed forces after the 1941 war with Peru, which culminated in the reopening of the war academy in 1956, clearly established the pre-eminence of the officers' identification with the military institution. As shown in chapter 11, this basic identification with the *institución armada* provides the underlying rationale for the specific set of decision criteria enumerated above. At this intermediate level of professionalization (five to seven years of specialized military education for most Ecuadorian officers) the institutional identity so established seems to be primarily corporate—a reification of collective self-interest—rather than a fully professionalized identity. The high levels of professionalization in Argentina, Brazil, and Peru (eight to ten years of specialized military training) have been accompanied by a professional identity strong enough to resist civilian practices in violation of professional norms, practices that were still accepted in Ecuador, even though they were disliked by most Ecuadorian officers.

Proposition Four: As the level of professionalization increases and basic psychological identification with the institution is strengthened, the social origins of civilian and military leaders become less important in determining perceptions of relative capabilities to govern.

Proposition Five: As the level of professionalization increases, the importance of respect for professional norms in rating government performance on protecting institutional interests is increased.

Finally, as indicated above, a very high level of professionalization also directly enhances perceptions of military capacity to govern, since the highest level of training in the more professionalized militaries is generally devoted to non-military problems, as in the Peruvian Centro de Altos Estudios Militares or the Brazilian Escola Superior de Guerra.

While the primary focus of the analysis thus far has been the explanation of the political behavior of individual officers, ultimately what matters is the collective military decision to support or overthrow the government. Historical case studies generally stress the key role played in that larger institutional decision-making process by conspiratorial movements, secret military lodges, and intrigue and counter-intrigue by the government and its opponents.[3] In an appealing attempt to distill a theoretical model from such case studies, Martin Needler has argued that the decision of the military to overthrow a government can be best described as the outcome of a process of coalition-building within the officer corps.[4] The procoup coalition typically begins with a hard core of instigators who are resolutely opposed to the government. As the situation develops, other officers—partial opponents of the government with a variety of motivations for favoring a coup d'état—may be added to the initial group of conspirators. Finally, conversions may be made among those officers whom Needler has termed the "reluctants." This group might include personal supporters of the president, but mostly consists of officers opposed in principle to military intervention in politics. The process of coalition-building continues with more partial opponents and reluctants joining the original conspirators. Finally, the procoup coalition reaches a "critical mass" with the conversion of a prestigious senior "swing man" who usually becomes the head of the postcoup government.[5]

In practice, institutional decision-making in the Ecuadorian coups did not follow the pattern of a gradually growing conspiracy that finally captures a commanding majority of individual officers and then moves to take over. In 1961, the arrest of the vice-president combined with popular discontent and a month of serious public disorders to produce a veritable explosion of military opposition and a rapid disintegration of the military hierarchy. Within a twenty-four-hour period, the Taura air base, the navy, the war academy, and the air force command all declared themselves to be in favor of the forced resignation of the president and the immediate succession of the vice-president. In the 1963 coup, none of the various conspiracies commanded, separately, even a bare majority of important officers, and contact between the groups was minimal. The final decision of the Nuevo Orden group to stage their coup was based largely on hopes of capturing the support of a large number of officers who were in favor of a change but who were not personally willing to take part in any conspiratorial efforts. The decision of the service commanders to act despite the fact that they owed their positions to the president's personal confidence in them made the whole movement institutional. The coup against Arosemena was thus made easier, since it did not involve any break in the existing military hierarchy. The 1966 coup presents still another variation in intramilitary alignments. Nearly the entire general staff opposed the government and the heads of several key departments were actively collaborating with opposition politicians. Two of the three service commanders favored the opposition plan for immediate installation of a civilian interim president. Most of the provincial commanders, especially in Guayaquil and El Oro, remained basically loyal to the junta. The troops that, in the end, decided matters were the Quito units, which refused to break the transport workers' strike, leaving the junta little choice but immediate resignation.

In summary then, it can be said that a different pattern of intramilitary coalitions characterized each of the four Ecuadorian coups. Contrary to Needler's predictions, pre-coup conspiracies did not play a major role in any of the three successful coups. (In almost all of the conspiracies that did take place, the nucleus of key leaders—Needler's instigators—lay outside the ranks of active duty officers. In two cases the key leaders were opposition politicians and in the rest they were retired officers.) Although institutional decision-making procedures varied in each of the cases, the general pattern seems to have been the taking of a general consensus of the officer corps after some crisis event (Velasco's flight to Guayaquil in 1954, the vice-president's arrest in 1961, the banquet incident in 1963, and the Central University attack in 1966) led a segment of the military (Quito garrison in 1954, Chimborazo battalion in 1961, Cuenca garrison in 1962, force commanders in 1963, and the general staff in 1966) to take a stand against the government. Once the crisis point was reached, open military caucuses were generally held at the unit, divisional, service, and general staff levels to discuss and decide what action should be taken. The Ecuadorian experience, then, clearly suggests that conspiratorial maneuvering and conversion of particular individuals to a procoup position were less important factors in determining the outcome of politico-military crises than was the general sentiment for or against the government among the middle and upper ranks of the armed forces.

An examination of the frequency distributions of attitudes in the different coup samples likewise suggests that the attitudes of the "typical" officer rather than of any particular officer were the crucial factor in determining whether or not the government survived that particular crisis. In each of the four crises, the winning side was supported by at least two-thirds of the participants in our samples. Still, the proportion of officers on the winning side may be less important in determining the certainty of the outcome than is the intensity of that support or opposition, specifically the number of officers strongly supporting or strongly opposing the coup. Here the nonrandomness of the sampling procedures used here makes it difficult to estimate what those proportions really were in the officer corps at large. Nevertheless, in 1961, when nearly half of the respondents strongly favored the coup, the coup was successful despite the determined resistance of the high command and the commander of the Quito

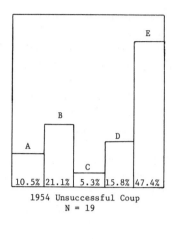

1954 Unsuccessful Coup
N = 19

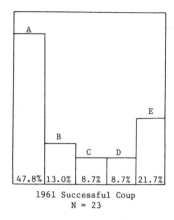

1961 Successful Coup
N = 23

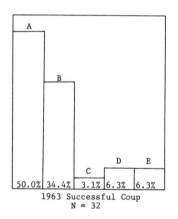

1963 Successful Coup
N = 32

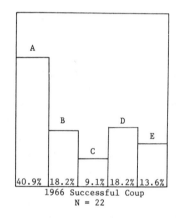

1966 Successful Coup
N = 22

A = Strongly Procoup
B = Procoup                    D = Progovernment
C = Neutral or ambivalent      E = Strongly progovernment

Figure 14.1.  Frequency Distribution of Attitudes toward Coup

garrison. In 1966, the median response was favorable to the coup, but not strongly so; it appears that the junta might have been able to muster enough support for at least a more graceful exit, had its members been more active in their own self-defense.

On the other hand, the internal composition of that procoup majority seems to have had relatively little impact on coup outcomes. As indicated above, in terms of the positions held by winning and losing officers, intramilitary alignments have been quite varied. Nevertheless, the army very clearly counts more than either of the other services, even though at the higher levels army, navy, and air force officers voice their opinions without any particular distinction by service. Although higher-ranking officers obviously carried more weight within the intramilitary caucuses, their command authority was limited in significance by the number of links between themselves and the troops that were theoretically at their command. Since the general rule in Ecuador was for troops to obey their most immediate and visible superiors, the decision of a high-ranking officer to support or oppose the government could be negated at any of these links by the refusal of a lower-ranking officer to accept his orders.[6]

Likewise, the distribution of personal ties appears to have little impact on collective decisions to intervene. Personal relationships—the lifelong friendship and family ties of one officer with President Arosemena, the deep personal allegiance of another to Lieutenant Colonel Varea in 1954, a military engineer's anger at being passed over in the junta's decision to name a nonengineer to the Public Works Ministry, or the bitter resentment of a senior officer chastised as "an ill-mannered child" by a member of the junta—deeply affected the attitudes of individual officers, but at the aggregate level these personal factors tended to cancel each other out. Generally, the government had as many friends as it had enemies. Its friends usually remained loyal, and its personal enemies were, as one would expect, implacable in their opposition; thus the critical margin was provided by those who had no important personal ties to the government or to the opposition. So when Velasco lost the support of the majority of officers in the middle and upper ranks, his friends could not save him, despite their control over the high command and many strategic garrisons.

The various combinations of political outcomes that would be sufficient to generate a majority of procoup officers or a majority of strongly procoup officers in the relevant ranks can, in principle, be determined; in practice, the sufficient conditions will vary according to the proportion of officers subscribing to each type of role definition. For analytical purposes, disaggregation by role definition would facilitate understanding situations like that of 1961 where both the professionalist and developmentalist minorities allied in defense of Velasco, but had rather different reasons for doing so.[7] In most cases, then, the likelihood of a collective military decision to intervene will depend upon the predominant attitude within the politically relevant ranks, which in turn will reflect the political conditions prevailing at the time and the frequency distribution of role definitions within those ranks.

This revised model of the process of individual and collective military decision-making in political crises highlights the complexity of the Ecuadorian military's response to the changes in its political environment. That response was, first of all, conditioned by the increased professionalization of the armed forces during the late forties and early fifties. As indicated in chapter 2, during the previous two decades of political instability the military had played a rather secondary role. With perceptions of their relative capacity to govern derived primarily from their inferior social and educational status, most officers were content either to be individually co-opted by competing elite factions or, as "professionalists," to remain on the sidelines while the shifting coalitions among civilian factions determined the rise and fall of a rapid succession of governments. With the increased sense of corporate identity with and loyalty to the institution that resulted from the military reforms and reorganizations instituted by the 1941 generation of officers, the decision to uphold or overthrow the government became increasingly a military decision made in accordance with the military's own standards for measuring government performance. Nevertheless, during the 1948–1960 interlude, as a result of favorable economic conditions and the low level of political mobilization, political crises were infrequent. At no point was there a serious "national crisis" according to the decision criteria of the constitutionalists who constituted the dominant military faction. As long as the civilian political arena remained relatively calm, the armed forces remained politically quiescent. The only repercussions of these institutional reforms that were immediately apparent were the decreased susceptibility to co-optation of individual officers by the political opposition and the resultant decline in the number of politically inspired barracks revolts.

The deteriorating economic conditions and the rise of populism and the radical left shattered the surface political calm of the patrician democracy of the 1950s. However, these changes led to more than just an increase in the frequency of irregular changes of government. The decreased importance of social origins in perceptions of relative capability to govern also permitted a rapid military role expansion in response to the inability of civilian leaders to generate sufficient support to keep the level of "crisis" within acceptable limits or to provide credible guarantees that the military's institutional interests and survival would not be endangered. With the shift away from professionalist and constitutionalist role definitions, not only were the armed forces less constrained by doctrinal inhibitions against direct military intervention in politics, but the relative salience of the coup decision criteria defining the level of crisis was also altered to give greater weight to those criteria that were directly related to the maintenance of institutional security in an unstable political environment. Ultimately, the military response to the threats inherent in this unstable environment was to shift toward the developmentalist role definition. According to developmentalist doctrines, the armed forces have a responsibility to guarantee national security and, therefore, a responsibility to intervene directly through a military government to restructure the civilian political arena and the socioeconomic context within which it operates. While this trend toward role expansion was slowed by the absence of a superior war college and reversed itself after the failure of the military junta, that reversal proved to be only temporary, as the junta's civilian successors proved incapable of providing more than a return to the political status quo ante of the early 1960s. As a result of the moderate level of professionalization achieved during the previous decade, the unstable politics of the 1960s led to changes in the frequency, direction, and duration of military intervention, and in military capability perceptions and role definitions—a process which led, in 1973, to the establishment of the Institute for Higher National Studies in ironic recognition of the need for greater professionalization to give the armed forces the non-military expertise required by their new role as the key actors in Ecuadorian politics.

Much more research will be needed in order to fully appraise the system-level consequences of the interaction of the military subsystem with the larger economic and political system within which the armed forces are located. Nevertheless, this analysis suggests that the institutionalization of the coup d'état in the Ecuadorian political process has had a major impact on that larger system.

Since 1948, Ecuador has experienced a modest but steady trend toward socioeconomic modernization, a doubling of the rate of political participation, and a twelve-year interlude of relative political peace, followed by nine governments in the last seventeen years. Yet, in a basic sense, Ecuador has changed very little. After more than three decades of modernization, the basic social structure remains intact, the economy remains wedded to externally controlled markets for primary products, and the political system still lacks legitimacy and institutions capable of mobilizing support on a sustained basis. Ecuador clearly conforms to the general rule (noted by Charles Anderson and others)[8] that Latin American political systems change very little despite high rates of surface political instability. For all its importance as a seminal work in the emergence of a revisionist interpretation of Latin American politics,[9] Anderson's explanation of the conservative bias in Latin American political systems is not fully satisfying, since it depends heavily on the imputation of an unwritten set of rules for political conflict to a reified set of actors ("power contenders") that more detailed research has shown to be frequently lacking in strong group or class consciousness or cohesiveness.[10] The model elaborated in these concluding chapters suggests a partial alternative to Anderson's explanation of instability without change and a new perspective on the role of the coup d'état in political development.[11]

Ecuador, like many Third World countries, is a politically underdeveloped society whose history has been marked by a succession of weak, ineffective, and often short-lived governments. Given the absence of any mass belief in the legitimacy of the system, most governments have been unable to survive even minor crises. Samuel Huntington has argued that the only escape from this "praetorian syndrome" lies in the creation of strong political institutions.[12] More recently, other political scientists have argued that prior creation of a strong central government and development of a sense of national identity should precede the establishment of institutions for mass political participation.[13] What such prescriptions share is an implicit assumption that institution-building, nation-building, and state-building are narrowly political concerns, issues that can be divorced from the question of for whom political parties, the nation, and the state are being built. The contrasting fates of Ayub Khan, Kwame Nkrumah, Ho Chi Minh, and Julius Nyerere suggest that something more than the will to build political institutions is required. In considering why Nyerere has succeeded thus far while Nkrumah failed, and why the Mexican Party of the Institutional Revolution has retained its dominant position while Ataturk's accomplishments in Turkey proved transitory, it would appear that the crucial difference lies in the greater attention given to the key questions of mass participation and redistribution of values in Mexico and Tanzania.[14] Within Latin America, the striking contrast in mass attitudes toward the regimes in Mexico and Cuba[15] with those prevailing elsewhere again suggests that developing countries caught in the "praetorian syndrome" will continue to lack legitimacy as long as they do not provide a sense of meaningful mass participation in the political process and a clear and visible change in the economic and/or social status of the mass of the population. If these are the prerequisites for political development, then at least in those countries where the military has achieved a moderate level of professionalization, the combination of the military coup and periodic elections makes it quite unlikely that those prerequisites will be attained.

First of all, once a moderate level of professionalization is achieved, the corporate military identity and a primary loyalty to the military institution are fairly well established for the large majority of officers. In turn, this corporate identification provides the underlying rationale for a set of coup decision criteria through which, in effect, the military protects itself from the institutional costs of maintaining an unpopular government through a period of political crisis. The conservative military reaction against governments or political organizations that seem to threaten the institutional survival of the armed forces is only one obvious consequence of this identification. These decision criteria also generally lead to intervention whenever sufficient public opposition emerges against a government that has become too harshly dictatorial or repressive, too socially retrograde, or simply too inept. Whatever its origins, if the crisis is sufficiently severe and if the government has lost public support, the result is generally a coup d'état, which removes the offending administration, restores public calm, and installs a new government, to the applause of those antagonized by its predecessor.

Likewise populist parties, by responding periodically in a personalistic, charismatic, and therefore comprehensible fashion to the discontents and demands of the newly participant, but economically marginal masses, also act as a depressurizing mechanism. As mass political participation rises, populist leaders—promising jobs, public services, and a government responsive to the forgotten people of society—come to dominate the electoral arena at the expense of both the traditionally and ideologically oriented parties. Yet once they are in power, nonideological, nonprogrammatic populist leaders like Velasco concentrate on public works and patronage instead of on changing the basic social and economic structures underlying the economic marginality of their constituents. In the end, however, the supply of particularistic payoffs is limited by the weakness of government finances, and when the export recession strikes, the government loses its support. A crisis emerges—as it did in 1961—and is eventually resolved in a military coup that installs a new government with a popular mandate to avoid the errors of its predecessor.

As the case of the Arosemena government suggests, civilian reformist governments are usually hamstrung by a lack of political organization, by constitutional constraints, and by the military's fear of communism. They are, therefore, unlikely to be any more successful in achieving basic reforms than are their populist counterparts. Gradually the participant citizenry becomes disillusioned with civilian rule. At the same time, the inability of civilian leaders to provide a politically secure environment for the armed forces usually generates a movement toward military adoption of the developmentalist role definition, which legitimizes direct military intervention to restructure that environment. Given the antipolitical, bureaucratic mentality of the moderately professionalized officer and his aversion to ideologies of social and partisan conflict, most military governments are also not likely to pursue policies conducive to mass mobilization or radical redistribution, and hence, most of them will also culminate in a military coup.

If one could measure the trends in public support for and opposition to the government, one would find an erratic but persistent cycle of gradually eroding support and rising opposition, periodically cut short and then restarted by coups or new elections. Military governments will alternate with civilian governments[16] and periods of high instability will be interspersed with periods of "normalcy" as the state of the economy varies. Over time, cynicism and apathy may grow, but rarely to the point of endangering the system. Thus the *institutionalization* of the coup d'état as part of a political process that also includes periodic elections may be profoundly inimical to true social and political development. Underlying the high degree of surface instability are mechanisms for the release and limitation of discontents generated by unjust social and economic structures. These structures are nevertheless ultra-stable, because the periodic release of these tensions prevents them from accumulating and, more important, prevents them from being transformed into revolutionary convictions of the illegitimacy of the status quo. In Ecuador and in Latin America generally, "succession, programmatic reform, and palace revolutions function as substitutes for political and social revolutions. . . . Less fundamental changes have the (proximate) consequence of reducing the intensity of predispositions to more fundamental ones. . . . Opposition perspectives in the mass are not ordinarily directed toward the adoption of fully specified policies but . . . are in

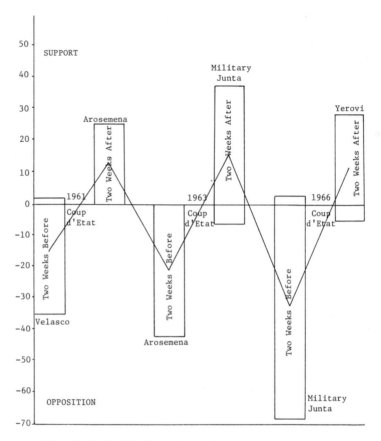

Figure 14.2.   Stabilization by Coup d'Etat: Combined Editorial
Analysis Scores: 1961, 1963, 1966

NOTE: Scores are based on the sum of *El Comercio* and *El Universo* editorial analysis
scores for the two-week periods preceding and following each coup. The trend line connects
the mid-points of each column, and thus represents the overall balance of positive/negative
appraisals.

considerable degree simply demands for 'a change.' "[17] The military coup d'état
satisfies those demands without changing the structures generating the discontent.

If this analysis is correct, then a large share of the credit for the Cuban
Revolution should be given to the conditions prevailing in the Cuban armed
forces—in particular to the low level of professionalization therein prior to
1959.[18] By the arguments presented above, the inability of the Cuban army to
overthrow Batista in late 1957 or early 1958—as the Ecuadorian military surely
would have in the same political situation—was a crucial factor in preventing the

premature termination of the anti-Batista struggle. If that coup had occurred, in all likelihood Fidel Castro's quixotic adventures in the Sierra Maestra would have amounted to no more than a curious historical footnote in the transition from Batista's reign to a Cuban Balaguer.[19]

While much research remains to be done, the Ecuadorian experience clearly suggests that the coup d'état is more than merely a symptom of political decay. The institutionalization of the coup d'état as a political process has, in fact, become a major barrier to political development and to basic changes in social and economic structure.

# chapter fifteen

# Ecuador since 1966: Testing the Model

Events that have occurred in Ecuador since 1966 provide the basis for a preliminary test of the theoretical model summarized in chapter 14. The test is "preliminary" in the sense that the real proof of the utility of that model will come in testing it in countries other than Ecuador. This is also a preliminary test in the sense that another book would be required to do full justice to the events that have given Ecuador six governments in the past eleven years. Nevertheless, the armed forces have played a key role in all of these events, and some in particular—the progovernment coup of 1970, the military revolt of 1971, and the 1972 coup re-establishing military rule, the unsuccessful coup of September 1975, and the replacement of General Rodríguez as the head of the military government—provide new insights into the complexities of the coup d'état as a political process.

Following the fall of the military junta in 1966, Clemente Yerovi faithfully complied with the terms of the political pact that had brought him to power. Within six months, elections were held for a Constituent Assembly to elect a new president and write a new constitution. With the assembly evenly divided between Liberals and Conservatives, the latter made a deal to back the leader—Otto Arosemena Gómez—of a small splinter party in exchange for Cabinet posts and support in the presidential elections of 1968. As provisional president, Arosemena Gómez was notable for his independent foreign policy and a budgetary emphasis on education that left his successor with an empty Treasury.

The initial frontrunner in the electoral race for the presidency was Camilo Ponce, candidate of the conservative coalition and chief architect of the 1966 coup. The Liberals nominated Dr. Andrés F. Córdova. Despite the poor showing of *velasquista* candidates in the assembly and municipal elections, José María Velasco Ibarra returned to Ecuador to proclaim his candidacy for yet another term as president. With total disregard for both his age and his previous record,

Velasco waged another fiery campaign in which he denounced the oligarchy and the secret campaign pact that existed between Ponce and Arosemena Gómez.[1] This time, however, the margin of Velasco's victory was only 2 percent over Ponce and even less over Córdova, who finished a very close second.[2]

Governing once again proved more complicated than campaigning. Congress was firmly in the hands of the opposition, after an attempt to form a coalition with the Liberals failed. Declining banana exports and a growing budget deficit contributed to the short tenure of a series of finance ministers. Foreign exchange reserves fell by two-thirds and the government found it increasingly difficult to meet its own payrolls—a situation that was temporarily solved by using 1970 revenues to pay 1969 salaries.

By March 1970 the projected budget deficit exceeded 155 million dollars in a 295 million dollar budget. Civic strife and protests over the lack of funds for provincial public works competed for attention with student demonstrations that turned into riots following the assassination of a prominent student leader. After sharp government losses in the June congressional elections, Velasco sent to Congress a series of measures designed to consolidate the national debt, increase taxes, and reduce expenditures—and thereby cover most of the deficit. Congress, with characteristic abandon, approved only the debt consolidation before adjourning for the summer. Denouncing congressional irresponsibility in the harshest terms, Velasco published his initial proposals as emergency decree laws without any clear legal authority to do so. Inasmuch as the decrees included a substantial increase in import tariffs, the Guayaquil Chamber of Commerce immediately brought suit before the Supreme Court, which ruled in mid-June that the decrees were unconstitutional.

Denouncing the 1967 constitution's new restrictions on executive powers, Velasco repeatedly declared that he would govern or resign. Faced with a total impasse in Congress and in the courts, Velasco was encouraged by the minister of defense (his nephew) and his military intimates to seek the support of the armed forces.[3] Renewed student protests became violently antimilitary after the bombing of the Central University Press—an act that was widely attributed to elements of the Escuela de Paracaidistas. Military officers in uniform were accosted on the street and, in one instance, were seized by student demonstrators.[4] At the height of the crisis Velasco was called to a special meeting with the high command, key Cabinet ministers, and selected military officers, who "demanded" that Velasco assume dictatorial powers to save the country from total ruin.[5] Velasco quickly agreed that there was no other alternative. After closing Congress and assuming the power to rule by decree, his first act as dictator was to order the occupation and indefinite closure of all state universities. Although initially it promised to use its special powers to bring about a variety of important reforms, in actuality the government did little more than reissue its previous decrees.

Following a 50 percent drop in foreign reserves during the next month, the government also decreed a 28 percent devaluation of the sucre.[6] The devaluation brought rising prices to the general public, windfall profits to exporters, and gradual but substantial budgetary improvements through the remainder of the year. Opposition attacks were met alternately with arrests and with promises to hold a plebescite on a modified version of the 1946 Constitution. In addition, Velasco publicly promised to step down in 1972—the end of his elected term.

With the students deprived of their usual base of operations and the budget deficit reduced to manageable proportions, the political situation stabilized. The government, though hardly popular, appeared to be in full control. Nevertheless, discontent was building within the armed forces over other matters. Following the June coup, General Julio Sacoto Montero had been promoted to army commander over the heads of numerous officers with greater seniority. Shortly thereafter twenty high-ranking officers were forcibly retired, mostly because they had drawn constitutionalist conclusions from their experiences with the military junta. Added to the large number of officers who had been retired since 1966, these new purges gave rise to renewed complaints against political interference in the military. In particular, there was a growing fear that the minister of defense, Jorge Acosta Velasco, through his highly partisan use of promotions and assignments, was building a personal power base in the key garrisons of Quito and Guayaquil. The issue finally came to a head in late March 1971, when Acosta tried to force the resignation of General Luís Jácome Chávez, the director of the army war academy.[7] Jácome challenged his dismissal and denounced both Acosta and Sacoto as threats to the professional integrity of the armed forces.[8] Virtually the entire faculty and student body of the war academy and the Escuela de Perfeccionamiento rebelled, calling for the immediate resignations of the army commander and the minister of defense. The first group of paratroopers sent to squelch the revolt joined it, but with the quick show of support for Acosta from key garrison commanders and the immediate seizure of the communications media by the government, the rebels remained isolated. Key army units in Quito remained loyal to the high command, although the air force again declared itself neutral and refused to attack the rebel headquarters.[9] That night, following negotiations mediated by the navy and air force commanders, the rebels agreed to return home and pursue their case through regular channels. However, under pressure from an indignant president, Acosta decided that he could afford not to negotiate. The following morning rebel leaders were individually arrested, taken to the penitentiary, and publicly denounced for their politically inspired insubordination.[10]

Though several days passed without event, Acosta had placed himself in a precarious position. Coupled with the existing shortage of senior officers, Acosta's decision to retire the 29 rebel leaders would have left the army with virtually no academy-trained officers. Sensing the clear threat of becoming a personal vehicle of the defense minister, the army began to resist. Informally this time, low-ranking officers began to determine the consensus in each garrison. As copies of the academy manifesto reached the provincial garrisons, it was Acosta's personal *camarilla* of commanders that was left without troops to command.[11] In a coordinated counter-coup on the night of 5 April, the division of El Oro declared itself opposed to Acosta. The next morning the military college in Quito emerged as the head of the rebel movement and rapidly received declarations of support from all major garrisons. The president, defense minister, and members of the government were immediately summoned to an open military meeting at the Colegio Militar that was headed by its director, General Guillermo Rodríguez Lara. While no one spoke against the president, a series of officers denounced the actions of Acosta and demanded his immediate resignation. After twice declaring he would resign rather than submit to such an imposition, Velasco heeded those senior officers who argued that there was no intention to take over or to be disloyal to his government.[12] Acosta was immediately replaced.[13]

That same night, however, Velasco appeared on nationwide television to deliver a vitriolic personal attack on General Jácome that led to a new revolt by younger, more radical officers who had, earlier, favored accepting Velasco's resignation. In an angry, all-night meeting of more than three hundred officers in the Ministry of Defense, a sizable faction proposed that Velasco be immediately removed and then replaced by Rear Admiral Jorge Cruz Polanco, the chief of the general staff. However, Cruz refused to accept the position. As the discussion and debate dragged on, it began to lessen in intensity. Again it was Rodríguez and a small group of colonels who prevailed, arguing that to make a political move at this point would tarnish what had been a purely institutional, professional movement "in defense of institutional solidarity."[14] The next day Sacoto was retired and, in accordance with the manifesto issued by the El Oro division, Colonel Rodríguez was named the new army commander—the first commander ever to be named by the army itself rather than by the president.[15]

The government survived the 1971 revolt and the political scene showed no more than normal levels of crisis, but the position of Rodríguez was a major source of tension within the Velasco regime. Rodríguez refused to promote Acosta's clique of progovernment officers and in fact, he began removing them from their posts. Unaccustomed to dealing with an autonomous army, Velasco desperately wanted to rid himself of Rodríguez, but he was warned on various occasions that firing him would probably cause an immediate coup.[16] Sensing the conflict, the leaders of the war academy revolt did indeed begin to prepare to counter any attempt by Velasco to reassert his control over the armed forces. At later academy meetings and discussions it was agreed that "if the armed forces had to intervene, it would have to be different this time. There would be no temporary interventions just to turn power over to the same old politicians, the same old parties. If circumstances should force the military to act, this time it would be to totally transform the entire country."[17]

In the midst of these continuing institutional tensions, the government announced in July that the plebescite on the reformed 1946 Constitution would be held concurrently with the general elections of 1972. In the presidential contest Asaad Bucaram, still popular after his tremendous victory in the 1970 election for provincial prefect of Guayas, was nominated by the Concentration of Popular Forces. Bucaram's candidacy (which some observers likened to that of the "young Velasco")[18] sparked an intense but unsuccessful campaign by the minister of the interior, Jaime Nebot, to prove that Bucaram was born in Lebanon and was, therefore, ineligible to run. Ex-presidents Camilo Ponce and Carlos Julio Arosemena also entered the race, along with a variety of other candidates. Jaime Nebot received the nomination of the *velasquista* party, but no endorsement from the president, who strongly favored Ponce as the candidate most likely to defeat Bucaram.[19] Ponce, however, refused to commit himself to enter a race against Bucaram. Velasco then tried to have the Supreme Court bar Bucaram, but it refused to rule on the question.

The prospect of a Bucaram victory—deemed certain by virtually all observers in light of the total disarray in the other parties[20] —brought dismay, not only to those who would lose, but also to the Guayaquil elite, who had already had a taste of Bucaram's populism during his term as mayor of the port city. Those who opposed Bucaram began to actively seek military support for some sort of preventive coup. In early February, President Velasco publicly expressed his willingness to let the voters decide; privately, he strongly urged the military to intervene to stop Bucaram—a move that was completely rejected by the military commanders and in particular by Rodríguez, who argued that the only beneficiaries of that action would be the old politicians.[21] The defense minister favored outright cancellation of the elections, but very few officers were sympathetic to either Velasco or to his minister.[22]

Meanwhile the war academy group was working nights, reviewing these events and preparing contingency plans, aided in part by retired General Victor Aulestia, now a member of the army and naval war academy staffs. The increasingly apparent political decomposition and the evident inability of the civilians to manage the succession problem served to accelerate plans for the coup.[23] Contingency now became presumption, if not certainty, although it is doubtful that these plans involved more than a minority of senior officers in and around Quito. Velasco made another bid for a military veto of Bucaram, by-passing his defense minister, who immediately resigned.[24] His successor proposed that Velasco resign and turn power over to the Supreme Court; this move would be rejected by the armed forces, who would then take over the government.[25] General Rodríguez agreed to the proposal, but Velasco could not bring himself to resign. At the last minute he fled to Guayaquil to seek

Bucaram's support under the assumption that, together with Bucaram, he could mobilize the masses to defend the government and the September elections.[26] Within the military, however, news of Velasco's new move was interpreted as further evidence of his "demagoguery and insincerity."[27] General Rodríguez ordered Velasco's immediate arrest, declaring, "The armed forces will not lend themselves to a political game of this nature."[28]

Rodríguez's decision to act found many officers unprepared. Since there had been few overt signs of crisis, no clear military consensus had been formed. Still, confronted with the *fait accompli,* there was no interest in a countermovement to support Velasco. Quickly establishing an almost all-military government that balanced moderates, *peruanistas* and the "Brazilian" faction led by Aulestia, Rodríguez promised a government that would be nationalist, revolutionary, humanist, and disciplined. "The situation of the country has become [totally] chaotic. To the problems of a society that is economically underdeveloped, socially unjust, and politically dependent is added the collective frustration produced by the irresponsible management of the affairs of state. . . . It is, therefore, imperative to create a revolutionary government under the leadership of the armed forces."[29]

While each of these more recent coups differed from the coups previously analyzed, their outcomes were generally consistent with the list of coup decision criteria developed earlier. In most respects the political crisis in June 1970 had all the elements of a classic coup situation—high levels of public disorders, negative public opinion in the midst of an economic crisis, a fear of "subversive" student groups, frustrated budgetary aspirations, criticism of the armed forces, and an impasse between Congress and the president. Unlike the situation in 1961, however, the chief source of the disorders and of the subversive threat was the radical student groups that both the government and the armed forces were anxious to suppress. While public opinion was generally divided on the merits of the Velasco government, when confronted with the rising level of disorders, the Quito middle class began to opt for some immediate change.[30] Moreover, Velasco had been working for over a year to shift the blame for the financial crisis and related problems onto Congress.[31] Nevertheless, this crisis might well have ended in the overthrow of the government had it not been for the military's vivid memories of the negative consequences of the previous military government.

On the other hand, the military revolt of 1971 (like the unsuccessful coup of 1954) was, essentially, an intramilitary, one-issue crisis, primarily centered on institutional grievances and personality clashes among the senior officers. Given the eventual emergence of a solid antigovernment majority on the issue of institutional autonomy, the outcome of the crisis rested largely on the balance between the proponents of the arbiter and developmentalist role definitions. In the end the government survived largely because of the older officers' preference for dealing only with the immediate crisis.

Table 15.1 Military Appraisal of
the Political Situation: 1970–1976

| Coup decision criteria | 1970 | 1971 | Crisis 1972 | 1975 | 1976 |
|---|---|---|---|---|---|
| Personal ties | +,- | +,- | +,- | +,- | +,- |
| Communist threat | -† | | | | |
| Public opinion | - | | - | - | - |
| Institutional interests | -† | * | - | | |
| Socioeconomic reform | - | - | * | * | |
| Public disorders | *† | | | | - |
| Constitutionality | | | | | * |
| Electoral veto | | | | | |

*Indicates the key issue in that crisis.
†The government was not perceived to be the source of the problem in these cases.

Despite the heated electoral campaign, it appears that in 1972 there was no crisis atmosphere as there had been in earlier successful coups. In fact, the situation was in some ways similar to that of 1971, except that the institutional interests at stake here were much less immediate. On the other hand, judging by *El Comercio* editorials, public opinion was rather hostile toward the Velasco government and even more critical of the political and economic situation of the country as a whole.[32] Nevertheless, Bucaram could hardly be labeled a communist; nor were there any significant public disorders. This suggests that after 1971 there was a significant shift toward the developmentalist role definition that predisposed large numbers of officers to intervene regardless of the circumstances.[33]

It seems that the electoral veto of Bucaram was not the key element differentiating the political situation in 1972 from that of 1971. While it is clear that the pre-election maneuvering played a large role in the political confusion with which the military was becoming increasingly impatient, it is not clear how many officers were acting to prevent a likely Bucaram victory or to what degree Bucaram really entered into military decisions to support or oppose the coup. Knowledgeable civilian and military observers reported some military distaste for Bucaram, although the commonly mentioned objections were not his populist or possibly radical policies,[34] but, rather, his humble origins and lack of formal schooling, which some officers feared would adversely affect Ecuador's international prestige.[35] Nevertheless, the leaders, both civilian and military, who were most intimately involved in the coup itself, unanimously agreed that the electoral issue was a pretext.[36] Even though the sample is small, it appears to indicate that, for most officers, Bucaram was important only as an indication of the failure of the civilian regime to offer any prospects for anything but a continuation of the same disorganized, ill-planned, and frequently corrupt politics that characterized the Velasco administration. Given their previous records, Camilo Ponce, Carlos Julio Arosemena, and Velasco were no more acceptable to the war academy than Bucaram was. Once this group had decided to proceed with the coup, the question facing most officers was not whether to stop Bucaram, but whether there was any reason to fight to maintain a thoroughly discredited status quo.[37]

If the above analysis is correct, the key to the 1972 coup was not Bucaram, but a shift in role definitions within the relevant ranks of officers. As indicated previously, the failure of the military junta had reversed a trend toward adoption of the developmentalist role definition. The strong reprisals against the armed forces after the fall of the junta heightened military sensitivity to the limitations of their training and experience in nonmilitary affairs, but the reprisals also led to even more hostile attitudes toward the civilian leadership. Nevertheless, even though initially there was little confidence in either military or civilian capacity to govern, over time the junta's failures became more remote, whereas Velasco soon ran into the same problems that had beset previous civilian administrations. Thus the balance of role definitions shifted again.

The successful revolt against Acosta Velasco played an important role in this process by generating a new sense of military confidence, especially among the senior officers who had been closer to the previous military government. The fact that the army had finally fought back by refusing to accept political interference in its professional affairs sharply boosted previously sagging military egos. Having won that battle, having set their own house in order, most officers were inclined to believe that they could do the same for the government.[38] While confidence levels varied considerably among individual officers, there was a consensus that it would be hard for a military government to do any worse than the civilians had done.

In most respects the political and economic processes that were shaping the political environment remained the same until 1972. However, with the completion of the trans-Andean pipeline in that year, Ecuador began to export approximately two hundred thousand barrels of oil daily. Export earnings more than tripled in less than two years and government revenues increased accordingly.[39] In addition to generating record increases in GNP and inflation, the oil boom significantly changed the societal distribution of economic power. The sharp growth in the economic resources of the state decreased the ability of the Guayaquil commercial oligarchy to manipulate the economy, thus significantly reducing the relative power of that traditional elite. With the bulk of the petroleum-related activities concentrated in Esmeraldas, Quito, and the Oriente, Guayaquil as a whole suffered a serious economic decline, which was reflected in a reversal of Quito's and Guayaquil's traditional population growth rates. Whereas the Guayaquil elite was forced to play a lesser role in national politics, foreign corporations—particularly the oil companies—became major political actors. Oil policy, in fact, occupied a central place on the agenda of the new government, which was especially anxious not to let its inexperience render it vulnerable to the bitter nationalist criticism that had been used so effectively against the military junta. The political equation also changed somewhat, in that the economy was not quite the zero-sum game it had traditionally been. As in Venezuela, the influx of substantial oil revenues raised hopes that elite acquiescence in the government's reforms might be purchased.

Despite the changes in the economic sphere, there were relatively few significant political changes. Like the military junta, the new military government chose to rule without any organized base of political support. Political parties were not outlawed, but remained more or less moribund until 1974. The Rodríguez government pursued a nationalist foreign policy, allying itself with the Organization of Petroleum Exporting Countries on oil questions[40] and with Peru, Cuba, and Mexico on hemispheric concerns.[41] However, in domestic matters, the Rodríguez government tended to adopt the rhetoric of Peru's "revolutionary military government" without adopting any of the structural reforms being carried out by the Peruvians.

In part, the lack of any strong attempt to effect domestic reforms was a consequence of the close balance among opposing factions within the armed forces. While the *peruanistas* were surprisingly strong in the navy[42] and, to a lesser extent, among the younger generation of army officers, they were opposed by the so-called "Brazilian faction" led by General Aulestia, who had become the new minister of defense.[43] The deciding vote was thus generally held by the small but senior group of moderates and careerists for whom Rodríguez reserved most of the key positions in the government. The moderates were, in general, much more concerned with orderly administration and avoidance of crises than they were with domestic reforms. The military leadership's lack of nonmilitary training, its memories of the mistakes of the military junta, and the generally low salience of the counterinsurgency problem[44] all contributed to a prevailing atmosphere of caution. Despite occasionally bold talk, the government was not willing to accept the political or psychological risks of undertaking any radical changes.

Nowhere were the limitations of the government's commitment to structural change more apparent than in the area of agrarian reform. Despite its initial pledge that the agrarian structure would be "radically changed,"[45] it took the government nearly a year and a half to produce a new agrarian reform law, which was in some respects weaker than the old law that had been decreed by the military junta. No limits were set on the maximum size of land holdings, and the existing owners were given a two-year delay in which to bring their properties up to the required minimum of 80 percent efficient cultivation.[46] Still, uncertainty about the government's intentions before and after the 1974 decree led to strong counterattacks from both Chambers of Agriculture and a virtual boycott of any further investment in agriculture, despite the soaring urban demand that tripled the previous rate of inflation. Characteristically, the government's response was to replace several progressive agriculture ministers and to offer even more generous production incentives to the land-owning class. Finally, faced with stiff resistance from land-owners, the government abandoned agrarian reform in favor of colonization. Whereas the colonization program was 64 percent completed by 1975, less than 6 percent of the agrarian reform target acreage had actually been expropriated by that date.[47]

Given the government's refusal to pursue radical egalitarian policies or to mobilize mass support, the new military government enjoyed no more legitimacy than its predecessors had. Despite the initially favorable public reaction to its reformist promises and to its nationalist foreign policy, the government—in the end—remained at the mercy of the economy. After two years of rapidly rising oil revenues and a fast-growing GNP, the oil boom suddenly faded. With the weakening of world demand for petroleum, various companies gave up their concessions rather than accept tough new government policies governing oil contracts. In 1974 Ecuador, as a marginal producer, came under increasingly strong pressure from the Texaco-Gulf consortium to cut its prices below the OPEC minimum. Citing marketing difficulties and problems with the trans-Andean pipeline, Texaco-Gulf cut back production from 200,000 to just over 100,000 barrels a day. As a result, government revenues and exports declined sharply, presenting the government with a growing budget deficit, a large balance of payments deficit, and popular protests that prices were now rising more rapidly than wages were.[48]

Not surprisingly, the government's economic troubles and the lack of any signs of public support gave new life to the opposition.[49] In May of 1975 ex-Presidents Camilo Ponce and Carlos Julio Arosemena, along with the leaders of various parties, announced the formation of a new Frente Civilista modeled on the constitutionalist fronts that had spearheaded the campaign against the military junta.[50] Strikes by oil workers, tuna fishermen, and professional groups were interspersed with strong land-owner protests against the Agrarian Reform Law and merchant objections to the government's tariff policies and favoritism toward the industrialists. Strongly worded manifestos demanding an end to the military government coincided with increasingly critical editorials in the major newspapers and outside pressure for concessions on oil prices and the 200-mile fishing limit.

As the opposition chorus reached a crescendo, the chairman of the joint chiefs of staff, General Raúl González Alvear decided that it was time to heed the appeals of civilian leaders for an interim military government to prepare for a return to civilian rule. With the support of a few similarly inclined senior officers in Quito including the zone commander and the head of the war academy, General González surrounded the presidential palace with antigovernment troops. Nevertheless, President Rodríguez managed to escape and the presidential guard refused to surrender. At dawn, fighting broke out. Although the rebels controlled the downtown area, the air force remained loyal and dropped warning bombs at one nearby rebel barracks. Meanwhile General Rodríguez found refuge in the military garrison of Ambato. Rodríguez then began a countermarch at the head of a column of armored vehicles while a key supporter, General Carlos Aguirre Asanza, organized a counterforce in Quito that surrounded the rebel forces shortly after they had finally made their way into the presidential palace. Vastly outnumbered the rebels surrendered, although González and several civilian supporters managed to escape to foreign embassies. By midnight the revolt was over and General Rodríguez triumphantly returned to what was left of the presidential palace.

Undaunted by the failure of the coup and unimpressed by the government's concessions on oil prices and import duties, the opposition forces merely stepped up their attacks on the military administration. When the government demanded punishment for the rebels in an attempt to capitalize on its new "tough guy" image, Ponce, Arosemena, and ex-Ministers Aulestia and Latorre offered themselves as defense counsel for officers accused of participating in the revolt, turning the government's plan for a quick court-martial into a victory for its opponents. Seriously embarrassed by the mishandling of the trial, several of the president's key supporters presented him with an ultimatum stating that he should either act or resign. Eleven antigovernment officers (including four generals) were immediately deported with no visible impact on the government's public credibility.[51] Encouraged by the evident disarray in military ranks, the Frente Civilista redoubled its efforts to promote a coup, despite its earlier failure. New arrests were followed by the deportation of both Arosemena and the head of the Conservative party, which did not prevent various bombings or a 12-hour nationwide general strike demanding a 50 percent wage hike. Vague government statements about a plan to "institutionalize" the government only increased the uncertainty. Contrary to the expectations of many observers, the rising tide of right-wing opposition did not lead to a closer government alliance with the left or to a more decided reform orientation.

Finally, in the face of strong antigovernment riots and several new strikes, including a major transport workers strike, the government collapsed. On 10 January 1976 the three service commanders notified Rodríguez that he would have to resign, though they agreed to wait until after the president's daughter's wedding, which was to take place the next day. Despite stiff resistance to the presence of former Army Commander General Durán Arcentales in the new military junta, he emerged as the pivotal figure in the new government.[52] Nevertheless, the new government generally reflected the same moderate outlook that characterized its predecessor. The lack of any clear sense of priorities was immediately apparent in the junta's pledges to carry out the reforms to which the military had committed itself in 1972 and at the same time execute a secret plan to return power to the civilians by 1977.

Given the internal division between those favoring reforms and those advocating a quick return to the barracks, and given the predictably intense opposition to its plan to eliminate all of the old leaders by banning presidential re-election, the political future of the new military junta is uncertain at best. It is likely that the current military government will end like its predecessors—in a military coup d'état.

Thus the Ecuadorian military's political behavior since 1966 generally seems to conform to the model of the coup d'état elaborated in chapter 14. There has been little change in the basic patterns of civil-military interaction described earlier, despite the occurrence of several different forms of military intervention, such as the progovernment coup of 1970 and the ultimatum-revolt against Jorge Acosta in 1971. The decision criteria for the several coups since 1966 are nearly identical to those previously identified, with the single exception of the constitutional norm, which has now ceased to be a salient concern. Role definitions continue to shift—mostly between the arbiter and developmentalist doctrines—in accordance with the fluctuations in the balance of perceived capabilities to govern. Given the failure of both civilian and military governments to attack the structural problems underlying Ecuador's repeated political crises, these crises have continued to occur, and, as expected, the coup d'état continues to be a key element in the Ecuadorian political process.

Nevertheless, a number of important research questions remain. Clearly the most important is the generality of this model. To what extent can it be used to explain coup behavior in other contexts? Despite many apparent parallels in other Latin American countries, some discrepancies are also apparent. For example, the electoral veto of certain parties appears to have been an important decision criterion in Peru and Argentina, but not in Ecuador. Further research is needed to explain why some civilian groups and not others, in some countries but not in others, come to be viewed by the military as illegitimate political forces. What other additions or modifications might be required to account for cross-national differences among Latin American militaries or between those of Latin America and other Third World areas?

More research will also be required to test the arguments made here concerning the impact of organizational variables, such as the level of professionalization, on civil-military relations. In particular, there is a need for more direct evidence of a causal linkage between the intensity and duration of the military socialization process and the strength of the individual officer's psychological identification with the military institution. In general, more attention needs to be given to comparative studies of organizational factors, especially in the smaller, less professionalized military forces. Precisely because cases like Bolivia, Nicaragua, and prerevolutionary Cuba are militarily as well as economically and politically more akin to Africa and Asia, these may prove the most important for cross-regional analyses and for the development of a more broadly comparative theory of the coup d'état process.[53]

There is also a need for further refinement and specification of the concept of the developmentalist role definition. Within the ranks of those espousing the basic security and development doctrine, there has been no real agreement on what development is or how it is to be achieved. Some officers have favored relatively radical reforms like those of General Velasco in Peru, while others have advocated policies more like those of the military government in Brazil.[54] It is not clear whether or not these different interpretations of the security and development doctrine figured directly in decisions to support or oppose a given government. Nevertheless, the conflict between these factions appears to have been a significant factor underlying the rather uncertain course of Ecuadorian military governments since 1972.

Finally, this model of the coup d'état needs to be integrated with the emerging literature on military regimes and military rule.[55] The research to date on the military in power has revealed a wide variation in policy orientations and policy outcomes, even in countries with relatively similar military institutions.[56] Part of the explanation for this variation clearly lies in the different initial conditions in which military governments came to power. The experience of the Rodríguez government in Ecuador also suggests that policy choices are affected by the internal distribution of role definitions among those officers in the government itself and among those left commanding the troops. The coup d'état model elaborated here may thus help identify some of the larger processes that shape the policy orientations of military governments. Many other factors—institutional, societal, and situational—will be required to adequately explain the behavior of the military in power. Nevertheless, a clear understanding of the process by which such governments are initiated is an essential part of any analysis of the consequences of coup decisions. This model of the coup d'état as a political process is, therefore, a first step toward a more comprehensive analysis of the political behavior of the Latin American armed forces.

# Notes

## Acknowledgments

1. See the comment by Frank Bonilla, quoted in Lyle N. McAlister, "Recent Research and Writings on the Role of the Military in Latin America," *Latin American Research Review* 2 (Fall 1966):33.

2. Material from individual interviews is generally cited to coded interview numbers. A key to the code is available upon written request from any properly accredited scholar with a professional interest in this information. Several officers still on active duty are not listed in the acknowledgments or in the key.

## Chapter 1: The Military Coup d'Etat: A Theoretical Framework

1. See Lyle N. McAlister, "Recent Research and Writings on the Role of the Military in Latin America," *Latin American Research Review* 2 (Fall 1966):5–36; José Enrique Miguens, "The New Latin American Coup," in *Militarism in Developing Countries,* ed. Kenneth Fidel (New Brunswick, N.J.: Transaction Books, 1975), pp. 99–123; Richard Rankin, "The Expanding Institutional Concerns of the Latin American Military Establishments: A Review Article," *Latin American Research Review* 9, no. 1 (Spring 1974):81–108; and Abraham Lowenthal "Armies and Politics in Latin America: A Review of the Recent Literature," *World Politics* 27, no. 1 (October 1974):107–30.

2. Victor Villanueva, *¿Nueva mentalidad militar en el Perú?* (Lima, Peru: Editorial Juan Mejía Baca, 1969), p. 194.

3. See Samuel P. Huntington, "Civilian Control of the Military: A Theoretical Statement," in *Political Behavior: A Reader in Theory and Research,* ed. Heinz Eulau, Samuel Eldersveld, and Morris Janowitz (Glencoe, Ill.: The Free Press, 1956), pp. 380–85.

4. Samuel P. Huntington, *Political Order in Changing Societies* (New Haven: Yale University Press, 1968), pp. 1–92.

5. Mario Grandona, "La estructura cívico-militar del nuevo estado argentino," *Aportes* 6 (October 1967):70. Unless otherwise noted, all translations from Spanish are by the author.

6. Edwin Lieuwen, *Generals vs. Presidents: Neo-Militarism in Latin America* (New York: Frederick A. Praeger, 1964), pp. 102, 104–9.

7. Edwin Lieuwen, *Arms and Politics in Latin America* (New York: Frederick A. Praeger, 1960), p. 123.

8. John J. Johnson, *The Military and Society in Latin America* (Stanford, Calif.: Stanford University Press, 1964), p. 120.

9. Dr. Rafael Caldera, quoted in Robert Gilmore, *Caudillism and Militarism in Venezuela 1810–1910* (Athens: Ohio University Press, 1964), p. 13.

10. See James Payne, *Labor and Politics in Peru* (New Haven: Yale University Press, 1964), pp. 9–10.

11. Lieuwen, *Generals,* p. 98.

12. Egil Fossum, "Factors Influencing the Occurrence of Military Coups d'Etat in Latin America," *Journal of Peace Research* 3 (Fall 1967):p. 234.

13. Liisa North, *Civil-Military Relations in Argentina, Chile, and Peru* (Berkeley, Calif.: Institute of International Studies, 1966), p. 52.

14. Samuel E. Finer, *The Man on Horseback: The Role of the Military in Politics* (New York: Frederick A. Praeger, 1962), p. 196.

15. Martin Needler, *Anatomy of a Coup d'Etat: Ecuador 1963* (Washington, D.C.: Institute for the Comparative Study of Political Systems, 1964), p. 44.

16. José Nun, "The Middle Class Military Coup," in *The Politics of Conformity in Latin America,* ed. Claudio Veliz (New York: Oxford University Press, 1967), pp. 72–74.

17. Lieuwen, *Generals,* p. 98.

18. Robert C. Case, "El entrenamiento de los militares latinoamericanos en los Estados Unidos," *Aportes* 6 (October 1967):55.

19. See Alfred C. Stepan, *The Military in Politics: Changing Patterns in Brazil* (Princeton, N.J.: Princeton University Press, 1971), p. 327; Needler, *Anatomy,* p. 41.

20. Martin Needler, "Political Development and Military Intervention in Latin America," *American Political Science Review* 60, no. 3 (September 1966):620.

21. J. Lloyd Mecham, "Latin American Constitutions: Nominal and Real," *Journal of Politics* 21, no. 2 (May 1959):264.

22. Victor Alba, "The Stages of Militarism in Latin America," in *The Role of the Military in Underdeveloped Countries,* ed. John J. Johnson (Princeton, N.J.: Princeton University Press, 1962), pp. 165–83; Lieuwen, *Arms and Politics,* pp. 151–53.

23. North, *Civil-Military Relations,* pp. 13, 37, 59.

24. Alfred C. Stepan, "The 'New Professionalism' of Internal Warfare and Military Role Expansion," in *Authoritarian Brazil: Origins, Policies, and Future,* ed. Alfred C. Stepan (New Haven: Yale University Press, 1974), pp. 47–68.

25. See Martin Needler's excellent review article, "Military Motivations in the Seizure of Power," *Latin American Research Review* 10, no. 3 (Winter 1975):62–78.

26. Johnson, *Military and Society,* p. 250; Morris Janowitz, *The Military in the Political Development of New Nations* (Chicago: University of Chicago Press, 1964), p. 56.

27. Lieuwen, *Generals,* p. 104.

28. José Nun, *Latin America: The Hegemonic Crisis and the Military Coup* (Berkeley, Calif.: Institute of International Studies, 1969), p. 48.

29. Stepan, *Military in Politics,* pp. 42–47 and 153–71.

30. Robert Price, "A Theoretical Approach to Military Rule in New States: Reference Group Theory and the Ghanaian Case," *World Politics* 13 (April 1971):399–430.

31. Huntington, *Political Order,* pp. 1–6.

32. Mauricio Solaún and Michael Quinn, *Sinners and Heretics: The Politics of Military Intervention in Latin America* (Urbana: University of Illinois Press, 1973), pp. 190–95.

33. Huntington, *Political Order,* pp. 32–56; Solaún and Quinn, *Sinners and Heretics,* pp. 19–43.

34. Guillermo O'Donnell, *Modernization and Bureaucratic Authoritarianism: Studies in South American Politics* (Berkeley, Calif.: Institute of International Studies, 1973), pp. 1–52; Gino Germani and Kalman Silvert, "Politics, Social Structure, and Military Intervention in Latin America," *European Journal of Sociology* 2 (1961):62–81.

35. Huntington, *Political Order,* pp. 8–32.

36. Martin Needler, *Political Development in Latin America: Instability, Violence, and Evolutionary Change* (New York: Random House, 1968), pp. 98–116.

37. Robert Putnam, "Toward Explaining Military Intervention in Latin American Politics," *World Politics* 20 (October 1967):83–110; Merle Kling, "Toward a Theory of Power and Political Instability in Latin America," *Western Political Quarterly* 9, no. 1 (March 1956):21–35.

38. Jacques Lambert, *Latin America: Social Structures and Political Institutions*, trans. Helen Katel (Berkeley: University of California Press, 1969), pp. 229, 239–42; Nun, *Hegemonic Crisis,* pp. 22–33.

39. Douglas Chalmers, "Developing on the Periphery: External Factors in Latin American Politics," in *Linkage Politics*, ed. James Rosenau (New York: The Free Press, 1969), pp. 67–93; Harry Magdoff, "Militarism and Imperialism," *American Economic Review* 60 (May 1970):237–42.

40. Putnam, "Explaining Military Intervention"; Douglas Bwy, "Political Instability in Latin America: The Cross Cultural Test of a Causal Model," *Latin American Research Review* 3, no. 2 (Spring 1968):17–87; Phillips Cutwright, "National Political Development," in *Politics and Social Life*, ed. N. W. Polsby, R. A. Dentler, and P. A. Smith (Boston: Houghton Mifflin, 1963), pp. 569–82; David Collier, "The Timing of Development and Political Outcomes in Latin America," (Paper presented to the American Political Science Association convention, Washington, D.C., 1972); Warren Dean, "Latin American Golpes and Economic Fluctuations, 1823–1966," *Social Science Quarterly* 51, no. 1 (June 1970):70–80; William R. Thompson, "Regime Vulnerability and the Military Coup," *Comparative Politics* 7, no. 4 (July 1975):459–87.

41. Ronald D. Brunner and Garry D. Brewer, *Organized Complexity: Empirical Theories of Political Development* (New York: The Free Press, 1971), pp. 1–7.

42. Specifically, prior specification of the independent variables, minimal interaction, no feedback, and simple, linear relationships. Brunner and Brewer, *Organized Complexity*, pp. 162–76. In addition, such analyses are invariably forced to treat the degree of military intervention for any given country as a constant over a fairly long period. The absurdity of an "average score" for the years 1948–1966 in Ecuador is readily apparent from the following chapters.

43. John J. Johnson, *Political Change in Latin America: The Emergence of the Middle Sectors* (Stanford, Calif.: Stanford University Press, 1958), p. 94.

44. For example, the debate over explanations of military intervention that stress the military "push" as opposed to the "pull" of weak democratic institutions. Framed in this fashion the distinction is meaningless, since no coup could occur without a military belief that certain political outcomes are intolerable. Yet these political outcomes are obviously caused by other factors (such as weak political institutions) that are not under military control. In terms of this framework, coups result from both situational and structural causes, the former presumably grounded in the latter. Cf. McAlister, "Role of the Military," and Needler, "Political Development," p. 620 n. See also Martin Needler, "The Latin American Military: Predatory Reactionaries or Modernizing Patriots? " *Journal of Inter-American Studies* 11, no. 2 (April 1969):239.

## Chapter 2: The Ecuadorian Armed Forces

1. Samuel P. Huntington, *Political Order in Changing Societies* (New Haven: Yale University Press, 1968), p. 194. Cf. Morris Janowitz, *The Military in the Political Development of New Nations* (Chicago: University of Chicago Press, 1964).

2. In the case of the Latin American military, the major exceptions are: Lyle N. McAlister, Anthony P. Maingot, and Robert A. Potash, *The Military in Latin American Sociopolitical Evolution: Four Case Studies* (Washington, D.C.: Center for Research in Social Systems, 1970); Alfred C. Stepan, *The Military in Politics: Changing Patterns in Brazil* (Princeton, N.J.: Princeton University Press, 1971); Guillermo O'Donnell, "Modernización y golpes militares: teoría, comparación, y el caso argentino," Documento de trabajo, Instituto Torcuato di Tella, Centro de Investigaciones en Administración Pública (Buenos Aires, Argentina, 1972).

3. This argument is developed in greater depth and detail in John Samuel Fitch III, "Civil-Military Relations in Prewar Ecuador" (Manuscript).

4. On the colonial history of Ecuador, see John Leddy Phelan, *The Kingdom of Quito in the Seventeenth Century: Bureaucratic Politics in the Spanish Empire* (Madison:

University of Wisconsin Press, 1967), and Federico González Suárez, *Historia General de la República del Ecuador* 7 vols. (Quito, Ecuador: Imprenta del Clero, 1901).

5. See Alfredo Costales Samaniego and Piedad de Costales, *Historia Social del Ecuador* (published as issue no. 17 of *Llacta*, Quito, Ecuador, 1964), 1:298; Comité Interamericano de Desarrollo Agrícola (CIDA), *Tenencia de la tierra y desarrollo socio-económico del sector agrícola: Ecuador* (Washington, D.C.: Pan American Union, 1965), pp. 155–56.

6. Oscar Efren Reyes, *Historia de la República, esquema de ideas, y hechos del Ecuador, al partir de la Emancipación* (Quito, Ecuador: Imprenta Nacional, 1931), pp. 32–97; idem, *Breve historia general del Ecuador* 7th ed. (Quito, Ecuador: Editorial "Fray Jodoco Ricke," 1967):2, 3:70–96.

7. The term comes from J. M. Ots Capdequi's description of the Spanish colonizers, who, like the Ecuadorian political elite of the nineteenth century, were "the *segundones hijosdalgo* . . . a marginal class, claimants of social prestige to whom the primogeniture system denied economic security and for whom only bureaucratic, military, or ecclesiastical careers were acceptable." J. M. Ots Capdequi, quoted in Richard Morse, "The Heritage of Latin America," in *The Founding of New Societies*, ed. Louis Hartz (New York: Harcourt, Brace, and World, 1964), p. 127. Cf. Leopoldo Benites Vineuza, *Ecuador: drama y paradoja* (Mexico City: Fondo de Cultura Económica, 1950), pp. 51–53.

8. Although Merle Kling's classic essay on the sources of Latin American instability stresses foreign control over channels of economic mobility, the net result was the same in Ecuador, where there were no readily available natural resources to attract foreign exploitation. Ostensibly, Kling was describing contemporary events, though his argument is more relevant to the nineteenth century than to the twentieth. Merle Kling, "Toward a Theory of Power and Political Instability in Latin America," *Western Political Quarterly* 9, no. 1 (March 1956):21–35. Cf. James Payne, *Patterns of Conflict in Colombia* (New Haven: Yale University Press, 1968).

9. The most interesting exception was the Conservative patriarch Gabriel García Moreno, who had tried his hand in military conflicts with a conspicuous lack of success. Learning from his past failures, García Moreno brought General Flores out of exile to lead his military forces for him. García Moreno was the only nonmilitary figure among the major caudillos of the 1830–1916 period. See Richard Pattee, *Gabriel García Moreno y el Ecuador de su tiempo* (Mexico City: Editorial Jus, 1962).

10. For a general economic history of Ecuador, and this period in particular, see Augustín Cueva, *El proceso de dominación política en el Ecuador* (Quito, Ecuador: Ediciones Crítica, 1972), pp. 3–11; CIDA, *Tenencia de la tierra*, pp. 104–12; North American Congress on Latin America, "Ecuador: Oil Up for Grabs," *Latin America and Empire Report* 9, no. 8 (November 1975):2–13.

11. *Informe del Ministro de Guerra y Marina al Congreso Nacional de 1900* (Quito, Ecuador: Imprenta Nacional, 1900), pp. 1–9, 16, 18, 22–23; *Informe del Ministro de Guerra y Marina al Congreso Nacional de 1901* (Quito, Ecuador: Imprenta Nacional, 1901), pp. vii, xiv–xxi, xxiii, tables 9, 23, 27; *Memoria del Ministro de Guerra y Marina presentada al Congreso Nacional de 1904* (Quito, Ecuador: Imprenta Nacional, 1904), pp. iv, 345, 469, 529; *Memoria del Ministro de Guerra y Marina presentada al Congreso de 1905* (Quito, Ecuador: Imprenta Nacional, 1905), pp. iv, vii, x–xi, xxii–xxiii; *Informe del Ministerio de Guerra y Marina presentada a la Asamblea Nacional de 1906* (Quito, Ecuador: Imprenta Nacional, 1906), pp. v–vi.

12. Reyes, *Breve historia*, pp. 223–26. Cf. Pattee, *Gabriel García Moreno*, p. 364. See William F. Sands, *Our Jungle Diplomacy* (Chapel Hill: University of North Carolina Press, 1944), pp. 205–10, for an outsider's description of the intra-Liberal struggles; Luis Larrea Alba, *La campaña de 1941: la agresión peruana al Ecuador y sus antecedentes históricos, políticas y militares* (Quito, Ecuador: Editorial Casa de la Cultura Ecuatoriana, 1964), p. 231. See also, idem, *La campaña de 1906: antecedentes de la revolución alfarista, su desarrollo, y sus consecuencias, el conflicto de 1910* (Quito, Ecuador: Gráficos Cyma, 1962); Julio Muñoz, *Doctrinas militares aplicadas en el Ecuador: historia y pedagogía militar* (Quito, Ecuador: Imprenta del Estado Mayor General, 1949), p. 218.

13. Oscar Efren Reyes, *Los últimos siete años* (Quito, Ecuador: Talleres Gráficos Nacionales, 1933), pp. 48–52.

14. Reyes, *Breve Historia,* pp. 274–317.

15. See Robert Gilmore, *Caudillism and Militarism in Venezuela 1810–1910* (Athens: Ohio University Press, 1964), pp. 121–59. See also Abraham Lowenthal, "The Dominican Republic: The Politics of Chaos," in *Latin America: Reform and Revolution,* ed. Arpad von Lazar and Robert Kaufman (Boston: Allyn and Bacon, 1969), pp. 50–53.

16. *Ley de planta y sueldos del personal del ejército permanente* (Quito, Ecuador: Imprenta Nacional, 1912), pp. 1–2; *Memorial de Infantería (España),* cited in "Organización de los ejércitos americanos," *El Ejército Nacional* 3, no. 20 (1924):466–70; Remigio Romero y Cordero, "El ejército en cien años de vida republicana," *El Ejército Nacional* 12, no. 67 (1933):209–10; "Criterio económico del ejército," *El Ejército Nacional* 11, no. 61 (1932):4.

17. Mayor von Behring, "Evolución cultural de nuestro ejército," *Revista Militar* 2, no. 6 (February–March 1934):4; Luis Larrea Alba, "El ejército y la política," *El Ejército Nacional* 10, no. 55 (1931):36–38; Angel Isaac Chiriboga, "El ejército y el Congreso de 1930," *El Ejército Nacional* 10, no. 55 (1931):1–6; interview with Ingeniero Federico Páez, Presidente de la República 1935–1937, Quito, Ecuador, 19 August 1970.

18. Daniel Hidalgo, *El militarismo: sus causas y remedios* (Quito, Ecuador: R. Racines, 1913), pp. 148–50.

19. Cf. Anthony P. Maingot, "The Colombian Military: A Case of Inconsistent Status," in McAlister, Maingot, and Potash, *Sociopolitical Evolution,* pp. 127–70.

20. Mayor von Behring, *Evolucion cultural,* p. 5. From 1900 to 1925, there were three major sources of officers: the Escuela Militar, direct promotion of subofficials, and incorporation of politically appointed reserve officers. (Interview with General Luis Larrea Alba, Quito, Ecuador, 25 August 1970.)

21. N=85. Source: *Libro de solicitudes de ingreso 1928, 1929, 1930,* Archive of Colegio Militar Eloy Alfaro, Quito, Ecuador. Use of the archive requires written authorization by the commander general of the army.

22. The Escuela Militar, which, in 1935, was renamed the Colegio Militar, required for admission at least a primary education and entrance exams, although most of the *cadetes* entered with 1–6 years of high school. Given the extremely small number of public schools, especially at the secondary level, this level of education was beyond the reach of all but the most dedicated of poor families. Pedro Moncayo, "Breve historia del Colegio Militar" (unpublished manuscript, Quito, Ecuador, 1970), pp. 6–7.

23. Angel F. Araujo, *Episodios de campaña y relatos históricos* (Quito, Ecuador: Imprenta Nacional, 1922), pp. 51–52; Pattee, *Gabriel García Moreno,* pp. 363–64.

24. Illiterates are constitutionally disenfranchised. There was only one free election in the nineteenth century and only two between 1900 and 1948. By my calculations, only 6 percent of the adult population voted in 1931, and even fewer voted in 1933.

25. Francisco Urrutia Suárez, *Apuntes para la historia: la agresión peruana* (Quito, Ecuador: Editorial Ecuatoriana, 1968), pp. 233–34.; Larrea Alba, *La campaña de 1941;* Interview with Ing. Victor Marchán Aguirre, Quito, Ecuador, October 1969. Marchán was in his last year of the Colegio Militar in 1941 and participated in the 1944 revolution and in the 1947 countercoup against Colonel Mancheno.

26. Interview with General Luis Larrea Alba, Quito, Ecuador, 25 August 1970; Larrea Alba, *La compaña de 1941,* pp. 233–36. According to another officer of the day, military assignments were made by the Arroyo del Rio government without consulting the high command. Urrutia Suárez, *Agresión peruana,* pp. 11–18.

27. Even this coup came only after Arroyo had added insult to injury by placing the entire blame for the 1941 defeat on the military high command and by building up the paramilitary *carabineros* as a counterbalance to the army. Reyes, *Breve historia,* pp. 299–301. Another indication of the institutional weakness of the army during the early twentieth century is the strength attained by the *carabineros,* who had their own training school, enjoyed military *fuero,* and were, in some respects, better equipped than the regular army. The hostility between the army and the *carabineros* came to a head in the 1944 revolution, where the issue was bloodily resolved in favor of the army. Interview 20; J. Gonzalo

Orellana, "Resúmen histórico-político de la República," in *Resúmen histórico del Ecuador, 1830–1930, 1947–8,* ed. J. Gonzalo Orellano (Quito, Ecuador: Editorial "Fray Jodoco Ricke," 1948), p. 133.

28. Interview with Ing. Marchán.

29. Olarte A., "Función democrática de las fuerzas armadas," *Revista Militar de las Fuerzas Armadas Ecuatorianas* 2 (September–October 1943):4. See also "La institutión armada y los partidos políticos," editorial in *Revista de las Fuerzas Armadas Ecuatorianas* 3, no. 146 (September 1944):3–8; Cromwell [pseud.], "Apoliticismo bien entendido," *El Comercio,* 12 March 1962, p. 4.

30. In 1970, a major reorganization of the Colegio Militar was begun. Recruitment of army officers will henceforth be the work of two institutions—the Colegio Militar, which will include the six grades of secondary education, and the Escuela Superior Militar, which will take graduates of the Colegio Militar and other high schools for a four-year program combining military subjects with the equivalent of the first three years of university training in engineering, economics, or education. Thus all future officers will have the equivalent of a junior college degree when they graduate from the Escuela Superior as second lieutenants. A preliminary analysis of applications for the beginning course of the new military high school suggests that the reorganization will accelerate the trend toward the Quito lower-middle and lower classes as the modal source of new officers. Data relative to the various military educational institutions were obtained in a series of informal interviews with members of their respective staffs.

31. "Colegio Militar," *El Comercio,* 16 August 1970, p. 5.

32. Pedro Menéndez Gilbert, *Informe a la Nación 1954–1955* (Quito, Ecuador: Editorial Santo Domingo, 1955), p. 1. Although this and the following statement were ostensibly written by civilians, they were chosen as representative of sentiments expressed on various ceremonial occasions at the military college and in the public statements of a variety of military officers.

33. Alejandro Ponce Luque, *Informe a la Nación 1955–1956* (Quito, Ecuador: Editorial Santo Domingo, 1956), p. iv.

34. Cf. Luigi Einaudi and Alfred C. Stepan, *Latin American Institutional Development: Changing Military Perspectives in Peru and Brazil* (Santa Monica, Calif.: The Rand Corporation, 1971), pp. 11–14; Robin Luckham, *The Nigerian Military: A Sociological Analysis of Authority and Revolt 1960–1967* (New York: Cambridge University Press, 1971), pp. 279–86.

35. Between 1950 and 1965, nearly 3,000 Ecuadorian officers received training abroad, 1,200 in the United States. Robert C. Case, "El entrenamiento de los militares latinoamericanos en los Estados Unidos," *Aportes* 6 (October 1967):55.

36. After ten years on the planning board, the Instituto de Altos Estudios Nacionales began operation in September 1972.

37. Even in 1970, after a major revision of the war academy curriculum resulting from the addition of "cooperation in socioeconomic development" to the constitutional definition of the military's functions, only about 200 out of 1,350 hours of instruction were devoted to nonmilitary topics.

38. Interviews 68 and 52. Four of the seventy-two officers in the initial sample were directly promoted from the ranks and another seven entered directly into the Artillery and Engineering School.

39. Enrique Ponce Luque, *Informe a la Nación 1960–1961* (Quito, Ecuador: Industrias Gráficas CYMA, 1961), p. 30. Interview 88.

40. René Lemarchand, "Civil-Military Relations in Former Belgian Africa: The Military as a Contextual Elite," in *Soldiers in Politics,* ed. Steffen Schmidt and Gerald Dorfman (Los Altos, Calif.: Geron-X, Inc., 1974), p. 76.

41. Interview 9. *Presupuesto General del Gobierno Nacional de la República,* 1950, 1955, archives of the Junta Nacional de Planificación, Quito, Ecuador; Joseph Loftus, *Latin American Defense Expenditures, 1938–1965* (Santa Monica, Calif.: The Rand Corporation, 1968), p. 95.

42. David Wood, *Armed Forces in Central and South America,* Adelphi Papers no. 34 (London: The Institute for Strategic Studies, 1967). 13. Document 63 states the air force share of the defense budget as 14.5 percent in 1955.

43. Loftus, *Defense Expenditures,* p. 36.

44. From 1948 to 1972 the only exceptions to this rule were Lieutenant Colonel Varea, who was promoted, retired, and named minister of defense in 1954 after having served as subsecretary, and Generals Naranjo and Coba, who served under the military junta from 1963 to 1966.

45. Also attached to the Ministry of Defense is the National Security Council, administered by another high-ranking officer, which theoretically has considerable defense policy powers, but has, in fact, been largely ignored.

46. A new reorganization in 1971 replaced the Estado Mayor de las Fuerzas Armadas with a Commando Conjunto.

47. Luigi Einaudi has analyzed the same process beginning at a somewhat earlier date in Peru. See Einaudi and Stepan, *Changing Military Perspectives,* pp. 43–44.

48. Stepan, *Military in Politics,* pp. 44–45.

49. The transfer of the offices of budget and personnel from the Ministry of Defense to the general staff in 1956 was another important step in reducing the extent of political penetration by the government. (Interview 51.)

50. All data on geographic and social recruitment of army officers were obtained by the author from the personal data supplied by each entering cadet on his initial application form. These are collected in the yearly volumes of *Libro de solicitudes de ingreso* (Archive of the Colegio Militar Eloy Alfaro).

51. Interviews with Capitán de Navío Alejandro Cajas Vallejo, ex-personnel director of the navy, Quito, 11 January 1971; Contralmirante Gonzalo Calderón Noriega, Quito, 18 January 1971; General de Aviación Jorge Salgado Murillo, Quito, 10 January 1971; and General de Aviación José Banderas Román, Quito, 25 May 1971. Salgado and Banderas are both ex-commanding generals of the air force. Cf. José Imaz, *Los que mandan* (Buenos Aires, Argentina: Editorial Universitaria, 1964), pp. 55–56, and Lyle McAlister, "Peru," in McAlister, Maingot, and Potash, *Sociopolitical Evolution,* pp. 34–35.

52. Thus actual recruitment from the middle class consists not only of the second group, but undeterminable fractions of the first and third groups as well.

53. Using the same classification scheme, recruitment to the Colegio Militar has been somewhat more open to the middle and lower strata than has been recruitment to Quito's Central University.

Father's Profession of Entering Students

|  | Upper, Upper-middle | Middle | Lower-middle, Lower |
|---|---|---|---|
| Central University (1967) | 25.2% | 62.6% | 11.0% |
| Colegio Militar (1966) | 12.2% | 64.3% | 23.5% |

SOURCE: Instituto de Investigaciones Económicas y Financieras de la Universidad Central, *Estadísticas Universitarias* no. 8 (1967–1968): 51.

NOTE: Figures are adjusted to eliminate a 4.6% "Others" category.

54. A member of the staff of the Colegio Militar noted that in recent years many "agriculturalists" have in fact been overseers rather than owners. (Interview 98.)

55. Assuming that the proportion of sons of officers who wish to follow in their fathers' footsteps is a constant, the substantial growth of the Ecuadorian armed forces after 1952 has increased the number of cadets relative to the pool of available officers' sons. The fact that internal recruitment has not fallen suggests that the inbreeding tendency, while masked, still exists for the reasons originally suggested by Stepan: more attractive possibilities for qualified young men in other careers, along with an educational system that denies to the large majority of the population the prerequisites for admission into the military academy. Stepan, *Military in Politics,* pp. 40–41.

56. See chapter 8.

57. Paul Goodfriend, "The Ecuadorian Army, Poor but Proud," *Infantry Journal* 61, no. 5 (October 1947):23.

58. Interview 23.

59. Kenneth Ruddle and Mukhtar Hamour, eds., *Statistical Abstract of Latin America* (Los Angeles: Latin American Center of the University of California, 1971), p. 96.

60. José Endara Erazo, "Aviso para los ciudadanos remisos al servicio militar," *El Universo,* 13 September 1969, p. 16. Students who have completed the premilitary training are considered members of the army reserves, subject to call-up in a general mobilization. Both the air force and the navy are served entirely by volunteers.

61. See Lucian W. Pye, "Armies in the Process of Political Modernization," in *The Role of the Military in Underdeveloped Countries,* ed. John J. Johnson (Princeton, N.J.: Princeton University Press, 1962), pp. 69–90.

62. Almost all were relatively senior retired officers. Additional information on the interviews and the sample is given in chapter 7.

63. Ruddle and Hamour, *Statistical Abstract,* p. 298. Figure cited is for 1968.

64. See Gobierno del Ecuador, *Registro Oficial* no. 964, 15 November 1951, p. 7881, for an earlier example of how the bonus system worked.

65. "Ley de pensiones de las Fuerzas Armadas," in *Leyes militares de la República* (Quito, Ecuador: Editorial "Fray Jodoco Ricke," 1961), pp. 135–36, 151–52; "Decreto 488," "Decreto 489," and "Decreto 490," *Registro Oficial,* 3 April 1969, pp. 1150–51.

66. Junta Militar de Gobierno, "Decreto supremo 16," *Registro Oficial* no. 157, 18 January 1964, pp. 1388–91.

67. Based on conversations with members of the clubs in question.

68. Interview 40.

69. Purely attitudinal definitions of professionalization as concentration on military matters frequently end in the circular argument that as professionalization increases, military intervention in politics will decline. Cf. Edwin Lieuwen, *Arms and Politics in Latin America* (New York: Frederick A. Praeger, 1960), pp. 151–53. Professionalization as used here is conceptually distinct from the classic professionalist military role definition as articulated, for example, by Samuel P. Huntington in *The Soldier and the State* (Cambridge: Harvard University Press, 1957), pp. 61–79. See chapter 12 for evidence that the two have been inversely related in the development of the Ecuadorian military. See also Einaudi and Stepan, *Changing Military Perspectives,* p. 123.

70. Imperfect because of differences in accounting definitions and incomplete or inaccurate data, and because it also reflects cross-national differences in military salaries as military officers "keep up with the Joneses" in their respective societies. Thus expenditure per man is also highly correlated with per capita GNP.

71. For a comparative interpretation of table 2.9, 1970 per soldier expenditures were $25,384 in the United States, $8,417 for NATO as a whole, but $2,981 for Greece, $4,146 in Spain, $2,255 in the Philippines, and $9,000 in the Republic of South Africa. United States Arms Control and Disarmament Agency, *World Military Expenditures 1971* (Washington, D.C.: Bureau of Economic Affairs, 1971), pp. 10–12. Unfortunately, the measure ceases to be valid for most of the African militaries because of the small number of soldiers.

72. Except for the distortion introduced by the "Kuwait effect" on Venezuelan expenditures, the rank orderings on both indicators of military professionalization are closely correlated with each other and with the ranks on total GNP. The rank order

correlation between number of journals and per soldier expenditure is .70. Both journals and expenditure have a lower correlation with per capita GNP ($r_s$ = .65 and .71 respectively) than with total GNP ($r_s$ = .74 and .83 respectively). GNP is, in turn, a relatively good measure of the general level of modernization of Latin American societies. Guillermo O'Donnell, *Modernization and Bureaucratic Authoritarianism: Studies in South American Politics* (Berkeley, Calif.: Institute of International Studies, 1973). The most interesting deviation from this pattern is the Peruvian military, which suggests that actual participation in armed conflicts acts as a stimulus to professionalization independent of the general relationship between modernization and military professionalization. Thus the Leticia conflict between Peru and Colombia in 1932 appears to be the point of divergence in the evolution of the Ecuadorian and Peruvian militaries, setting the stage for the reinforcement of Peruvian professionalization and an impetus toward the same in Ecuador in the latter's defeat by Peru in 1941.

73. Jacques Lambert, *Latin America: Social Structures and Political Institutions,* trans. Helen Katel (Berkeley, Calif: University of California Press, 1969), p. 246.

74. It is, in fact, doubtful that the military has that much autonomy anywhere in Latin America except in Argentina, Brazil, and Peru—and even in these cases, Lambert's statement is somewhat exaggerated. Nevertheless, in discussing civilian opposition to the creation of a center for higher studies, one Ecuadorian officer addressed the point directly, saying "We are not like some other Latin American countries where the armed forces can impose their will." Interview 97.

75. Stepan, *Military in Politics,* p. 51.

76. *Libro de Vida Militar, Academia de Guerra,* n.p. The first and only exception since the academy reopened in 1956 was General Guillermo Rodríguez Lara who, in 1971, was also the first army commanding general to be imposed by the army rather than chosen by the government. He later became president of the military government which took over in 1972.

77. *Nuevo Orden Nacional,* n.p., n.d., p. 14. This was one of several manifestos published by a group of retired officers conspiring against President Arosemena in 1963. See chapter 5.

78. All of the numerous officers with whom this problem was discussed recognized its seriousness, yet all had at several points in their careers failed to demand an end to such practices—an inconsistency that none ventured to explain.

79. Interview 97.

80. Interview 48.

81. "Codigo penal militar," in *Leyes militares de la República* (Quito, Ecuador: Editorial "Fray Jodoco Ricke," 1961), p. 29.

82. Interview 97.

83. Interview 3.

84. As defined by Huntington in terms of adaptability, complexity, autonomy, and coherence, in *Political Order,* pp. 12–24.

85. Abraham Lowenthal, in his recent review of the literature, argues that the relative balance "between the level of military institutionalization and the institutionalization of civilian political procedures may be a key determinant of the varying political roles military officers play." Abraham Lowenthal, "Armies and Politics in Latin America: A Review of the Recent Literature," *World Politics* 27, no. 1 (October 1974):107–30. See also Robin Luckham, "A Comparative Typology of Civil-Military Relations," *Government and Opposition* (Winter 1971), pp. 5–36.

## Chapter 3: Peace, Prosperity, and Constitutional Stability: 1948-1960

1. This criticism also applies to several interesting attempts to catalogue cross-nationally the situational antecedents of military coups. See Mauricio Solaun and Michael Quinn, *Sinners and Heretics: The Politics of Military Intervention in Latin America* (Urbana: University of Illinois Press, 1973), pp. 44–121 and John Michael Collins, "The

Successful Coup d'Etat in Modern Politics" (Ph.D. dissertation, Rutgers University, 1968). See William R. Thompson, *The Grievances of Military Coup Makers,* Sage Professional Papers in Comparative Politics 4, nos. 01–047 (Beverly Hills, Calif.: Sage Publications, 1973), which includes successful and unsuccessful coups.

2. Unless otherwise noted, information concerning events preceding each coup is drawn largely from the relevant issues of the major Ecuadorian newspapers, *El Comercio* of Quito and *El Universo* of Guayaquil, and of the *Hispanic American Report,* published by the Stanford Seminar on Hispanic World Affairs.

3. Ramiro Borja y Borja, *Las constituciones del Ecuador* (Madrid: Ediciones Cultura Hispánica, 1951), p. 634.

4. Georg Maier, *The Ecuadorian Presidential Election of June 2, 1968: An Analysis* (Washington, D.C.: Institute for the Comparative Study of Political Systems, 1969), pp. 26, 74.

5. The discovery of the Rio Cenepa in 1947 created an ambiguity in the Rio Protocol landmarks for a 60-mile stretch of the southern border. This brought demarcation to a halt and gave Ecuador an opening to demand renegotiation of the entire treaty.

6. Interview 59.

7. According to official estimates, the value of agricultural production for export jumped 57 percent from 1950 to 1952. During the same period, production for internal consumption also increased by 25 percent. Banco Central del Ecuador, *Series estadísticas básicas para el análisis económico* (Quito, Ecuador: Imprenta del Banco Central, 1962), p. 78.

8. Interviews 48 and 88.

9. Interview 91.

10. Interviews 88 and 86.

11. Maier, *Ecuadorian Presidential Election,* pp. 27, 75.

12. In the 1933 election and in the Revolution of 1944. It is generally conceded that only systematic fraud prevented him from winning the 1940 election as well–the only electoral defeat in his long political career.

13. Although rather outdated, George Blanksten's *Ecuador: Constitutions and Caudillos* (Berkeley: University of California Press, 1951) is the best portrait of Velasco available in English. A more detailed biography by Robert Norris is still unpublished. By far the best analytic treatment of *velasquismo* is Agustín Cueva, *El proceso de dominación política en el Ecuador* (Quito, Ecuador: Ediciones Crítica, 1972). See also John D. Martz, *Ecuador: Conflicting Political Culture and the Quest for Progress* (Boston: Allyn and Bacon, 1972), pp. 69–76, 121–23, and 147–63. For an introduction to Velasco's political philosophy, see José María Velasco Ibarra, *Conciencia o barbarie* (Medellín, Colombia: Editorial Atlántida, 1936).

14. Junta Nacional de Planificación, *Indicadores económicos,* 1, no. 3 (Quito, Ecuador, July 1967):H–11; and Banco Central del Ecuador, *Memoria del Gerente General, 1960* (Quito, Ecuador: Imprenta del Banco Central, 1961), Appendice II, Cuadro 7, p.x.

15. *Hispanic American Report* 7, no. 9 (October 1954): 24.

16. Interview 9.

17. Among other officers, they were unaffectionately labeled "los Che." Interview 26.

18. Interviews 26 and 44.

19. Interviews 85 and 44. The official version of these events is contained in Visitaduría General de la Administración, *El delito de 22 de diciembre y el constitucionalismo nacional* (Quito, Ecuador: Talleres Gráficos Nacionales, 1955).

20. Quoted in Interview 74.

21. Interviews 70 and 72.

22. Quoted in interviews 86 and 15.

23. In his long and controversial career, General Victor Aulestia Mier has been involved in virtually every major civil-military crisis of the postwar period. Since he appears as a key actor in three of these four chapters, a brief introduction is in order. Born in a small community outside of Guayaquil, Aulestia grew up in the interior and attended public high school in the small town of Latacunga. His father, grandfather, and great great-grandfather

were military officers. In 1929 he dropped out of school, and, at the age of 16, enrolled in a local military regiment. Although he never attended the Colegio Militar, he was commissioned in 1937 and fought in the 1941 war as a lieutenant in charge of a small frontier garrison. As a major stationed in the south, he supported the 1944 revolution but took no active role in it. His first political encounter came in 1946 when Velasco closed Congress and began to rule by decree—Aulestia was arrested when he and thirty-one other young officers opposed the dictatorship. All were released after they started a hunger strike, and were reinstated to their ranks when Velasco's government fell in 1947. In 1951 he was sent to the war academy in Brazil and later returned there to attend the superior war college. Aulestia's shortness and studious appearance conceal a strong-willed, aggressive nature that has proven costly to him on more than one occasion. (Shortly after the 1954 coup attempt, Aulestia was wounded in a shoot out with several Varea sympathizers who attempted to take him prisoner.) Although his career is in many respects atypical, his political evolution is illustrative of the changing attitudes of the whole 1941 generation of officers.

24. Interview 9.

25. Interview 15.

26. Interviews 53, 29, 74, and 44.

27. Interviews 41 and 80.

28. These efforts did produce a classic, cabled order to the second zone to arrest Velasco: "Capturen al Loco." Interviews 74 and 72.

29. Interviews 48 and 68.

30. The interview sample and questions used to derive these data are described in detail in chapter 7. The names of the officers interviewed are given in the acknowledgments.

31. The Ecuadorian press, particularly *El Comercio* of Quito and *El Universo* and *El Telégrafo* of Guayaquil, has traditionally been independent from the government. Except on rare occasions when the major papers have been temporarily closed, there has been no censorship, even under the military junta.

32. "Vigencia de lo constitucional," editorial in *El Comercio,* 23 December 1954, p. 4.

33. "Afirmación del orden democrático," editorial in *El Universo,* 25 December 1954, p. 4.

34. Varea was permitted to resign and, after being held for ten months, the five ringleaders were released shortly after the beginning of their trial.

35. Maier, *Ecuadorian Presidential Election,* p. 76.

36. Interview 63. The 1956 revolt gave the air force its first real opportunity to participate in intramilitary politics. A few strafing runs by its newly acquired jets put the small rebel column to flight.

37. *Hispanic American Report* 9, no. 6 (July 1956):294.

38. Interviews 7, 9, and 83.

39. "Editorial," *Revista Militar de las Fuerzas Armadas Ecuatorianas* 1 (1957):8.

40. Junta Nacional de Planificación, *Indice de precios al consumidor, Quito y Guayaquil* no. 190 (March 1969).

41. Interviews 51 and 52.

## Chapter 4: The End of an Era: The Fall of Velasco Ibarra

1. Interview 79.

2. *Hispanic American Report* 13, no. 3 (April 1960): 193; Ibid., 13, no. 4 (May 1960):259–60.

3. Interview 7.

4. Velasco's new high command was composed of: General Víctor Aulestia, one of his supporters in 1954 and a recent graduate of the Brazilian superior war college who was named chief of the general staff; General Alfredo del Pozo Lagos, commanding general of the army; Captain Jorge Wolf Franco, commanding general of the navy; General Víctor

Suárez Haz, commanding general of the air force; and Colonel Eudoro Naranjo, subsecretary of defense. All were known to be "professional" military men sympathetic to Velasco.

5. *Hispanic American Report* 13, no. 10 (December 1960); 718–19; Ibid. 13, no. 12 (February 1961):903.

6. Denouncing the persecution of the Church in Cuba, the cardinal archbishop of Quito flatly declared, "One cannot be a good Catholic and still sympathize with that regime." (Quoted in *El Comercio*, 4 July 1961, p. 1.) For information on CIA activities during this period, see Phillip Agee, *Inside the Company: CIA Diary* (Harmondsworth, England: Penguin Books, 1975), pp. 138–207.

7. David P. Hanson, "The Influence of Business Groups in Ecuadorian Politics between 1959 and 1962" (Ph.D. dissertation, University of Florida, 1971), pp. 233–68.

8. *Hispanic American Report* 14, no. 7 (September 1961):629.

9. Clarence Zuvekas, "Ecuador: Selected Economic Data" (Mimeographed. Quito, Ecuador: USAID, 1970), pp. 15, 40, 94.

10. Interview 36.

11. Perhaps misled by his huge electoral margin, Velasco waited too long before deciding to heed the counsel of a military supporter who advised him to seek an alliance with the Conservatives before it was too late. In early October, Velasco was warned that "the armed forces by themselves [could not] guarantee the survival of [his] government." (Interviews 9A and 79, and Francisco Salazar Alvarado, *Mensaje a la asamblea general del Partido Conservador Ecuatoriano* [Quito, Ecuador: 1961], pp. 7–9.

12. *El Comercio*, 2 September 1961, p. 1.

13. One eyewitness recalls that as *velasquistas* jeered and whistled at antigovernment legislators, the speeches against the government became even more heated. The gallery responded by throwing paper, eggs, and rotten fruit down to the legislative floor. As what was interpreted as a gunshot was heard from the gallery, a number of legislators (including the vice-president) drew their pistols and began firing, using desks and tables as shields against the return fire from the galleries. Meanwhile, oblivious to the gunplay, two legislators engaged in a vigorous fist fight. Dozens of bullet holes were later counted in the chamber. By some miracle no one was wounded. The police were conspicuous by their absence. The confrontations ended when Arosemena announced his intention to appeal directly to the armed forces for protection.

14. Interviews 75, 9A, and 5.

15. *El Comercio*, 7 November 1961, pp. 1, 3, 11.

16. Interview 5. A subsequent vote of Congress defended Arosemena against the accusation.

17. Interviews 90 and 45.

18. Quoted in interview 84.

19. Interviews 5 and 9B.

20. Quoted in interview 9B.

21. Document 8; Interview 8.

22. Document 22; Interview 22; Document 22B.

23. Interview 84.

24. Interviews 22 and 84.

25. *El Comercio*, 8 November 1961, p. 20.

26. Interview 76.

27. Interview 67. The decision was communicated by the commander of the second air zone to General Suárez, who, nevertheless, argued that only Congress had the legal authority to judge the constitutionality of Velasco's actions.

28. Interview 76.

29. Gonzalo Almeida Urrutia, "El Congreso de la República del Ecuador," *El Universo*, 7 November 1961, p. 7.

30. "Miembros de la Fuerza Aérea Ecuatoriana," *El Universo*, 7 November 1961, p. 7.

31. Guillermo Bossano, *Trances de la libertad* (Quito, Ecuador: Talleres Gráficos "Minerva," 1961), pp. 19–26; Document 22.

32. Interviews 43 and 6.

33. Interview 9B.

34. Interview 45.
35. Interview 76.
36. Interviews 67 and 76.
37. Interviews 34 and 11.
38. Interviews 66 and 11.
39. General Bolívar Pico Santos was called by Velasco to replace General Suárez as air force commander—though he was left with no more than an office to command.
40. Interview 21.
41. Interviews 80 and 52.
42. Interview 75.
43. Interviews 38, 78, 17, and 92. By the time decisions were being made in the provincial garrisons, Velasco's abdication was already a fact and little consideration was given to the Gallegos thesis.
44. Interview 21.
45. Interview 34.
46. Interview 21.
47. Interview 52. In a classic example of Ecuador's politicized military personnel policies, Velasco and Gallegos supporters—Generals Aulestia, Del Pozo, Villacís, Zurita, and Pico, Navy Captains Wolf and Cajas, and Colonels Naranjo and Tamayo—were all promptly retired by the new Arosemena government. Retired Colonel Andrés Arrata Macías, who had been active in the anti-Velasco movement, was named chief of the general staff. Colonel Carlos Arregui, who had also been forcibly retired by Velasco and who had joined in the Chimborazo revolt, became commanding general of the army. Former Squadron Commander Captain Northia became commanding general of the navy, while General Suárez was temporarily confirmed as air force commander. Another Chimborazo veteran (the former head of the Geographic Institute) was named subsecretary of defense. Lieutenant Colonel Vega became chief of the first zone and Lieutenant Colonel Vélez, chief of the second zone. Colonel Francisco Tamariz, a retired officer and opposition *velasquista* deputy from Cuenca, became Arosemena's minister of defense.
48. In calculating cumulative scores, when disorder event score totals passed a threshold of what might be considered normal, the score above that margin is carried over into subsequent periods until forgotten. Forgetting is assumed to occur exponentially, so that half of the carryover score is retained in the first subsequent period, one-fourth in the next, one-eighth in the next, etc.

## Chapter 5: The Fall of Carlos Julio Arosemena

1. Interviews 59 and 5. Despite the events of 1961 and despite Velasco's applause for Arosemena's overthrow in 1963, Arosemena supported Velasco in the 1968 campaign only to emerge later as an opponent of the government and of Velasco's seizure of dictatorial powers in 1970.
2. Interview 90. In a personal interview, Dr. Arosemena spoke of receiving a personal order from President Kennedy that demanded Ecuador's vote on the Cuban question at Punta del Este "or else." He then explained that it was actually the formal diplomatic note delivered to the presidents of all OAS member nations, but "a letter from the president of the United States, as polite as it may be, is still an order." (Interview, 12 May 1971 in Guayaquil.)
3. Phillip Agee, *Inside the Company: CIA Diary* (Harmondsworth, England: Penguin Books, 1975), pp. 206–94.
4. Ibid., p. 223.
5. *El Comercio,* 3 March 1962, pp. 1, 3.
6. Interviews 64 and 75.
7. Quoted in Interview 59.
8. Interviews 46 and 3. This course "opened the eyes of representatives from fourteen countries to the true dangers of communism and its methods of infiltrating the clergy, students, labor unions, and even the armed forces." (Interview 3.)

9. Interview 19.

10. Open letter of Army Commanding General Colonel Carlos Arregui Viteri in *El Comercio,* 30 March 1962, p. 3.

11. See the *El Comercio* editorials, 29 March 1962, p. 4 and 30 March 1962, p. 4.

12. *Hispanic American Report* 15, no. 3 (May 1962):249.

13. Ibid. 15, no. 4 (June 1962):344.

14. Interview 65. Most of those captured were released then and deported by the Supreme Court two months later.

15. Interview 64.

16. Francisco Salazar Alvarado, *Mensaje a la asamblea general del Partido Conservador* (Quito, Ecuador, 1963), p. 25.

17. Interview 1.

18. All figures cited in constant currency. United States Agency for International Development, "Ecuador: Review of Financial Developments 1960–1969" (Airgram. Quito, Ecuador: Department of State, 1969), Appendix tables 1, 2, 3, 9, 12, 22, and 24.

19. Banco Central del Ecuador, *Memoria del Gerente General, 1961,* and idem, *Memoria del Gerente General, 1964,* cited in Charles Gibson, "The Role of Foreign Trade in Ecuadorian Economic Development" (Ph.D. dissertation, University of Pennsylvania, 1968), p. 368.

20. United States Agency for International Development, *Financial Developments 1960–1969,* Appendix table 10.

21. Gibson, "Role of Foreign Trade," p. 127.

22. Interviews 87 and 59.

23. Interviews 52, 1, 9, and 66; "Programa del Nuevo Orden Nacional" (Mimeographed. Quito, Ecuador, 1963).

24. *Programa,* p. 3.

25. Contrary to what one would expect, the individual political parties did not simply support their "favorite" conspiratorial group. Instead, each conspiracy generally had permanent contact with all the major parties. In most cases, the nucleus of conspirators was composed of retired officers.

26. Interviews 3, 9, 52, 70, and 78.

27. Personal communication 98.

28. Interview 40 and Agee, *CIA Diary,* p. 142. Agee's memoirs also indicate that there was only minimal CIA penetration of the armed forces. Nevertheless, Dr. Arosemena says that he has documentary proof of the involvement of the American ambassador in a conscious policy aimed at his overthrow. (Interview, 12 May 1971.)

29. Quoted in Interview 2.

30. Interview 90.

31. Agee, *CIA Diary,* pp. 218, 220–21, 229, 239–40, 277–81, 283–86.

32. Quoted in *Hispanic American Report* 16, no. 6 (August 1963), p. 594.

33. Ibid.

34. Carlos Palacios Sáenz, "¿Que dictadura prefiere? ," *El Universo,* 19 June 1963, p. 4.

35. "Las Fuerzas Armadas," editorial in *El Universo,* 3 July 1963, p. 4.

36. Francisco Salazar Alvarado, Director of the Conservative party, quoted in *El Comercio,* 6 July 1963, p. 13.

37. After receiving a tip from a civilian member of the Nuevo Orden Nacional that a date had been set, the chief of army intelligence spent the entire night of 10 July trying to locate his close friend Army Commander Cabrera (who was scheduled to leave the country the next day), in order to urge him to take immediate pre-emptive action. By the next morning the message was superfluous. Colonel Arrata, chief of the general staff, was in Rome attending the coronation of Pope Paul VI. Prior to his departure, Colonel Gandara had assured him that no move against Arosemena was likely to occur during his absence.

38. In his remarks to the U.S. ambassador, Arosemena appears to have had in mind the May incident that was the opening round in what later became the great "tuna war" over Ecuadorian claims to 200 miles of territorial waters. Three U.S. tuna boats were captured by the Ecuadorian navy off the Ecuadorian coast. The minister of public works,

who was in Washington to complete negotiations for a loan from the Reconstruction and Development Bank, was informed that the negotiations would be suspended pending release of the captured vessels. (Carlos Julio Arosemena Peet, "El modus vivendi y las 200 millas marítimas," *El País,* February 1971, p. 33.) Two weeks later the boats were released after payment had been made, "under protest," of a $26,000 fine imposed by the Ecuadorian courts. Agee, *CIA Diary,* pp. 206–95, makes no connection between these events and the CIA's anti-Arosemena campaign.

39. Widely circulated and widely believed reports of even more indecorous behavior were both confirmed and disputed in interviews with eyewitnesses.

40. Interviews 73, 69, and 42.

41. Marcos Gándara Enríquez, "De la revolución militar a la restauración oligárquica" (Manuscript. Buenos Aires, Argentina, 1970), p. 42. Gandara's conception of this book as an unqualified defense of the junta and of his own personal actions limits its utility as a historical source. Nevertheless, when published, it will be the only document of its kind written by a leading Ecuadorian officer, and an important source of insight into the changes occurring in military attitudes in the 1960s.

42. Interview 43.

43. Interview 57. The leaders of that group, caught flat-footed by the unexpected conversion of the service commanders who had been Arosemena's closest collaborators, resolved to try to get Gándara included in the junta in order to execute an immediate counter-coup. (Interview 9.) Gándara later declined the plan for a counter-coup as impractical under the circumstances. (Interview 52.)

44. The shooting left two soldiers and two civilians dead.

45. Martin Needler, *Anatomy of a Coup d'Etat: Ecuador 1963* (Washington, D.C.: Institute for the Comparative Study of Political Systems, 1964), p. 1.

46. Ibid., p. 48.

47. See chapter 11.

48. See chapter 1, note 44. Cf. Lyle N. McAlister, "Recent Research and Writings on the Role of the Military in Latin America," *Latin American Research Review* 2 (Fall 1966):5–36; Martin Needler, "Political Development and Military Intervention in Latin America," *American Political Science Review* 60, no. 3 (September 1966):620 n.

49. Except in 1963, there were relatively few public invitations to intervene published in the national press. Ecuador thus did not manifest one of the key elements of the moderator pattern of civil-military relations as described by Stepan for the years 1945 to 1964 in Brazil. Alfred C. Stepan, *The Military in Politics: Changing Patterns in Brazil* (Princeton, N.J.: Princeton University Press, 1971), pp. 99–115. The difference appears to be a consequence of the large size differential in the two systems–Brazil required greater institutionalization of civil-military interaction in the coup process than did Ecuador.

50. Cromwell [pseud.], "Ideas claras y planes sencillos," in *El Comercio,* 18 July 1963, p. 4.

51. Needler, *Anatomy,* pp. 21, 48.

## Chapter 6: The Fall of the Military Junta

1. Interviews 32 and 13.

2. Interview 42.

3. Even so, Castro was not from Guayaquil, but from Esmeraldas, which has traditionally been linked to the sierra as much as to the other coastal provinces. Like Freile and Gándara, Castro attended public high school at the Colegio Mejía in Quito.

4. United States Agency for International Development, "Ecuador: Review of Financial Developments, 1960–1969" (Airgram. Quito, Ecuador: Department of State, 1969), Appendix table 22.

5. Junta Militar de Gobierno, *Plan político de la Junta Militar de Gobierno* (Quito, Ecuador: Talleres Gráficos Nacionales, 1963), pp. 3–4. See also the initial manifestos of the junta, reprinted in Martin Needler, *Anatomy of a Coup d'Etat: Ecuador 1963* (Washington, D.C.: Institute for the Comparative Study of Political Systems, 1964), Appendices A, B, and

C. Like the passage cited, these statements primarily reflect Colonel Gándara's view of these events.

6. Reviewing the history of economic planning in Ecuador, Clarence Zuvekas, a former AID official in Quito, notes that the junta was the first and only government to pay any attention to the Planning Board since its creation in 1954. ("Economic Planning in Ecuador: An Evaluation," *Inter-American Economic Affairs* 25, no. 4 [Spring 1972]:39–69.)

7. The maximum limits were set generously at 2,000 and 6,250 acres in the sierra and on the coast respectively, with some exceptions and additional reserves allowed. Instituto Ecuatoriano de Reforma Agraria y Colonización, *Ley de reforma agraria y colonización* (Quito, Ecuador: Talleres Gráficos "Minerva," 1964), p. 40 and *passim.*

8. The land-owners were not opposed to the abolition of the *huasipungo* system–this much they had accepted in principle in 1962. Indeed, recent research has shown that many of the peasants affected were, on the whole, worse off on the free market (even with the higher wages they received there), since the old system had at least assured them of priority in hiring in an oversupplied labor market. See Carlos Paredes Barros, "Incidencia económico y social del proceso de liquidación del huasipungo en la provincia de Pichincha" (Master's thesis, Catholic University of Ecuador, 1967). Still, the administrative priority of *huasipungo* abolition was less a concession to the land-owners than it was a reflection of the limited technical knowledge of the law's authors and of the disrepute of the *huasipungo* system in intellectual circles resulting from Jorge Icaza's famous protest novel, *Huasipungo* (in English translation by Bernard Dulsey. Carbondale: Southern Illinois University Press, 1964), and Pío Jaramillo Alvarado's *El Indio Ecuatoriano,* (4th ed. Quito, Ecuador: Editorial Casa de la Cultura Ecuatoriana, 1954). In contrast to the Peruvian military's agrarian reform program, the junta's plan was a political time bomb. Its provision for limitation of maximum holdings and elimination of most rental and sharecropping arrangements in 3 to 8 years established the legal and administrative machinery for a major attack on the socioeconomic power base of the landowning classes without doing anything to impede their capability for a political counterattack.

9. Interviews 28 and 69.

10. Document 79.

11. Marcos Gándara Enríquez, "De la revolución militar a la restauración oligárquica" (Manuscript. Buenos Aires, Argentina, 1970), p. 116.

12. Interview 33.

13. United States Agency for International Development, *Financial Developments 1960–1969,* Appendix tables 21 and 22.

14. "Resoluciones que la comisión política presenta como sugerencias a la Junta Militar de Gobierno," Quito, Ecuador, n.d. (Personal archive 81). In an unsuccessful attempt to open a dialogue with the opposition parties, General Mora Bowen, who had made a number of enemies as minister of the government, was replaced by an ex-Director of the Liberal party. (Interview 28.)

15. "Resoluciones."

16. Personal as well as regional and class interests played an important role in the conflict over tariffs and protection of "false industries." The president of the Guayaquil Chamber of Commerce, who was the chief spokesman for the merchants, held the General Electric distributorship for the country and was thus in direct competition with a Quito firm that had been established under the Industrial Development Law to manufacture refrigerators locally. (Interview 77.)

17. Interviews 69 and 28.

18. Interviews 70 and 9.

19. Junta Militar de Gobierno, "A la Nación," *El Comercio,* 11 July 1965, p. 1.

20. "Planteamientos que hacen los partidos políticos al pueblo ecuatoriano y a la junta militar de Gobierno, para el retorno del país al estado de derecho," Quito, Ecuador, 6 August 1965 (Personal archive 81).

21. Interviews 13 and 42.

22. *El Comercio,* 4 December 1965, pp. 1, 14.

23. Interviews 13 and 81.

24. Interviews 70 and 40.

25. Interview 27.
26. Interviews 94, 13, 17, and 62.
27. "Solución política inevitable," editorial in *El Comercio,* 29 March 1966, p. 4.
28. Interviews 30 and 92.
29. Interviews 37, 73, and 50.
30. Interviews 32 and 57.
31. The opposition strategy was to contact all the higher-ranking officers (even supporters of the government) with offers to back an interim government (headed by that officer) as a means of extricating the country from the political crisis. In the end, practically everyone suspected everyone else of having betrayed the junta.
32. Gándara, "De la revolucion militar," pp. 152–53.
33. Interview 17.
34. Despite the formal resignation of the junta, this was a coup d'état in the sense that the junta's departure was occasioned by the withdrawal of military support and that it occurred according to the opposition's timetable and on its terms, rather than according to either the junta's original or accelerated plans for the return to civilian government.
35. Interview 7.

## Chapter 7: Individual Decisions to Support or Oppose a Coup d'Etat

1. Supplementary information on military attitudes and behavior was provided by interviews with eighteen civilian leaders, generally key participants in the various crises.
2. Despite the inclusion of all three services in the sample, on the one variable for which comparable information is available—region of birth—the interview sample is quite similar to the population of army cadets entering the Colegio Militar between 1930 and 1939. The observed differences across five regional categories are small enough to have happened by chance ($.5 < p < .7$).
3. Since the questionnaire was largely open-ended, the duration of the interviews for a single coup varied from one to six hours, although most ran slightly less than two hours. The interview request was directly refused by only seven officers and indirectly by another four—a rejection rate of approximately 13 percent.
4. This procedure obviously assumes that ratings on the individual decision criteria are additive in relationship to coup attitudes. Strong support for this assumption can be found in the Ecuadorian officers' comments about their reasoning processes. Several officers mentioned feeling cross-pressured by divergent ratings on separate criteria—particularly in 1963, where support for Arosemena as the constitutional president had to be weighed against distaste for his personal behavior. (Interviews 22, 13, 54, 4, and 81.) A number of officers also indicated that their decisions in 1963 reflected the cumulative impact of various events that culminated in the famous presidential banquet, which was "the drop that made the glass overflow." (Interviews 17, 81, 90, and 32.) That event "exhausted the patience of the armed forces" (interview 92), and "marked the limit of what the public would stomach" (interview 42). In a similar fashion, a senior officer explained that in 1966 "the disastrous attack on Central University was the last straw" for the officers who had not wanted to insist on the immediate removal of the military junta. (Interview 62.) These comments indicate that negative ratings on these criteria are balanced against the positive features of the government and that, as negative factors accumulate, the officers finally decide that they "cannot tolerate anymore." (Interview 60.) This index construction procedure also contains an assumption (dropped later) that each of the decision criteria were weighted more or less equally.
5. Albert Pierce, *Fundamentals of Nonparametric Statistics* (Belmont, Calif.: Dickenson Publishing Co., 1970), pp. 113–22; Eugene Edgington, *Statistical Inference: The Distribution-Free Approach* (New York: McGraw-Hill, 1969), pp. 109–15. Cumulative probabilities for the significance tests are taken from Gerald Lieberman and Donald Owen, *Tables of the Hypergeometric Probability Distribution* (Stanford, Calif.: Stanford University Press, 1961). The more familiar Chi-square test is not used here, since the samples are small, nonrandom, and drawn without replacement.

6. These ratings were based on the respondent's actions in the coup and on his own statement of his position. Prior to the data analysis, one officer was purged from the sample when cross-checking revealed that he had misrepresented his position in the 1961 coup. Distinguishing between the moderate and strong categories of attitudes toward the coup does present obvious problems in coding from open-ended data. In a preliminary check, a graduate student with experience in Ecuador coded 15 randomly selected interviews on attitudes toward the coup. The Pearson correlation with the author's ratings was .954. A second student with no Latin American background coded this variable for all of the respondents, resulting in a correlation of .821 with the author's ratings. See Kathleen Crittenden and Richard Hill, "Coding Reliability and the Validity of Interview Data," *American Sociological Review* 36, no. 6 (December 1971):1073–80.

7. The reader should be forewarned that several of the standard assumptions for correlation and regression analysis are not met by these data. Neither the measure of positions taken in the coups nor the composite performance ratings are true interval scale measures, although the results thus far suggest that both are strong ordinal scales. In addition, neither the values of these variables nor of others to be introduced are normally distributed. On the other hand, there are also serious problems in the use of cross-tabulation, where the underlying variables are theoretically conceptualized as interval scales, as is the case here. (Hubert Blalock, *Causal Inferences in Nonexperimental Research* [Chapel Hill: University of North Carolina Press, 1964], pp. 30–35 and 119–34.) On the robustness of regression techniques when these are applied to interval data, see Sanford Labovitz, "Some Observations on Measurement and Statistics," *Social Forces* 46, no. 2 (December 1967):151–60. Given the highly similar results of the cross-tabular, rank-order, and correlational analyses made thus far, the difficulties presented by violations of the standard assumptions seem less serious than does the loss of information involved in foregoing the use of more powerful statistical techniques.

8. Although not reported here, the same test was applied prior to the revision of the initial hypotheses to include the constitutionality and personal ties criteria.

9. The problems of the real meaning of these left-right statements and of a meaningful classification of Ecuadorian parties on such a scale are beyond the scope of the present study.

10. Even this correlation is purely coincidental; a group of progovernment general staff officers in 1961 formed the nucleus for a conspiratorial movement against Arosemena that *later* emerged as a fledgling party.

11. The degree of belief in the legitimacy of military intervention was also tested as an explanation of the residual variance in coup positions. It was initially hypothesized that, given equivalent ratings of government performance, those officers whose abstract role definition legitimated frequent military intervention would be more likely to favor a coup than those advocating stricter limits on military involvement in political matters. Again, in three of the four cases, the data do not support the hypothesis. This is true in large part because the complex nature of the impact of abstract role definition on coup decisions is not compatible with the standard regression model. The significance of military role definitions is discussed in detail in chapter 12.

12. See Hubert Blalock, *Social Statistics* (New York: McGraw-Hill, 1960), pp. 236–58 for a standard explanation of multiple regression. See also Ronald Brunner and Garry Brewer, *Organized Complexity: Empirical Theories of Political Development* (New York: The Free Press, 1971), pp. 162–70 for a convincing demonstration of the dangers of using simple multiple regression techniques when the standard linear, additive regression equation is not an accurate representation of the causal processes generating the data being analyzed. As a partial check against the inclusion of criteria that were not significant in that particular coup, the independent variables were entered into the regression in order of their F-values with all six included, until none of the coefficients for the remaining variables was significant at the .05 level.

13. Given what we know about the level of professionalization of the Ecuadorian military and the emphasis on particularistic ties in Ecuadorian political culture, the high salience attributed to personal ties by the regression analysis, when these were not stressed

as self-explanations, increases our confidence in the basic reliability of the statistical analysis.

14. Interviews 53, 26, and 29.

15. In comparing relative impact across the four cases, we have to take into consideration that we are comparing military actions in four rather distinct temporal contexts. It is difficult to assume, for example, that a negative rating given to Velasco in 1954 on the question of institutional interests is quite the same as a negative rating given to the military junta twelve years later. The perceived threat to institutional interests may have been much stronger in one case or the other, yet the value of the "institutional interests rating" variable is the same. Hence for comparison across cases (i.e., out of context) standardized regression coefficients (BETA) are preferable, so that each variable is measured, not in terms of its absolute value, but in terms of deviations from the average value for that coup sample.

16. The negative coefficients are explained in chapter 12.

17. Additional evidence on these two factors is presented in chapters 9 and 12.

18. Mauricio Solaun and Michael Quinn, *Sinners and Heretics: The Politics of Military Intervention in Latin America* (Urbana: University of Illinois Press, 1973), p. 46-47.

19. William R. Thompson, *The Grievances of Military Coup Makers,* Sage Professional Papers in Comparative Politics 4, no. 01-047 (Beverly Hills, Calif.: Sage Publications, 1973), pp. 27, 30, 33, 38, 46, 48, 66-67.

20. Cf. Martin Needler, "Political Development and Military Intervention in Latin America," *American Political Science Review* 60, no. 3 (September 1966):620.

## Chapter 8: Personal Backgrounds and Coup Decisions

1. Edwin Lieuwen, *Generals vs. Presidents: Neo-Militarism in Latin America* (New York: Frederick A. Praeger, 1964; John Saxe-Fernández, "The Central American Defense Council and *Pax Americana,*" in *Latin American Radicalism,* ed. Irving Horowitz, Josue de Castro, and John Gerassi (New York: Random House, 1969), pp. 75-96; Miles Wolpin, "External Political Socialization as a Source of Conservative Military Behavior in the Third World," *Studies in Comparative International Development* 8, no. 1 (January 1973):3-23.

2. Victor Alba, "The Stages of Militarism in Latin America," in *The Role of the Military in Underdeveloped Countries,* ed. John J. Johnson (Princeton, N.J.: Princeton University Press, 1962), pp. 165-83.

3. John J. Johnson, *The Military and Society in Latin America* (Stanford, Calif.: Stanford University Press, 1964), p. 107.

4. José Nun, "A Latin American Phenomenon: The Middle-Class Military Coup" in *Latin America: Reform or Revolution,* ed. James Petras and Maurice Zeitlin (Greenwich, Conn.: Fawcett Publications, 1969), pp. 146-85; Idem., *Latin America: The Hegemonic Crisis and the Military Coup* (Berkeley, Calif.: Institute of International Studies, 1969). For competing hypotheses on the significance of social origins, cf. Morris Janowitz, *The Professional Soldier: A Social and Political Portrait* (New York: The Free Press, 1960), p. 81, and C. Wright Mills, *The Power Elite* (New York: Oxford University Press, 1959), p. 192.

5. Alfred C. Stepan, *The Military in Politics: Changing Patterns in Brazil* (Princeton, N.J.: Princeton University Press, 1971), pp. 229-52.

6. Martin Needler, *Political Development in Latin America: Instability, Violence, and Evolutionary Change* (New York: Random House, 1968), p. 66.

7. William Quandt, *The Comparative Study of Political Elites,* Sage Professional Papers in Comparative Politics, no. 01-004 (Beverly Hills, Calif.: Sage Publications, 1970), p. 2.

8. See Donald Searing, "The Comparative Study of Elite Socialization," *Comparative Political Studies* 1 (January 1969):471-99. Cf. Steve C. Ropp, "The Military and Urbanization in Latin America: Some Implications of Trends in Recruitment," *Inter-American Economic Affairs* 24, no. 2 (Autumn 1970):27-35.

9. For the cross-tabulation of birth year and coup position, p = .20 for 1954, p = .08 for 1961, and, using three age categories for 1963, p < .05.

10. In part because politically based promotions create strong personal and professional resentments among those officers who are passed over. See chapters 11 and 12. Stepan reaches a similar conclusion regarding the Brazilian military in *Military in Politics*, pp. 165–68.

11. One partial exception is a correlation in three of the four coups between regional origins and the direction of one's personal ties for or against a particular government. Only in 1963 was there a substantive relationship. In the other two cases, it reflects the progovernment bias in the small sample of naval officers.

12. See chapter 11.

13. Stepan, *Military in Politics*, pp. 167–68. In neither Ecuadorian case, however, is there any definite relationship with final positions taken in the coup.

14. In recent years in Mexico, only 19 percent of the military academy applicants, and in Colombia, only 23 percent of the new cadets, have been sons of military officers, as compared with 32.5 percent of new cadets in Argentina and 34.9 percent of new cadets in Brazil. These figures refer to 1955, 1965, 1965, and 1962–1966 respectively. Lyle N. McAlister, Anthony P. Maingot, and Robert A. Potash, *The Military in Latin American Sociopolitical Evolution: Four Case Studies* (Washington, D.C.: Center for Research in Social Systems, 1970), pp. 97, 158, 219; Stepan, *Military in Politics*, p. 40.

15. Hence the general Latin American trend toward greater recruitment of officers from urban areas may not be significant, particularly if it does not imply a change in the pattern of primary socialization experiences. Cf. Ropp, "Military and Urbanization."

16. Because of the bias in the sample of naval officers toward those whose political reliability made them eligible for high command positions in Quito, a three-way comparison would be misleading. In any case, following the general rule of countries where the capital city is far removed from the coast, the Ecuadorian navy had only the most marginal influence in any of the four coups.

17. Combining the samples does entail a risk that differences that were important in individual coups may be lost in the combined sample. Nevertheless, only in 1961 would this seem to be an important problem. Overall, the results are highly congruent with the other evidence presented.

18. While the tabular breakdowns are omitted to conserve space, "substantial differences" means significance levels of less than .05, except for Rank at Coup (.079) and Expressing Political Preference (.051), using the Fisher Exact Test where possible, or ignoring the small cell frequency restriction on Chi-square. Distortions introduced by the latter procedure are inconsequential for our purposes, since what matters here is not the confidence level, but the comparison with political attitude differences using the same procedures.

19. Using a two-tailed Chi-square test, in the latter case, .10 < p < .20. On the other two issues, there is a 30–50 percent possibility that the observed differences could have occurred by chance and on the remaining four issues, there is at least a 70 percent possibility that these were only chance differences.

20. On these two variables, .30 < p < .50. For the remaining decision criteria ratings, p > .70.

21. See Abraham Lowenthal, "The Dominican Republic: The Politics of Chaos," in *Latin America: Reform and Revolution*, ed. Arpad von Lazar and Robert Kaufman (Boston: Allyn and Bacon, 1969), pp. 39–42; idem, "The Political Role of the Dominican Armed Forces: A Note on the 1963 Overthrow of Juan Bosch and the 1965 'Revolution'," *Journal of Inter-American Studies and World Affairs*, 15 (August 1973):355–62.

22. See also chapter 14.

23. In what has been perhaps the most comprehensive attempt to test the relationship between social backgrounds and elite attitudes, Donald Searing also fails to find clear evidence of any consistent linkage in five different samples of political elites. While most background characteristics were found to be correlated with one or more attitudes and vice versa, most of the correlations were limited in scope and inconsistent across samples.

Moreover, the correlations observed were not theoretically predictable and many, judging from the results of the same kind of analysis in this chapter, may have been spurious. However, those background variables that did predict a relatively large number of attitudes were generally those related to *adult* socialization experiences—especially, present occupation and party affiliation. The attitudes that these variables predicted also tended to be those involving highly salient political issues. In addition, nationality was found to be far more important than any other background variable, including present occupation. (Searing, "Elite Socialization," pp. 471–500.) See also Lewis Edinger and Donald Searing, "Social Background in Elite Analysis: A Methodological Inquiry," *American Political Science Review* 61, no. 2 (June 1967):428–45. While Searing interprets the nationality variable in terms of cultural and subcultural variations in the meaning of elite socialization experiences from one country to the next, the arguments presented above suggest an alternative interpretation. According to this view, the nationality variable is highly significant because it captures the variance from country to country in the contexts to which these elites are responding. For example, French military leaders may show a greater attitudinal similarity to French political leaders than to German military leaders because the French elites are both responding to the same context. Despite certain background similarities, French and German officers may have very different attitudes toward their respective political systems simply because the groups with which they identify are being indulged in one case and suffering deprivation in the other. Thus it is not so much the cultural meaning of a given socialization experience that varies from country to country, but rather the political context within which a given elite operates. Controlling for variations in the political context would probably reveal a spurious correlation between political attitudes and nationality. The analogous procedure in this study would be to take "coup year" (1954, 1961, etc.) as an independent explanation for the attitudes of Ecuadorian officers. As a surrogate for the different contexts to which the military was reacting, coup year would also "explain" a fairly large number of military attitudes.

24. See part iv.

## Chapter 9: The Armed Forces and the Constitution

1. Ramiro Borja y Borja, *Las constituciones del Ecuador* (Madrid: Ediciones Cultura Hispánica, 1951), p. 679. In accordance with Article 153's further injunction that the military was not a deliberative body, in 1961 the constitutional purists duly stated their position as one of opposition to the executive's attempt to impede the (hostile) Congress from ruling on the constitutionality of the vice-president's arrest.

2. If anything, the two previous constitutions were even more explicit in enjoining individual officers against obeying unconstitutional orders from any authority. Borja y Borja, *Las constituciones,* pp. 497, 544, *passim.*

3. J. Lloyd Mecham, "Latin American Constitutions: Nominal and Real," *Journal of Politics* 21, no. 2 (May 1959); 264. Cf. Lyle N. McAlister, Anthony P. Maingot, and Robert A. Potash, *The Military in Latin American Sociopolitical Evolution: Four Case Studies* (Washington, D.C.: Center for Research in Social Systems, 1970), pp. 28, 87, 207.

4. Interviews 90, 45, 84, 5, and 9.

5. Interview 29.

6. Interview 86. In some respects this response reflects the institutional weakness of the Ecuadorian military that existed even after the postwar reforms, since political interference in military affairs could easily have been ended if enough officers had agreed not to obey orders contrary to professional norms.

7. Interviews 86 and 76; Document 8.

8. Interview 29.

9. Interviews 59 and 44.

10. "Libro de vida militar, Academia de Guerra y Escuela de Comando y Estado Mayor," Manuscript. War Academy Archive, Quito, Ecuador.

11. The one exception was the small group of officers in 1954 who had been strongly influenced by the pro-interventionist doctrines in vogue in Argentina during the Peron administration. (Interview 44.)

12. Interview 88.

13. Interview 59.

14. Interviews 86 and 19. It should be noted, however, that the military's concern for the constitution did not deny the president considerable leeway for minor violations thereof as long as these infractions did not seem to indicate an attempt to entirely jettison constitutional forms. Less than a month before the 1961 coup the government announced that it had discovered a "subversive plot" allegedly led by a retired colonel who, along with several legislators from a coastal province, was accused of conspiring to overthrow Velasco and install Arosemena. Colonel Paredes and two congressmen were arrested. Both houses of Congress immediately denounced the arrests as violations of constitutional guarantees of legislative immunity. After several days the alleged conspirators were released. (*Hispanic American Report* 14, no. 10 [December 1961]:916.) Despite its temporal proximity to the coup, this incident was never mentioned in the interviews. The arrest of the vice-president was an entirely different matter, since, as all his military advisors warned, Velasco could not arrest Arosemena without closing Congress and assuming dictatorial powers.

15. Guillermo Bossano, *Trances de la libertad* (Quito, Ecuador: Talleres Gráficos "Minerva," 1961) is a representative eulogy by the war academy's professor of constitutional law. Cf. leading editorials of *El Comercio* and *El Universo.*

16. See chapter 12.

17. Interview 35.

18. The motives of the Conservative-dominated 1946 Constituent Assembly in making the military guarantors against (Liberal) electoral fraud are clear, though the rationale for giving the internal order function solely to the civilian police is not.

19. Interviews 22, 11, 17; Document 22.

20. Interviews 34 and 43.

21. Interview 30.

22. Interview 73; Indirect quote in Interview 33.

23. Only external defense is more widely accepted.

24. Document 8.

25. Interview 86.

26. Without further information for distinguishing gradations in how serious different officers perceived the problem to be, no correlation is possible.

27. Interview 15.

28. James Payne, "Scoring System for Compiling Strike-Demonstration (Opposition) Score in the Dominican Republic," Mimeographed. n.p., n.d. Included in the Payne index are all strikes and "all demonstrations which make an overt appeal for some social, economic, or political end." Each occurrence of one of these events is scored according to the number of people involved in it, its duration, whether it occurred in the capital city, the degree of violence involved in it, and whether university students were the primary participants in it. Scores of individual events are combined into two-week totals. The cumulative impact of particularly large-scale and/or violent disorders is incorporated by carrying these individual scores into the following periods for four or twelve weeks, depending on the magnitude of the event.

29. Interviews 32, 23, 19, 65, and 57B.

30. Interview 57B.

31. Interviews 83 and 52.

32. Interview 20.

## Chapter 10: The Influence of Public Opinion

1. Interview 62.

2. Interview 63.

3. Interview 50.

4. Interview 70.

5. Interview 9.

6. Interview 5.

7. Interview 88.

8. Interview 86.

9. "The armed forces are a regulating force to provide the government that is desired by the people." (Interview 38.) "The armed forces are the arm [of the people] to enforce compliance with the popular will." (Interview 25.)

10. Interview 3. (Emphasis added.)

11. Interview 30. (Emphasis added.)

12. Explaining the lack of a coup attempt in 1962, one officer argued that "there was no popular sentiment in favor of a change [of government], as there was for breaking relations with Cuba. Any political change requires preparation of the national conscience or radical imposition by a unified military force." Neither condition was satisfied in 1962. (Interview 2.)

13. The only officer interviewed who denied any interest in or knowledge of public opinion did so in the process of denying that the 1954 revolt of the Quito garrison was an attempt to overthrow the government. (Interview 53.)

14. Interviews 81, 19, 32, 93, 84, and 20.

15. Interviews 65, 19, 54, and 23.

16. Interviews 63, 19, and 70.

17. Interviews 64, 50, and 62.

18. Interviews 81, 20, and 76.

19. The economic interests of the wealthy and prestigious Mantilla family, which controls *El Comercio,* would seem to be most closely linked, if linked at all, to the "new" entrepreneurial-industrial group beginning to emerge in Quito. Cf. David P. Hanson, "The Influence of Business Groups in Ecuadorian Politics between 1959 and 1962," (Ph.D. dissertation, University of Florida, 1971), p. 355.

20. "Propaganda in accord with predispositions strengthens them; propaganda counter to predispositions weakens them only if supported by factors other than propaganda." (Harold Lasswell and Abraham Kaplan, *Power and Society: A Framework for Political Inquiry* [New Haven: Yale University Press, 1950], p. 113.)

21. All editorials that praised or criticized some aspect of administration policy or performance were given the appropriate sign (+,-) and scored on three factors: whether it was the lead editorial of the day, whether the evaluation was phrased in strong or in mild terms, and whether it was devoted wholly or only partially to appraisal of the government. Taking the first reaction to a coup as a starting point, individual editorial scores were combined for each four-week period before and after the coup.

22. One of the two officers to *deny* that in November 1961 Velasco had lost every semblance of public support had been out of the country during the entire crisis-ridden month of October. (Interview 66.)

23. Interview 50.

24. Interviews 81 and 50.

25. Three days later an *El Comercio* editorial reaffirmed its belief that "the people were an indifferent spectator" to the fall of the junta. "La Posición del Pueblo," editorial in *El Comercio,* 1 March 1966, p. 4.

## Chapter 11: Anticommunism and Institutional Interests

1. Tad Szulc's *The Winds of Revolution* (New York: Frederick A. Praeger, 1963) is typical of the early post-Castro analyses of the future of Latin America that were taken quite seriously by friends and enemies of the Cuban Revolution, both of whom expected that there would be similar revolutions elsewhere. "The winds of social revolution are blowing over Latin America. Her soil is fertile and ready to receive the seeds of rebellion and nurse them in great movements of protest and deep change. Fidel Castro's call for a new Sierra Maestra to erupt in the Andes may not presage immediate outbreaks of guerilla

activities everywhere, but as a concept of insurgency and political warfare, this is infinitely more than a rabble-rousing figure of speech." Ibid., p. 18.

2. Interview 2. To critics of his nonalignment policies, Arosemena proclaimed his willingness to negotiate with the devil if it were necessary to obtain better conditions for his country. (Ibid.)

3. Interview 14. This campaign was originally reported by Martin Needler, *Anatomy of a Coup d'Etat: Ecuador 1963* (Washington, D.C.: Institute for the Comparative Study of Political Systems, 1964), p. 19. See also *El Comercio,* 2 April 1962, p. 10; Ibid., 15 July 1963, p. 8. Phillip Agee, however, describes the bombings as the work of a group recruited from Ponce's Social Christian Movement. There is reason to believe that his after-the-fact "diary" errs on this point. (Phillip Agee, *Inside the Company: CIA Diary* [Harmondsworth, England: Penguin Books, 1975], pp. 220, 223, 229.)

4. Apart from the "terrorist bombings," the only concrete examples of "revolutionary" activities were the abortive guerrilla *foco* in Santo Domingo and the confiscation of $25,000 from a leftist book-dealer returning from a trip to Eastern Europe. Rather than calming military anxieties by demonstrating the efficiency of the existing control mechanisms, however, both incidents seem to have strengthened fears that similar activities were going on unchecked.

5. Agee, *CIA Diary,* pp. 206–95.

6. See Robert Price, "A Theoretical Approach to Military Rule in New States: Reference Group Theory and the Ghanaian Case," *World Politics* 13 (April 1971):399–430. As Price himself points out, however, the extremes of the Ghanaian case are not likely to be found in more established military institutions. In his reaction to student destruction of a U.S. military vehicle in 1966, one Ecuadorian officer took what was nearly an anti-anti-American position, but this was an atypical case. Several others, in their reaction to the Arosemena banquet incident, indicated a fear of antagonizing the United States, but this was not a reference group reaction.

7. Interviews 64 and 65. Like Goulart in Brazil, Arosemena's position in this regard was weakened by the fact that his succession to power was through the vice-presidency. Unlike Goulart, however, Arosemena never showed any intention of abandoning the constitution. See Thomas Skidmore, *Politics in Brazil, 1930–1964: An Experiment in Democracy* (New York: Oxford University Press, 1967), pp. 205–302.

8. *El Comercio,* 27 June 1963, p. 4.

9. Alejandro Carrión (Juan Sin Cielo), "Las Fuerzas Armadas y las instituciones democráticas," *Revista del Colegio Militar Eloy Alfaro* 25 (June 1962):81.

10. Martin Needler first noted this pattern in Needler, *Anatomy,* p. 41; Interviews 3 and 19.

11. Interview 90.

12. Interview 10.

13. Interview 17.

14. "Firme propósito institucional," Editorial in *Revista Militar de las Fuerzas Armadas Ecuatorianas* 2 (May–September 1970):4.

15. A category that, in military thinking, also includes the armed forces!

16. Interview 3.

17. Major purchases of military equipment are made through the National Defense Board, which has its own earmarked revenue sources that are not included in the Ministry of Defense share of the regular budget.

18. Interview 9.

19. Dr. José María Velasco Ibarra in an address to the National Congress. (Quoted in *El Comercio,* 11 August 1956, p. 12.)

20. Interview 83.

21. Interview 88.

22. Mayor Leonardo Granja. (Quoted in *El Comercio,* 4 July 1956, p. 1.)

23. Interview 17.

24. Interview 105.

25. Interview 65. While the government did not have a clear-cut majority in Congress, it did manage to muster enough votes in 1962 to survive two attempts to begin

impeachment hearings. Even though Arosemena denounced Congress for its irresponsibility and spoke highly of the qualifications of the officers involved, he could not explain why no other postwar government had ever had its promotions bill rejected. For over a year the highest-ranking officers in the country were colonels. See Carlos Enrique Carrión, "La verdad sobre los ascensos," *La Calle* 297 (November 1962), Reprinted in *El Comercio,* 28 November 1966, p. 16.

26. Arosemena's actions in the *chatarra* case were seen by some as a deliberate attempt to discredit the vice-president (interviews 81, 52, and 42) and to "separate the armed forces and public opinion" (interview 57).

27. Agee makes it clear that Arosemena was framed on this one too. The chief antimilitary agitators were, in fact, CIA plants. Agee, *CIA Diary,* p. 223.

28. Not a few officers viewed Arosemena's attitudes as "thinly disguised hatred for the armed forces." (Interview 55.)

29. Interview 64.

30. There was some feeling that the junta was biased against the air force. This complaint grew out of an attempt by the army-dominated government to eliminate special provisions for air force pilots in promotion regulations governing minimum service in grade, advanced training, examination scores, etc. (Interview 60.) Still, since only two air force officers are included in the 1966 sample (and only one of these criticized the junta's military policies), these service rivalries do not account for the junta's poor ratings.

31. One officer explicitly compared the junta and Velasco in terms of responsiveness to the military's economic needs, and concluded in favor of Velasco. (Interview 17.)

32. See Aaron Wildavsky's concept of a budgetary "fair share" in *The Politics of the Budgetary Process* (Boston: Little, Brown, 1964), p. 17.

33. See also Philippe C. Schmitter, "Military Intervention, Political Competitiveness, and Public Policy in Latin America: 1950–1967," in *On Military Intervention and Military Regimes,* ed. Morris Janowitz and Jacques van Doorn (Rotterdam: Rotterdam University Press, 1971), pp. 425–506; Eric Nordlinger, "Soldiers in Mufti: The Impact of Military Rule on Economic and Social Change in Non-Western States," *American Political Science Review* 64, no. 4 (December 1970):1131–48.

34. José Nun, *Latin America: The Hegemonic Crisis and the Military Coup* (Berkeley, Calif.: Institute of International Studies, 1969).

35. Ibid., p. 21.

36. Ibid., p. 47.

37. Ibid., p. 56.

38. Particularly, the characterization of the Latin American military as a cohesive and politically homogeneous force. Alfred C. Stepan, *The Military in Politics: Changing Patterns in Brazil* (Princeton, N.J.: Princeton University Press, 1971), pp. 44–56.

39. Darío Cantón, "Las intervenciones militares en la Argentina, 1900–1966," Documento de Trabajo no. 39, Instituto Torcuato di Tella, Centro de Investigaciones Sociales, Buenos Aires, Argentina, n.d.

40. Nun, *Hegemonic Crisis,* p. 48.

41. See Augustín Cueva, *El proceso de dominación política en el Ecuador* (Quito, Ecuador: Ediciones Crítica, 1972). His analysis of the inability of the middle class to consolidate its political position after the loss of political hegemony by the Liberal oligarchy in the military coup of 1925 is especially relevant.

42. There is some impressionistic evidence to the contrary, which suggests that most middle-class Ecuadorians resent the military's relatively high salaries and would prefer to cut, rather than expand, the military budget.

43. Indeed, in at least 200 hours of interviews with Ecuadorian officers (apart from answers given to the personal background questions), there were only three references to the middle class, and all of them were made in passing. Two indicated a secondary identification as members of the middle class and one treated middle-class opinion separately from public opinion in the 1966 coup. See also Stepan, *Military in Politics,* pp. 42–56.

44. Interview 94.

45. Interview 44.

46. Interview 45.

47. Interview 26.
48. Interview 26.
49. "Respeto para las instituciones fundamentales del estado," Editorial in *Revista Militar de las Fuerzas Armadas Ecuatorianas* 4, no. 14 (May–June 1950):1–2.
50. Interview 65.
51. Interview 2. Compare Huntington's description of the impact of strong political institutions on political leaders. "Politicians frequently remark that things 'look different' after they are in office than they did when they were competing for office. This difference is a measure of the institutional demands of office. It is precisely this difference in perspectives that legitimizes the demands of the officeholder on his fellow citizens." (Samuel P. Huntington, *Political Order in Changing Societies* [New Haven: Yale University Press, 1968], p. 27.)
52. Robert Price, "Military Rule in New States."
53. Oscar Efren Reyes, *Los últimos siete años* (Quito, Ecuador: Talleres Gráficos Nacionales, 1933), pp. 48–51.
54. See chapter 5.
55. See also Martin Needler, "Military Motivations in the Seizure of Power," *Latin American Research Review* 10, no. 3 (Winter 1975):62–78.

## Chapter 12: The Changing Role of the Ecuadorian Armed Forces

1. Cf. Samuel P. Huntington's description of the "professional military ethic" in *The Soldier and the State* (Cambridge, Mass.: Harvard University Press, 1957), pp. 61–79.
2. Document 63, p. 75.
3. Interview 6.
4. Interview 37.
5. Interviews 17 and 23.
6. Interview 69.
7. Interview 10.
8. Interview 38.
9. Interview 83.
10. Interview 42.
11. Interview 93.
12. Interview 9.
13. Interview 52.
14. Interview 17. According to another officer, the divisions within the Quito garrison resulted from Arosemena's arrest, "which split the armed forces between the duty to support the constituted order and their duty to the constitution." (Interview 5.)
15. Hence the insignificant correlation found in chapter 7 between coup attitudes and belief in military intervention. Abstract role definition is simply a nonscalar variable.
16. Cf. Robert A. Potash, *The Army and Politics in Argentina 1928–1945: Yrigoyen to Perón* (Stanford, Calif.: Stanford University Press, 1969), p. 283.
17. Liisa North, *Civil-Military Relations in Argentina, Chile, and Peru* (Berkeley, Calif.: Institute of International Studies, 1966), pp. 14–20, 26–31.
18. Even the oath taken by the military officer upon receipt of his commission was revised to reflect this change. The post-1941 oath included a promise to defend the constitution and the flag; in the 1930s, each officer was asked, "Do you swear by the fatherland and by your honor and promise *to the Government* to follow the flag constantly and defend it to the last drop of blood? " Angel Isaac Chiriboga, *Las fuerzas morales en el ejército* (Quito, Ecuador: Imprenta Nacional, 1932), p. 33. (Emphasis added.)
19. Interview 64.
20. Víctor Aulestia Mier, "Recuerdo de una tragedia y una orientación positiva para la sobrevivencia de la patria," *Revista de la Marina* 6 (February–March–April, 1968):16–21.
21. Marcos Gándara Enríquez, "De la revolución militar a la restauración oligárquica" (Manuscript. Buenos Aires, Argentina: 1970), p. 38.

22. Interview 90.
23. Interview 50.
24. Julio Montalvo Suárez. (Quoted in *El Comercio,* 5 December 1961, p. 11.)
25. Gándara, "De la revolucion militar," p. 40. (Emphasis in original.)
26. Interview 10. Indeed, in arguing against a congressional censure motion, one member of the high command warned Congress in 1962 that if the government were overthrown, it would not be to install one of the opposition parties, but to install a military dictatorship. (Interview 64.)
27. Interviews 13, 19, 69, and 73.
28. Interview 73.
29. See Richard Maullin, *Soldiers, Guerrillas, and Politics in Colombia* (Santa Monica, Calif.: The Rand Corporation, 1970), p. 81.
30. See Alfonso Littuma Arízaga, *La doctrina de seguridad nacional* (Caracas, Venezuela: Oficina Técnica del Ministerio de Defensa, 1966). The author was director of the Ecuadorian war academy from 1961 to 1963 and now teaches in the Escuela Superior de la Fuerza Aérea Venezolana.
31. Interview 11.
32. Interview 3. (Emphasis in interview.)
33. Interviews 9, 54, and 32.
34. Aulestia, "Recuerdo de una tragedia," p. 20.
35. On the linkage of development and national security, see Osiris Guillermo Villegas, *Políticas y estratégias para el desarrollo y la seguridad nacional* (Buenos Aires, Argentina: Editorial Pleamar, 1969); Ronald M. Schneider, *The Political System of Brazil* (New York: Columbia University Press, 1970), pp. 245–47; Thomas G. Saunders, "Development and Security are Linked in a Relationship of Mutual Causality," *American Universities Field Staff Reports,* East Coast South America Series 15, no. 3; Alfred C. Stepan, *The Military in Politics: Changing Patterns in Brazil* (Princeton, N.J.: Princeton University Press, 1971), pp. 173–87.
36. Gándara, "De la revolucion militar," p. 37.
37. Ibid., p. 11.
38. Interview 2.
39. Interview 9.
40. Gándara, "De la revolucion militar," p. 6.
41. The developmentalist demands for reform involved more than simply support for Civic Action programs. Such activities were generally accepted by proponents of all four role definitions as good public relations. Over 70 percent of the respondents listed "cooperation in the socioeconomic development of the country," (civic action) as part of the mission of the armed forces.
42. Gándara, "De la revolucion militar," pp. 116, 127.
43. Interview 4.
44. Interview 32.
45. Interview 81.
46. In explaining the divergent interpretations of the security-and-development doctrines in the policies of the current military regimes of Peru and Brazil, Luigi Einaudi and Alfred C. Stepan (*Latin American Institutional Development: Changing Military Perspectives in Peru and Brazil* [Santa Monica, Calif.: The Rand Corporation, 1971], pp. 123–30) stress differences in the socioeconomic context of decision-making in the two countries and differences in the political circumstances under which the military came to power. The Ecuadorian experience suggests that situational factors (especially the immediacy of the guerrilla problem relative to other political and economic problems) and the pattern of social relationships established in the military career (in particular the degree of contact with university intellectuals) may be the most important factors contributing to different interpretations of the developmentalist doctrine. See also Brady Tyson, "The Emerging Role of the Military as National Modernizers and Managers in Latin America: The Cases of Brazil and Peru," in *Latin American Prospects for the 1970's,* ed. David Pollock and Arch Ritter (New York: Frederick A. Praeger, 1973), pp. 107–30.

47. Those officers who cited the opposition campaign as a factor in the junta's downfall were more likely to *support* the junta if they also rated its reform policies *negatively*. Citations of opposition "subversion" were most common among developmentalists and were nil among those who reverted to the constitutionalist model. Similarly, those who had a preference for a political party or who defined their political orientation (mostly center-right) were more likely to have supported the junta's overthrow. Percentage differences for all of these cross-tabulations are, however, small.

48. Interview 30; Interviews 37, 23, and 55.

49. Interview 43; Interviews 50 and 81.

50. Interview 13.

51. Interview 69. One officer summarized the general disillusionment: "When we graduate from the Colegio Militar, we swear to respect the constitution, but then the time comes when the politicians begin coming to us with complaints against the government. As the citizens that we are, we become concerned with the welfare of the country. The public unrest strikes a responsive chord and the moment comes when we think we can resolve the situation, which we do in good faith, and not for capturing power or privilege. As the process culminates, when we step in and take over, the same civilians are our first enemies." (Interview 41.)

52. Carlos Julio Arosemena Monroy, *Cartas para la historia* (Quito, Ecuador: Editorial "Fray Jodoco Ricke," 1966), p. 27.

53. *El Comercio,* 22 November 1966.

54. Congreso Nacional, Ecuador, "Ley de personal de las fuerzas armadas," *Registro Oficial* no. 152 (7 April 1969), p. 1178.

55. Interview 64. In the words of an officer who had actively supported the overthrow of the junta, "[No one] was capable of defending the armed forces against the antimilitarist current. We saw that even the good works of the junta were criticized, . . . denied by the politicians. In Ecuador there cannot be democratic government. In the last fifty years, democracy has been only a still life in the name of the people while the rich get richer and the poor get poorer." (Interview 55.)

56. Interview 81.

57. "Filosofía y plan de acción del Gobierno Revolucionario Nacionalista del Ecuador" (Mimeographed. Quito, Ecuador, n.d.), pp. 1–2.

## Chapter 13: The Variable Political Environment

1. Interview 7; Alfredo Pareja Diezcanseco, *Historia del Ecuador* (Quito, Ecuador: Editorial Colón, 1962), pp. 373–75. In 1960 Edwin Lieuwen classified the Ecuadorian military as "one of several in transition from [being] political to non-political bodies." *(Arms and Politics in Latin America* [New York: Frederick A. Praeger, 1960], p. 163.)

2. 1950 is the earliest year for which the central bank has calculated national accounts statistics. In terms of growth rates, the 1940–1948 period was even more spectacular: exports soared from $10 million in 1940 to $55 million by 1948. However, most of this growth was merely a recovery to the economic levels achieved during the 1920s. In per capita terms, the recovery was not completed until 1950. Banco Central del Ecuador, *Memoria del Gerente General, 1955* (Quito, Ecuador: Imprenta del Banco Central, 1956), p. 22, XXVIII.

3. Banco Central del Ecuador, *Series estadísticas básicas para el análisis económico* (Quito, Ecuador: Imprenta del Banco Central, 1962), p. 78.

4. In the decade from 1950 to 1960, total public expenditures at constant prices increased by 122 percent. Ibid., p. 73. Cf. Helio Jaguaribe's description of the "estado cartorial" in Brazil before Vargas. "Political Strategies of National Development," in *Latin American Radicalism,* ed. Irving Horowitz, Josue de Castro, and John Gerassi (New York: Random House, 1969), pp. 390–439.

5. Samuel P. Huntington, *Political Order in Changing Societies* (New Haven: Yale University Press, 1969), p. 54, and Augustín Cueva, *El proceso de dominación política en Ecuador* (Quito, Ecuador: Ediciones Crítica, 1972), pp. 52–59.

6. In the 1954 sample, the questionnaire item dealing with the communist threat was answered negatively by all respondents. Most expressed surprise that anyone would ask such an obviously irrelevant question.

7. "Declining world market prices for bananas, coffee, and cocoa during the 1955–65 period reduced annual per capita Gross National Product growth [in Ecuador] some 56 percent." Charles Gibson, "The Role of Foreign Trade in Ecuadorian Economic Development" (Ph.D. dissertation, University of Pennsylvania, 1968), p. 314.

8. Even according to relatively optimistic government figures, from 1950 to 1960, the growth rate of total employment was approximately 10 percent less than the rate of population growth. César Robalino Gonzaga, *El desarrollo económico del Ecuador* (Quito, Ecuador: Junta Nacional de Planificación, n.d.), Apéndice Estadístico, Cuadro 64, reproduced as table 19 in Clarence Zuvekas's, "Ecuador: Selected Economic Data" (Mimeographed. Quito, Ecuador: USAID, 1970), p. 52. No reliable figures exist on unemployment, but whereas debate between the government and the trade unions centered on 5,000 vs. 7,000 in 1950, by 1961 the numbers had jumped to 150,000 vs. 200,000. *Hispanic American Report* 3, no. 5 (May 1950):23; Ibid., 16, no. 3 (May 1961):238.

9. Pedro Merlo, "Crecimiento de la población del Ecuador," *Indicadores Económicos* 1, no. 3 (July 1967):46.

10. Cueva, "Dominación política," p. 81. The second essay in this volume is the most perceptive analysis of a Latin American populist movement made to date. Its treatment of the symbolic dimensions of Velasco's relationship to his supporters is especially insightful.

11. The Liberal party's presidential candidate in 1968 was the head of a special commission of sierra landowners formed to fight the government's agrarian reform proposal. *Hispanic American Report* 15, no. 1 (March 1962):57.

12. Postwar elections have always been contested by three or more coalitions rather than by individual parties. The consistent preference for coalition labels that obscure, rather than identify, the parties in a given coalition is another indication that none of the existing parties possesses much of a stable following. (The National Velasquista Movement is a partial exception.) See James Payne, *Patterns of Conflict in Colombia* (New Haven: Yale University Press, 1968), pp. 130–33.

13. Junta Nacional de Planificación, *Síntesis estadística del Ecuador 1955–1962* (Quito, Ecuador, 1963), pp. 15, 26.

14. Marcos Gándara Enríquez, "De la revolución militar a la restauración oligárquica" (Manuscript. Buenos Aires, Argentina, 1970), p. 45.

15. Document 79.

16. In contrast, Juan Perón's rapid mobilization of the Buenos Aires working class in 1944–1945 was based on a straightforward delivery of tangible benefits that were clearly attributed to Perón's control of the Ministry of Labor. Peter Smith, *Politics and Beef in Argentina: Patterns of Conflict and Change* (New York: Columbia University Press, 1969), pp. 236–41.

17. Carlos Paredes Barros, "Incidencia económica y social del proceso de liquidación del huasipungo en la provincia de Pichincha" (Master's thesis, Catholic University of Ecuador, 1967).

18. Cueva, "Dominación política," pp. 80–81.

19. Marcos Gándara Enríquez, "La junta militar entiende a la política," *Con patriotismo y sin temor* (Quito, Ecuador: Talleres Gráficos Nacionales, 1964), p. 107.

20. Interview 69.

21. Huntington, *Political Order*, p. 245.

22. David P. Hanson, "The Influence of Business Groups in Ecuadorian Politics between 1959 and 1962," (Ph.D. dissertation, University of Florida, 1971), pp. 233–38.

23. Although the five coastal provinces contained nearly half the total population of Ecuador in the early sixties, they elected only 2 more senators than the 5 percent of the population living in the Amazon provinces.

24. Compare the congressional brawl described in n. 13 of chapter 4 with Weston Agor, *The Chilean Senate* (Austin: University of Texas Press, 1971).

25. As civilian dictator in 1970, Velasco kept the universities closed for over a year. Without their usual rallying ground, students found it difficult to organize demonstrations.

Student protests were practically nonexistent, and the universities remained relatively quiet even after their reopening in 1971.

26.  Zuvekas, "Selected Economic Data," p. 57.

27.  The minimal GNP response to the export recovery of 1957 is a partial exception, but can easily be explained by the conservative monetary policy of the Ponce government, which limited the increase in imports to $2.5 million—despite the $17 million rise in exports. Ibid., p. 101.

28.  Clarence Zuvekas, *A Note on Capital Flight from Ecuador* (Mimeographed. Quito, Ecuador: USAID, 1969), p. 3; United States Agency for International Development, *Ecuador: Review of Financial Developments 1960–1969* (Airgram. Quito, Ecuador: Department of State, 1969), Appendix table 19.

29.  Zuvekas, "Selected Economic Data," p. 57.

## Chapter 14:  The Systemic Interaction

1.  These proportions may, however, be modified where significant numbers of officers receive advanced military training in other countries.

2.  Elizabeth Hyman, "Soldiers in Politics: New Insights on Latin American Armed Forces," *Political Science Quarterly* 87, no. 3 (September 1972):416–17.

3.  Robert A. Potash's, *The Army and Politics in Argentina 1928–1945: Yrigoyen to Peron* (Stanford, Calif.: Stanford University Press, 1969), is perhaps the best example. The Institute for the Comparative Study of Political Systems series of monographs provides others.

4.  Martin Needler, "Political Development and Military Intervention in Latin America," *American Political Science Review* 60, no. 3 (September 1966), pp. 612–26.

5.  Ibid.

6.  The extreme case was the 1961 arrest of Army Commander Del Pozo by the majors who commanded the Chimborazo Engineering Battalion.

7.  Such a procedure would also allow for incorporation of recent arguments that, in highly professionalized militaries, the degree of factionalization itself becomes an important factor in changes in role definition. Guillermo O'Donnell, "Modernización y golpes militares," Documento de trabajo, Instituto Torcuato di Tella, Centro de Investigaciones en Administración Pública (Buenos Aires, Argentina, 1972).

8.  Charles Anderson, *Politics and Economic Change in Latin America* (Princeton, N.J.: Van Nostrand, 1967), pp. 87–114; Merle Kling, "Toward a Theory of Power and Instability in Latin America," *Western Political Quarterly* 9, no. 1 (March 1956):23–25; Kalman Silvert, *The Conflict Society* (New Orleans, La.: Hauser Press, 1961), p. 20.

9.  For example: Douglas Chalmers, "Parties and Society in Latin America" (Paper presented to the American Political Science Association convention, Washington, D.C., September 1968); Eldon Kenworthy, "Coalitions in the Political Development of Latin America," in *The Study of Coalition Behavior,* ed. Sven Groennings, E. W. Kelley, and Michael Leiserson (New York: Holt, Rinehart, and Winston, 1970), pp. 103–40; Alfred C. Stepan, *The Military in Politics: Changing Patterns in Brazil* (Princeton, N.J.: Princeton University Press, 1971); Philippe C. Schmitter, "The Portugalization of Brazil?" in *Authoritarian Brazil: Origins, Policies, and Future,* ed. Alfred C. Stepan (New Haven: Yale University Press, 1973), pp. 179–232. Though the works cited do not constitute a unified body of analysis, they all share Charles Anderson's "revisionist" premise that Latin American political systems can best be understood as a distinctive set of political systems rather than simply as variants of European systems that are subject to analysis through orthodox neoliberal or Marxian categories.

10.  See Philippe C. Schmitter, *Interest Conflict and Political Change in Brazil* (Stanford, Calif.: Stanford University Press, 1971), pp. 227–392; Nathaniel Leff, *Economic Policy-making and Development in Brazil: 1947–1964* (New York: John Wiley & Sons, 1968), pp. 107–31; Chalmers, "Parties and Society," pp. 5–8; and Markos Mamalakis, "The Theory of Sectoral Clashes and Coalitions Revisited," *Latin American Research Review* 6, no. 3 (Fall 1971):89–126. Anderson argues that the subordinate conflicts among the

contenders for any given power capability do not alter the rules or outcomes of the larger political game. (Anderson, *Politics and Economic Change,* pp. 91–92.)

11. This analysis is most applicable to those countries in Latin America that are in the intermediate ranks of modernization and military professionalization; it is less applicable to Paraguay, Nicaragua, Argentina, or Brazil. For a superb analysis of civil-military interaction in the special case of high modernization and professionalization, see Guillermo O'Donnell, *Modernization and Bureaucratic Authoritarianism: Studies in South American Politics* (Berkeley, Calif.: Institute of International Studies, 1973).

12. Samuel P. Huntington, *Political Order in Changing Societies* (New Haven: Yale University Press, 1968), pp. 8–32.

13. Leonard Binder et al., *Crises and Sequences in Political Development* (Princeton, N.J.: Princeton University Press, 1971). See also Gabriel Almond and Bingham Powell, *Comparative Politics: A Developmental Approach* (Boston: Little, Brown, 1966), pp. 34–41, 314–22.

14. For a compelling argument against current conventional thought on the optimal sequencing and policy priorities in confronting the "crises of development," see Raymond Hopkins, "Equality, Structure, and Legitimation: Alternative Political Paths in Kenya and Tanzania" (Paper presented to the American Political Science Association convention, Washington, D.C., September 1972). See also Ergun Ozbudun, "Established Revolution versus Unfinished Revolution: Contrasting Patterns of Democratization in Mexico and Turkey," in *Authoritarian Politics in Modern Society,* ed. Samuel P. Huntington and Clement Moore (New York: Basic Books, 1970), pp. 380–405; Egil Fossum, "Political Development and Strategies for Change," *Journal of Peace Research* 7, no. 1 (January 1970):17–32; Raymond Hopkins, *Political Roles in a New State: Tanzania's First Decade* (New Haven: Yale University Press, 1971); Huntington, *Political Order,* pp. 264–343.

15. See Richard Fagen, *The Transformation of Political Culture in Cuba* (Stanford, Calif.: Stanford University Press, 1969), pp. 148–65 and *passim;* Gabriel Almond and Sidney Verba, *The Civic Culture* (Boston: Little, Brown, 1965), pp. 414–28 and *passim.* See also, René Lemarchand's comparative analysis of Zaire, Rwanda, and Burundi in "Civil-Military Relations in Former Belgian Africa: The Military as a Contextual Elite" in *Soldiers in Politics,* ed. Steffen Schmidt and Gerald Dorfman (Los Altos, Calif.: Geron-X, Inc., 1974), pp. 69–96; idem., "Army Men and Nation-building in Former Belgian Africa: From Force Publique to Praetorian Guard," in *Political-Military Systems: A Comparative Analysis,* ed. Catherine Kelleher (Beverly Hills, Calif.: Sage Publications, 1974), pp. 87–104.

16. Even these shifts may mean relatively little. As David Ronfeldt has pointed out, in most Latin American countries the distinction between military and civilian governments is largely a question of the relative position of civilians and officers within mixed governmental coalitions. See David Ronfeldt, "Patterns of Civil-Military Rule," in *Latin America in the 1970s,* ed. Luigi Einaudi (Santa Monica, Calif.: The Rand Corporation, 1972), pp. 74–80.

17. Harold Lasswell and Abraham Kaplan, *Power and Society: A Framework for Political Inquiry* (New Haven: Yale University Press, 1950), pp. 276–77.

18. See Edward Gonzalez, *Cuba under Castro: The Limits of Charisma* (Boston: Houghton Mifflin, 1974), pp. 89–91, and D.E.H. Russell, *Rebellion, Revolution, and Armed Force* (New York: Academic Press, 1974), pp. 16–28.

19. In Castro's own words, "That which worried us most was the fear that a military coup would occur before we had sufficient forces to be masters of the situation." Fidel Castro, *Les Etapes de la révolution cubaine,* ed. Michel Merlier (Paris: François Maspero, 1964), p. 52. On the antirevolutionary effect of elections, see also Ernesto "Che" Guevara, *Guerrilla Warfare* (New York: Vintage Books, 1968), p. 5.

## Chapter 15: Ecuador since 1966: Testing the Model

1. John D. Martz, *Ecuador: Conflicting Political Culture and the Quest for Progress* (Boston: Allyn and Bacon, 1972), p. 147–53.

2. Velasco's failure to run away with this election as he had the election of 1960 was, nevertheless, less influenced by popular disenchantment with his past policies than by wholesale disenfranchisement of his supporters. During the revision of voter registration lists undertaken by the military junta, registration criteria were stringently applied, especially in working-class districts on the coast that had been *velasquista* strongholds. Reversing a clear trend in the three previous elections, the total vote from the coastal provinces remained almost constant from 1960 to 1968, despite the rapid increase in total population.

3. Interviews 102, 24, and 32.

4. Interviews 32 and 24. See also the military appeal "to avert civil war" following this incident, "A la Nación," *El Comercio,* 17 June 1970, pp. 1, 12.

5. Interviews 102 and 24.

6. Clarence Zuvekas, *The Ecuadorean Devaluation of 1970: Causes and Consequences* (State University of New York at Buffalo: Council on International Studies, Special Studies no. 33):6–12.

7. President Velasco especially disliked Jácome because his brother was a leader of the opposition Liberal party. Although the movement to defend Jácome was scrupulously apolitical, there is some evidence that Jácome himself had been involved in political discussions with the opposition. Interviews 154 and 40.

8. Carlos Aguirre and Luís Espinosa, "La Academia de Guerra del Ejército al Sr. Presidente de la República y a la Nación" (Manuscript. Quito, Ecuador, 29 March 1971).

9. Interview 58.

10. Interviews 102 and 20.

11. Retired officers, including veterans of Victor Aulestia's Nuevo Orden Nacional, played an important role in rallying support for the "defense of the institution" against Acosta Velasco. (Interviews 104 and 101.)

12. Interview 20.

13. There was, however, no resolution of the impasse over military demands for a military minister of defense. Later that day Velasco named a civilian to the post who immediately restored to active duty all those officers who had been fired by Acosta. The new minister also promised that Jácome would remain as director of the war academy. It was that pledge that infuriated Velasco again. (Interview 100.) Both Martz (*Conflicting Political Culture,* p. 102) and the *Latin America* newsletter (9 April 1971, p. 112–13) incorrectly describe the Acosta faction as *peruanistas* opposed to the victorious "traditionalist" officers. There is no basis in fact for any such characterization of Acosta. The academy group led by Jácome was "professionalist" and institutionalist in character, though it was the support of the younger officers that provided the basis for the eventual success of the revolt.

14. Interview 20; Interviews 102, 100, and 104.

15. Interviews 101 and 20.

16. Interview 100.

17. Interview 20.

18. *Latin America,* 5 November 1971, p. 357–58.

19. Interviews 85 and 100.

20. Ponce could not even persuade the Conservative party candidate (Dr. Carlos Arizaga Vega) to withdraw in his favor; nor could he bridge the gap to the center-left, which was also unable to form any stable coalition against Bucaram. See *El Comercio* reports on the political maneuvering during the first 10 days of February 1972.

21. Interviews 20 and 100.

22. Interviews 85 and 32.

23. Interviews 20 and 104.

24. Interview 100.

25. Interview 85.

26. Interview 102. Bucaram is reported to have refused to make any deal. (Interview 32.)

27. Interview 20.

28. Guillermo Rodríquez Lara, radio speech to the nation, (Quoted in *El Comercio,* 17 February 1972), p. 3.

29. "Filosofía y Plan de Acción del Gobierno Revolucionario Nacionalista del Ecuador" (Mimeographed. Quito, Ecuador: n.d.), pp. 1–2.

30. On at least two occasions the disorders led to panic buying in the supermarkets of the northern suburbs.

31. A content analysis of *El Comercio* editorials in the two weeks prior to the *autogolpe* shows a rather ambiguous attitude toward the Velasco government. Nevertheless, the overall balance was slightly positive, a sharp contrast to the series of consistently negative comments on the Congress. The day after the coup the lead editorial placed most of the blame on political extremists, reactionary pressure groups, and anachronistic parties, strongly implying that the government had no other choice but to act as it did. See "Ante la nueva situación," editorial in *El Comercio,* 23 June 1970, p. 4.

32. See, for example, "La nueva situación política," editorial in *El Comercio,* 17 February 1972, p. 4. See also the only slightly veiled calls for a "new politics" in "Política de disoluciones," editorial in *El Comercio,* 10 February 1972, p. 4.

33. The 1966 coup overthrowing the Illía government in Argentina also occurred in a noncrisis situation characterized by a strong military predisposition to act and a high civilian willingness to acquiesce in a military regime. Guillermo O'Donnell, *Modernization and Bureaucratic Authoritarianism: Studies in South American Politics* (Berkeley, Calif.: Institute of International Studies, 1973), pp. 115–65.

34. While some observers stressed the "conservative" military's fears of a "leftist" Bucaram government (See "Ecuador: Fifth Time Unlucky," *Latin America* 6, no. 7 [18 February 1972]:49), one key participant in the 1972 coup specifically noted that "Bucaram's populist, antioligarchical campaign had won him considerable prestige. As perhaps the only candidate who cared about anything other than his own ambitions, he had support. Still, we did not even analyze this. If we had thought that Bucaram had the full support of the people, we would have backed [an alliance of] the armed forces and the people in a new system of government. As it was, we thought of Bucaram only as a potential source of resistance [to the coup]." (Interview 20.)

35. Thus, even though Velasco was a populist, he was at the same time a university-educated intellectual and therefore, he was personally worthy of respect, regardless of what one might think of his politics or of his economic policies. The "lack of education" argument against Bucaram was fairly common among middle-class Ecuadorians and was particularly emphasized in two interviews—one with a retired officer and another with a civilian technocrat. (Interviews 32 and 103.) However, while both were relatively well-informed about political affairs, neither had any direct involvement in the 1972 coup or any close contact with anyone who had.

36. Interviews 104, 100, 85, and 20.

37. The few who hesitated to support the new regime were, as one might expect, those who had had strong personal connections to former Minister of Defense Acosta. Personal ties continued to be an important factor in individual coup decisions in all of the post-1966 coups.

38. Cf. O'Donnell, *Modernization and Bureaucratic Authoritarianism,* p. 158.

39. *Latin America,* 15 March 1975, p. 84.

40. See Carl F. Herbold, "The Ecuadorian Military: The Management of Oil Policy and Political Instability" (Paper presented to the Regional Conference of the Inter-University Seminar on Armed Forces and Society, Tempe, Arizona, 26–28 February 1976.

41. See Mary Jane Martz, "Ecuador," in *Latin American Foreign Policies: An Analysis,* ed. Harold Davis and Larman Wilson (Baltimore: The Johns Hopkins University Press, 1975), pp. 383–400.

42. The strongly nationalist orientation of the navy (which led to several clashes between the president and naval officers in the cabinet) appears to have been a by-product of Ecuador's fifteen-year conflict with the U.S. government and American tuna companies over Ecuador's 200-mile fishing limit.

43. Aulestia and several of his key supporters were removed from the government in 1973.

44. In 1970 the Ecuadorian war academy devoted less than 76 hours of its 1350-hour curriculum to guerrilla warfare, while its Brazilian equivalent spent "222 hours on internal

security, 129 hours on irregular warfare, and only 21 hours . . . on territorial defense."
(Alfred C. Stepan, *The Military in Politics: Changing Patterns in Brazil* [Princeton,
Princeton University Press, 1971], p. 181.) An analysis of the titles of theses written by
recent graduates of the Ecuadorian academy also reveals a clear preoccupation with
conventional warfare, rather than counterinsurgency.

45. "Filosofía y Plan de Acción, p. 9.
46. "Reforma agraria: entre el 'caos' y la justicia," *Nueva* 26 (January 1976):15.
47. "Entre la incertidumbre y la frustración," *Nueva* 19 (May 1975):39.
48. "Balanza comercial: Lecciones de una déficit," *Nueva* 20 (June 1975):22–26.
49. It should be pointed out that this account of the September and January coups is
based entirely on public sources, rather than on personal interviews. Previous experience
with journalistic accounts of military politics in Ecuador suggests that this reconstruction of
these events should be used with caution until more reliable data is available.
50. "Ecuador: Civilian Coup on the Way?" *Latin America* 9, no. 19 (16 May
1975):150–51. In typical Ecuadorian fashion, the government was accused of being
"communist-infiltrated" by the right at the same time that Carlos Julio Arosemena was
denouncing it as a tool of the CIA. "Civiles o militares," *Nueva* 21, (July 1975):24–26.
51. "Ecuador: Term of Trial," *Latin America* 9, no. 41 (17 October 1975):326–27.
52. In fact, the crisis was precipitated by the decision of General Durán to force the
resignation of Generals Vásconez and Puma, both of whom were members of the cabinet
who were known to be working with the civilian opposition; in turn, both denounced the
new military government. "Hay que volver a los cuarteles con la dignidad," *El Comercio,* 11
January 1976, p. 1.
53. René Lemarchand has suggested a number of intriguing possibilities in this
direction. See "Civil-Military Relations in Former Belgian Africa: The Military as a
Contextual Elite," in *Soldiers in Politics,* ed. Steffen Schmidt and Gerald Dorfman (Los
Altos, Calif.: Geron-X, Inc., 1974), pp. 69–96.
54. Interview 9.
55. In addition to various general treatises on military rule, see Eric Nordlinger,
"Soldiers in Mufti: The Impact of Military Rule on Economic and Social Change in the
Non-Western States," *American Political Science Review* 64, no. 4 (December 1970):
1131–48; Jerry Weaver, "Assessing the Impact of Military Rule: Alternative Approaches,"
in *Military Rule in Latin America: Functions, Consequences, and Perspectives,* ed. Philippe
C. Schmitter (Beverly Hills, Calif.: Sage Publications, 1973), pp. 58–116; Philippe C.
Schmitter, "Foreign Military Assistance, National Military Spending, and Military Rule in
Latin America," in Schmitter, *Military Rule,* pp. 117–87; idem, "Military Intervention,
Political Competitiveness, and Public Policy in Latin America," in *On Military Intervention
and Military Regimes,* ed. Morris Janowitz and Jacques van Doorn (Rotterdam: Rotterdam
University Press, 1971), pp. 425–506.
56. On these countries in particular, see Abraham Lowenthal, ed., *The Peruvian
Experiment: Continuity and Change under Military Rule* (Princeton, N.J.: Princeton
University Press, 1975); Alfred C. Stepan, ed., *Authoritarian Brazil: Origins, Policies, and
Future* (New Haven: Yale University Press, 1973); idem, *The Military in Politics: Changing
Patterns in Brazil* (Princeton, N.J.: Princeton University Press, 1971); idem, *State and
Society in Peru* (Princeton, N.J.: Princeton University Press, 1977); Kevin Middlebrook
and David Scott Palmer, *Military Government and Political Development: Lessons
from Peru,* Sage Papers on Latin America no. 01–054 (Beverly Hills, Calif.: Sage
Publications, 1975); Luigi Einaudi and Alfred C. Stepan, *Latin American Institutional
Development: Changing Military Perspectives in Peru and Brazil* (Santa Monica, Calif.: The
Rand Corporation, 1971); Barry Ames, "The Policy-making Process in a Militarized Regime:
Brazil after 1964", in *Soldiers,* ed. Schmidt and Dorfman, pp. 186–214; Julio Cotler,
"Political Crisis and Military Populism in Peru," in *Militarism in Developing Countries,* ed.
Kenneth Fidel (New Brunswick, N.J.: Transaction Books, 1975), pp. 219–57; O'Donnell,
*Modernization and Bureaucratic Authoritarianism;* idem, "Modernización y golpes militares:
teoría, comparación, y el caso argentino," Documento de trabajo, Instituto Torcuato di
Tella, Centro de Investigaciones en Administración Pública (Buenos Aires, Argentina, 1972.)

# Bibliographical References

## Bibliography of Works Cited

"Afirmación del orden democrático." Editorial in *El Universo,* 25 December 1954, p. 4.

Agee, Phillip. *Inside the Company: CIA Diary.* Harmondsworth, England: Penguin Books, 1975.

Agor, Weston. *The Chilean Senate.* Austin: University of Texas Press, 1971.

Aguirre, Carlos, and Espinosa, Luis. "La Academia de Guerra del Ejército al Sr. Presidente de la República y a la Nación." Manuscript. Quito, Ecuador, 29 March 1971.

"A la Nación." *El Comercio,* 17 June 1970, pp. 1, 12.

Alba, Víctor. "The Stages of Militarism in Latin America." In *The Role of the Military in Underdeveloped Countries,* edited by John J. Johnson, pp. 165–83. Princeton, N.J.: Princeton University Press, 1962.

Almeida Urrutia, Gonzalo. "El Congreso de la República del Ecuador." *El Universo,* 7 November 1961, p. 7.

Almond, Gabriel, and Powell, Bingham. *Comparative Politics: A Developmental Approach.* Boston: Little, Brown, 1966.

Almond, Gabriel, and Verba, Sidney. *The Civic Culture: Political Attitudes and Democracy.* Boston: Little, Brown, 1965.

Ames, Barry. "The Policy-making Process in a Militarized Regime: Brazil after 1964." In *Soldiers in Politics,* edited by Steffen Schmidt and Gerald Dorfman, pp. 186–214. Los Altos, Calif.: Geron-X, 1974.

Anderson, Charles. *Politics and Economic Change in Latin America.* Princeton, N.J.: Van Nostrand, 1967.

"Ante la nueva situación política." Editorial in *El Comercio,* 23 June 1970, p. 4.

"Aprobó el senado." *El Universo,* 25 September 1969, p. 3.

Araujo, Angel F. *Episodios de campaña y relatos históricos.* Quito, Ecuador: Imprenta Nacional, 1922.

Arosemena Monroy, Carlos Julio. *Cartas para la historia.* Quito, Ecuador: Editorial "Fray Jodoco Ricke," 1966.

Arosemena Peet, Carlos Julio. "El modus vivendi y las 200 millas marítimas." *El País,* February 1971, pp. 5–8, 33–38.

Aulestia Mier, Víctor. "Recuerdo de una tragedia y una orientación positiva para la sobrevivencia de la patria." *Revista de la Marina* 6 (February–March–April 1968):16–21.

"Balanza comercial: lecciones de una déficit." *Nueva* 20 (June 1975):22–26.

Banco Central del Ecuador, *Memoria del Gerente General, 1955.* Quito, Ecuador: Imprenta del Banco Central, 1956.

———. *Memoria del Gerente General, 1960.* Quito, Ecuador: Imprenta del Banco Central, 1961.

———. *Series estadísticas básicas para el análisis económico.* Quito, Ecuador: Imprenta del Banco Central, 1962.

Benites Vinueza, Leopoldo. *Ecuador: drama y paradoja.* Mexico City: Fondo de Cultura Económica, 1950.

Binder, Leonard; Coleman, James S.; La Palombara, Joseph; Pye, Lucian; Verba, Sidney; and Weiner, Myron. *Crises and Sequences in Political Development.* Princeton, N.J.: Princeton University Press, 1971.

Blalock, Hubert. *Causal Inferences in Nonexperimental Research.* Chapel Hill: University of North Carolina Press, 1964.

———. *Social Statistics.* New York: McGraw-Hill, 1960.

Blanksten, George I. *Ecuador: Constitutions and Caudillos.* Berkeley: University of California Press, 1951.

Borja y Borja, Ramiro. *Las constituciones del Ecuador.* Madrid: Ediciones Cultura Hispánica, 1951.

Bossano, Guillermo. *Trances de la libertad.* Quito, Ecuador: Talleres Gráficos "Minerva," 1961.

Brunner, Ronald D., and Brewer, Garry D. *Organized Complexity: Empirical Theories of Political Development.* New York: The Free Press, 1971.

Bwy, Douglas. "Political Instability in Latin America: The Cross Cultural Test of a Causal Model." *Latin American Research Review* 3, no. 2 (Spring 1968): 17–87.

Cantón, Darío. "Las intervenciones militares en la Argentina, 1900–1966." Documento de Trabajo no. 39, Instituto Torcuato di Tella, Centro de Investigaciones Sociales, Buenos Aires, Argentina, n.d.

Carrión, Alejandro. "Las fuerzas armadas y las instituciones democráticas." *Revista del Colegio Militar Eloy Alfaro* 25 (June 1962):79–83.

Case, Robert C. "El entrenamiento de los militares latinoamericanos en los Estados Unidos." *Aportes* 6 (October 1967):44–56.

Castro, Fidel. *Les Etapes de la révolution cubaine.* Edited by Michel Merlier. Paris: François Maspero, 1964.

Chalmers, Douglas. "Developing on the Periphery: External Factors in Latin American Politics." In *Linkage Politics,* edited by James Rosenau, pp. 67–93. New York: The Free Press, 1969.

———. "Parties and Society in Latin America." Paper presented to the American Political Science Association convention, Washington, D.C., September 1968.

Chiriboga, Angel Isaac. "El Ejército y el congreso de 1930." *El Ejército Nacional* 10, no. 55 (1931):1-6.

_____. *Las fuerzas morales en el Ejército.* Quito, Ecuador: Imprenta Nacional, 1932.

"Civiles o militares," *Nueva* 21 (July 1975):24-26.

Collier, David. "The Timing of Development and Political Outcomes in Latin America." Paper presented to the American Political Science Association convention, Washington, D.C., 1972.

Collins, John Michael. "The Successful Coup d'Etat in Modern Politics." Ph.D. dissertation, Rutgers University, 1968.

Comité Interamericano de Desarrollo Agrícola. *Tenencia de la tierra y desarrollo socio-económico del sector agrícola: Ecuador.* Washington, D.C.: Pan American Union, 1965.

Congreso Nacional, [Ecuador]. "Ley de personal de las fuerzas armadas." *Registro Oficial* no. 152 (7 April 1969):1163-81.

Costales Samaniego, Alfredo, and de Costales, Piedad. *Historia social del Ecuador.* 3 vols. Issued as nos. 17, 18, and 19 of *Llacta*, Quito, Ecuador, 1964.

Cotler, Julio. "Political Crisis and Military Populism in Peru." In *Militarism in Developing Countries,* edited by Kenneth Fidel, pp. 219-57. New Brunswick, N.J.: Transaction Books, 1975.

"Criterio económico del ejército." *El Ejército Nacional* 11, no. 61 (1932):4-7.

Crittenden, Kathleen, and Hill, Richard. "Coding Reliability and the Validity of Interview Data." *American Sociological Review* 36, no. 6 (December 1971):1073-80.

Cromwell [pseud.]. "Apoliticismo bien entendido." *El Comercio,* 12 March 1962, p. 4.

_____. "Ideas claras y planes sencillos." *El Comercio,* 18 July 1963, p. 4.

Crow, Edwin; Davis, Frances; and Maxfield, Margaret. *Statistics Manual.* New York: Dover Publications, 1960.

Cueva, Augustín. *El proceso de dominación política en el Ecuador.* Quito, Ecuador: Ediciones Crítica, 1972.

_____. "Sociología política ecuatoriana." Mimeographed. Quito, Ecuador: Escuela de Sociología y de Ciencias Políticas y Administrativas, Universidad Central del Ecuador, 1969.

Cutright, Phillips. "National Political Development." In *Politics and Social Life,* edited by N.W. Polsby, R. A. Dentler, and P. A. Smith, pp. 569-82. Boston: Houghton Mifflin, 1963.

Dean, Warren. "Latin American Golpes and Economic Fluctuations, 1823-1966." *Social Science Quarterly* 51, no. 1 (June 1970):70-80.

Dirección Nacional de Estadística. *Ecuador en cifras 1938-1942.* Quito, Ecuador: Imprenta del Ministerio de Hacienda, 1944.

"Ecuador: Civilian Coup on the Way?" *Latin America* 9, no. 19 (16 May 1975):150-51.

"Ecuador: Fifth Time Unlucky," *Latin America* 6, no. 7 (18 February 1972):49.

"Ecuador: Term of Trial." *Latin America* 9, no. 41 (17 October 1975):326-27.

Edgington, Eugene. *Statistical Inference: The Distribution-Free Approach.* New York: McGraw-Hill, 1969.

Edinger, Lewis, and Searing, Donald. "Social Background in Elite Analysis: A Methodological Inquiry." *American Political Science Review* 61, no. 2 (June 1967):428-45.

Einaudi, Luigi. *The Peruvian Military: A Summary Political Analysis.* Santa Monica, Calif.: The Rand Corporation, 1969.

Einaudi, Luigi, and Goldheimer, Herbert. "An Annotated Bibliography of Latin American Military Journals." *Latin American Research Review* 2, no. 2 (Spring 1967):95-122.

Einaudi, Luigi, and Stepan, Alfred C. *Latin American Institutional Development: Changing Military Perspectives in Peru and Brazil.* Santa Monica, Calif.: The Rand Corporation, 1971.

Endara Erazo, José. "Aviso para los ciudadanos remisos al servicio militar." *El Universo,* 13 September 1969, p. 16.

"Entre la incertidumbre y la frustración." *Nueva* 19 (May 1975):39.

Fagen, Richard. *The Transformation of Political Culture in Cuba.* Stanford, Calif.: Stanford University Press, 1969.

Feit, Edward. *The Armed Bureaucrats: Military-Administrative Regimes and Political Development.* Boston: Houghton Mifflin, 1973.

"Filosofía y plan de acción del Gobierno Revolucionario Nacionalista del Ecuador." Mimeographed. Quito, Ecuador: n.d.

Finer, Samuel. *The Man on Horseback: The Role of the Military in Politics.* New York: Frederick A. Praeger, 1962.

"Firme propósito institucional." Editorial in *Revista Militar de las Fuerzas Armadas Ecuatorianas* 2 (May–September 1970):4.

First, Ruth. *Power in Africa: Political Power in Africa and the Coup d'Etat.* London: Penguin Books, 1972.

Fitch, John S. "Civil-Military Relations in Prewar Ecuador." Manuscript.

————. "Toward a Model of the Coup d'Etat in Latin America." In *Political Development and Change: A Policy Approach,* edited by Garry D. Brewer and Ronald D. Brunner. New York: The Free Press, 1975.

Fossum, Egil. "Factors Influencing the Occurrence of Military Coups d'Etat in Latin America." *Journal of Peace Research* 3 (Fall 1967):228-51.

————. "Political Development and Strategies for Change." *Journal of Peace Research* 7, no. 1 (January 1970):17-32.

"Las fuerzas armadas." Editorial in *El Universo,* 3 July 1963, p. 4.

Gándara Enríquez, Marcos. "De la revolución militar a la restauración oligárquica." Manuscript. Buenos Aires, Argentina, 1970.

Germani, Gino, and Silvert, Kalman. "Politics, Social Structure, and Military Intervention in Latin America." *European Journal of Sociology* 2 (1961): 62-81.

Gibson, Charles. "The Role of Foreign Trade in Ecuadorian Economic Development." Ph.D. dissertation, University of Pennsylvania, 1968.

Gilmore, Robert. *Caudillism and Militarism in Venezuela 1810-1910.* Athens: Ohio University Press, 1964.

Gonzalez, Edward. *Cuba under Castro: The Limits of Charisma.* Boston: Houghton Mifflin, 1974.

González Suárez, Federico. *Historia general de la República del Ecuador.* 7 vols. Quito, Ecuador: Imprenta del clero, 1901.

Goodfriend, Paul. "The Ecuadorian Army is Poor but Proud." *Infantry Journal* 61, no. 4 (October 1947):23-25.

Grandona, Mariano. "La estructura cívico-militar del nuevo estado argentino." *Aportes* 6 (October 1967):66-76.

Guevara, Ernesto "Che." *Guerrilla Warfare.* New York: Vintage Books, 1968.

Hanson, David P. "The Influence of Business Groups in Ecuadorian Politics between 1959 and 1962." Ph.D. dissertation, University of Florida, 1971.

"Hay que volver a los cuarteles con la dignidad." *El Comercio,* 11 January 1976, p. 1.

Herbold, Carl F. "The Ecuadorian Military: The Management of Oil Policy and Political Instability." Paper presented to the Regional Conference of the Inter-University Seminar on Armed Forces and Society, Tempe, Arizona, 26-28 February 1976.

Hidalgo, Daniel. *El militarismo: sus causas y remedios.* Quito, Ecuador: R. Racines, 1913.

Hopkins, Raymond. "Equality, Structure, and Legitimation: Alternative Political Paths in Kenya and Tanzania." Paper presented to the American Political Science Association convention, Washington, D.C., September 1972.

_____. *Political Roles in a New State: Tanzania's First Decade.* New Haven: Yale University Press, 1971.

Huntington, Samuel P. "Civilian Control of the Military: A Theoretical Statement." In *Political Behavior: A Reader in Theory and Research,* edited by Heinz Eulau, Samuel Eldersveld, and Morris Janowitz, pp. 380-85. Glencoe, Ill.: The Free Press, 1956.

_____. *Political Order in Changing Societies.* New Haven: Yale University Press, 1968.

_____. *The Soldier and the State: The Theory and Politics of Civil-Military Relations.* Cambridge, Mass.: Harvard University Press, 1957.

Hyman, Elizabeth. "Soldiers in Politics: New Insights on Latin American Armed Forces." *Political Science Quarterly* 87, no. 3 (September 1972):401-18.

Icaza, Jorge. *Huasipungo.* Translated by Bernard Dulsey. Carbondale: Southern Illinois University Press, 1964.

Imaz, José. *Los que mandan.* Buenos Aires, Argentina: Editorial Universitaria, 1964.

"La institución armada y los partidos políticos." *Revista Militar de las Fuerzas Armadas Ecuatorianas* 3, no. 146 (September 1944):3-8.

Instituto de Investigaciones Económicas y Financieras de la Universidad Central. *Estadísticas Universitarias* 6 (1967-1968).

Instituto Ecuatoriano de Reforma Agraria y Colonización. *Ley de reforma agraria y colonización.* Quito, Ecuador: Talleres Gráficos "Minerva," 1964.

Jaguaribe, Helio. "Political Strategies of National Development." In *Latin American Radicalism,* edited by Irving Horowitz, Josue de Castro, and John Gerassi, pp. 390–439. New York: Random House, 1969.

Janowitz, Morris. *The Military in the Political Development of New Nations.* Chicago: University of Chicago Press, 1964.

———. *The Professional Soldier: A Social and Political Portrait.* New York: The Free Press, 1960.

Jaramillo Alvarado, Pío. *El indio ecuatoriano.* 4th ed. Quito, Ecuador: Editorial Casa de la Cultura Ecuatoriana, 1954.

Johnson, John J. *The Military and Society in Latin America.* Stanford, Calif.: Stanford University Press, 1964.

———. *Political Change in Latin America: The Emergence of the Middle Sectors.* Stanford, Calif.: Stanford University Press, 1958.

Junta Militar de Gobierno. "A la Nación." *El Comercio,* 11 July 1965, p. 1.

———. *Con patriotismo y sin temor.* Quito, Ecuador: Talleres Gráficos Nacionales, 1964.

———. *Plan político de la Junta Militar de Gobierno.* Quito, Ecuador: Talleres Gráficos Nacionales, 1963.

Junta Nacional de Planificación. *Indicadores Económicos* 1, no. 3 (July 1967).

———. *Indice de precios al consumidor, Quito y Guayaquil,* no. 190 (March 1969).

———. *Segundo censo de población y primer censo de vivienda* 1. Quito, Ecuador, 1964.

———. *Síntesis estadística del Ecuador 1955–1962.* Quito, Ecuador, 1963.

Kenworthy, Eldon. "Coalitions in the Political Development of Latin America." In *The Study of Coalition Behavior,* edited by Sven Groennings, E. W. Kelley, and Michael Leiserson, pp. 103–40. New York: Holt, Rinehart, and Winston, 1970.

Kling, Merle. "Toward a Theory of Power and Instability in Latin America." *Western Political Quarterly* 9, no. 1 (March 1956):21–35.

Labovitz, Sanford. "Some Observations on Measurement and Statistics." *Social Forces* 46, no. 2 (December 1967):151–60.

Lambert, Jacques. *Latin America: Social Structures and Political Institutions.* Translated by Helen Katel. Berkeley: University of California Press, 1966.

Larrea Alba, Luis. *La campaña de 1906: antecedentes de la revolución alfarista, su desarrollo, y sus consequencias, el conflicto de 1910.* Quito, Ecuador: Gráficos Cyma, 1962.

———. *La campaña de 1941: la agresión peruana al Ecuador y sus antecedentes históricos, políticos, y militares.* Quito, Ecuador: Casa de la Cultura Ecuatoriana, 1964.

———. "El ejército y la política." *El Ejército Nacional* 10, no. 55 (1931):36–38.

Lasswell, Harold, and Kaplan, Abraham. *Power and Society: A Framework for Political Inquiry.* New Haven: Yale University Press, 1950.

Leff, Nathaniel. *Economic Policy-making and Development in Brazil, 1947–1964.* New York: John Wiley & Sons, 1968.

Lemarchand, René. "Army Men and Nation-building in Former Belgian Africa: From Force Publique to Praetorian Guard." In *Political-Military Systems: A Comparative Analysis,* edited by Catherine Kelleher, pp. 87–104. Beverly Hills, Calif.: Sage Publications, 1974.

_____. "Civil-Military Relations in Former Belgian Africa: The Military as a Contextual Elite." In *Soldiers in Politics,* edited by Steffen Schmidt and Gerald Dorfman, pp. 69–96. Los Altos, Calif.: Geron-X, Inc., 1974.

*Ley de planta y sueldos del personal del ejército permanente.* Quito, Ecuador: Imprenta Nacional, 1912.

*Leyes militares de la República.* Quito, Ecuador: Editorial "Fray Jodoco Ricke," 1961.

*Libro de solicitudes de ingreso,* annual series. Archive of the Colegio Militar Eloy Alfaro, Quito, Ecuador.

"Libro de vida militar: Academia de Guerra y Escuela de Comando y Estado Mayor." Manuscript. War Academy Archive, Quito, Ecuador.

Lieberman, Gerald, and Owen, Donald. *Tables of the Hypergeometric Probability Distribution.* Stanford, Calif.: Stanford University Press, 1961.

Lieuwen, Edwin. *Arms and Politics in Latin America.* New York: Frederick A. Praeger, 1960.

_____. *Generals vs. Presidents: Neo-Militarism in Latin America.* New York: Frederick A. Praeger, 1964.

Littuma Arízaga, Alfonso. *La doctrina de seguridad nacional.* Caracas, Venezuela: Oficina Técnica del Ministerio de Defensa, 1966.

Loftus, Joseph. *Latin American Defense Expenditures, 1938–1965.* Santa Monica, Calif.: The Rand Corporation, 1968.

Lowenthal, Abraham. "Armies and Politics in Latin America: A Review of the Recent Literature." *World Politics* 27, no. 1 (October 1974):107-30.

_____. "The Dominican Republic: The Politics of Chaos." In *Latin America: Reform and Revolution,* edited by Arpad von Lazar and Robert Kaufman, pp. 34-58. Boston: Allyn and Bacon, 1969.

_____. ed. *The Peruvian Experiment: Continuity and Change under Military Rule.* Princeton, N.J.: Princeton University Press, 1975.

_____. "The Political Role of the Dominican Armed Forces: A Note on the 1963 Overthrow of Juan Bosch and the 1965 'Revolution'." *Journal of Inter-American Studies and World Affairs* 15 (August 1973):355-62.

Luckham, Robin. "A Comparative Typology of Civil-Military Relations." *Government and Opposition* (Winter 1971):5-36.

_____. *The Nigerian Military: A Sociological Analysis of Authority and Revolt 1960-1967.* New York: Cambridge University Press, 1971.

McAlister, Lyle N. "Recent Research and Writings on the Role of the Military in Latin America." *Latin American Research Review* 2, no. 1 (Fall 1966): 5-36.

McAlister, Lyle N.; Maingot, Anthony P.; and Potash, Robert A. *The Military in Latin American Sociopolitical Evolution: Four Case Studies.* Washington, D.C.: Center for Research in Social Systems, 1970.

Magdoff, Harry. "Militarism and Imperialism." *American Economic Review* 60 (May 1970):237-42.

Maier, Georg. *The Ecuadorian Presidential Elections of June 2, 1968: An Analysis.* Washington, D.C.: Institute for the Comparative Study of Political Systems, 1969.

Mamalakis, Markos. "The Theory of Sectoral Clashes and Coalitions Revisited." *Latin American Research Review* 6, no. 3 (Fall 1971):89-126.

Martz, John D. *Ecuador: Conflicting Political Culture and the Quest for Progress.* Boston: Allyn and Bacon, 1972.

Martz, Mary Jane. "Ecuador." In *Latin American Foreign Policies: An Analysis,* edited by Harold Davis and Larman Wilson, pp. 383-400. Baltimore: The Johns Hopkins University Press, 1975.

Maullin, Richard. *Soldiers, Guerrillas, and Politics in Colombia.* Santa Monica, Calif.: The Rand Corporation, 1970.

Mecham, J. Lloyd. "Latin American Constitutions: Nominal and Real." *Journal of Politics* 21, no. 2 (May 1959):258-75.

Merlo, Pedro. "Crecimiento de la población del Ecuador." *Indicadores Económicos* 1, no. 3 (July 1967):23-46.

_____. *Ecuador: Evaluación y ajuste de la población total del año 1960 al año 2000.* Centro Latinoamericano de Demografía, Series C, no. 113 (June 1959).

Middlebrook, Kevin, and Palmer, David Scott. *Military Government and Political Development: Lessons from Peru.* Sage Papers on Latin America, no. 01-054. Beverly Hills, Calif.: Sage Publications, 1975.

"Miembros de la fuerza aérea ecuatoriana." *El Universo,* 7 November 1961, p. 7.

Miguens, José Enrique. "The New Latin American Coup." In *Militarism in Developing Countries,* edited by Kenneth Fidel, pp. 99-123. New Brunswick, N.J.: Transaction Books, 1975.

Mills, C. Wright. *The Power Elite.* New York: Oxford University Press, 1959.

Ministerio de Educación Pública, Departamento de Planeamiento. "Tabla de sueldos básicos y funcionales del magisterio." Mimeographed. Quito, Ecuador: n.d.

Ministerio de Guerra (Ministerio de Defensa Nacional). *Memoria (Informe a la Nación),* annual series. Quito, Ecuador: 1839, 1846, 1847, 1849, 1855, 1871, 1888, 1900, 1901, 1904, 1905, 1906, 1942, 1943, 1948, 1952-1953, 1953-1954, 1954-1955, 1955-1956, 1960-1961.

Moncayo, Pedro. "Breve historia del Colegio Militar Eloy Alfaro." Manuscript. Quito, Ecuador, 1970.

Morse, Richard. "The Heritage of Latin America." In *The Founding of New Societies,* edited by Louis Hartz, pp. 123-77. New York: Harcourt, Brace & World, 1964.

Muñoz, Julio. *Doctrinas militares aplicadas en el Ecuador: historia y pedagogía militar.* Quito, Ecuador: Imprenta del Estado Mayor General, 1949.

"La Nación y las fuerzas armadas." Editorial in *El Comercio,* 5 March 1962, p. 4.

Needler, Martin. *Anatomy of a Coup d'Etat: Ecuador 1963.* Washington, D.C.: Institute for the Comparative Study of Political Systems, 1964.

_____. "The Causality of the Latin American Coup d'Etat: Some Numbers, Some Speculations." Paper presented to the American Political Science Association convention, Washington, D.C., September 1972.

_____. "The Latin American Military: Predatory Reactionaries or Modernizing Patriots." *Journal of Inter-American Studies* 11, no. 2 (April 1969):237-44.

_____. "Military Motivations in the Seizure of Power." *Latin American Research Review* 10, no. 13 (Winter 1975):62-78.

_____. "Political Development and Military Intervention in Latin America." *American Political Science Review* 60, no. 3 (September 1966):616-26.

_____. *Political Development in Latin America: Instability, Violence, and Evolutionary Change.* New York: Random House, 1968.

Nie, Norman; Bent, Dale; and Hull, Hadlai. *SPSS: Statistical Package for the Social Sciences.* New York: McGraw-Hill, 1970.

Nordlinger, Eric. "Soldiers in Mufti: The Impact of Military Rule on Economic and Social Change in Non-Western States." *American Political Science Review* 64, no. 4 (December 1970):1131-48.

North, Liisa. *Civil-Military Relations in Argentina, Chile, and Peru.* Berkeley, Calif.: Institute of International Studies, 1966.

North American Congress on Latin America. "Ecuador: Oil Up for Grabs." *Latin American and Empire Report* 9, no. 8 (November 1975):2-13.

"La nueva situación política." Editorial in *El Comercio,* 17 February 1972, p. 4.

*Nuevo Orden Nacional,* N.p., n.d.

Nun, José. *Latin America: The Hegemonic Crisis and the Military Coup.* Berkeley, Calif.: Institute of International Studies, 1969.

_____. "A Latin American Phenomenon: The Middle-Class Military Coup." In *Latin America: Reform or Revolution,* edited by James Petras and Maurice Zeitlin, pp. 146-85. Greenwich, Conn.: Fawcett Publications, 1969.

_____. "The Middle Class Military Coup." In *The Politics of Conformity in Latin America,* edited by Claudio Veliz, pp. 66-118. New York: Oxford University Press, 1967.

O'Donnell, Guillermo. "Modernización y golpes militares: teoría, comparación, y el caso argentino." Documento de trabajo, Instituto Torcuato di Tella, Centro de Investigaciones en Administración Pública, Buenos Aires, Argentina, 1972.

_____. *Modernization and Bureaucratic Authoritarianism: Studies in South American Politics.* Berkeley, Calif.: Institute of International Studies, 1973.

Olarte, A. "Función democrática de las fuerzas armadas." *Revista Militar de las Fuerzas Armadas Ecuatorianas* 2, no. 2-3 (September-October 1943):4-5.

"Organización de los ejércitos americanos." Reprint from *Memorial de Infantería (España), El Ejército Nacional* 3, no. 20 (1924):466-70.

Ozbudun, Ergun. "Established Revolution versus Unfinished Revolution: Contrasting Patterns of Democratization in Mexico and Turkey." In *Authoritarian Politics in Modern Society,* edited by Samuel P. Huntington and Clement Moore, pp. 380-405. New York: Basic Books, 1970.

Palacios Sáenz, Carlos. "¿Qué dictadura prefiere? " *El Universo,* 19 June 1963, p. 4.

Paredes Barros, Carlos. "Incidencia ecónomico y social del proceso de liquidación del huasipungo en la provincia de Pichincha." Master's thesis, Catholic University of Ecuador, 1967.

Pareja Diezcanseco, Alfredo. *Historia del Ecuador.* Quito, Ecuador: Editorial Colón, 1962.

Pattee, Richard. *Gabriel García Moreno y el Ecuador de su tiempo.* Mexico City: Editorial Jus, 1962.

Payne, James. *Labor and Politics in Peru.* New Haven: Yale University Press, 1965.

———. *Patterns of Conflict in Colombia.* New Haven: Yale University Press, 1968.

———. "Scoring System for Compiling Strike-Demonstration (Opposition) Score in the Dominican Republic." Mimeographed. N.p., n.d.

Phelan, John Leddy. *The Kingdom of Quito in the Seventeenth Century: Bureaucratic Politics in the Spanish Empire.* Madison: University of Wisconsin Press, 1967.

Pierce, Albert. *Fundamentals of Nonparametric Statistics.* Belmont, Calif.: Dickenson Publishing Co., 1970.

"Planteamientos que hacen los partidos políticos al pueblo ecuatoriano y a la junta militar de Gobierno, para el retorno del país al estado de derecho." Quito, Ecuador, 6 August 1965.

"Política de disoluciones." Editorial in *El Comercio,* 10 February 1972, p. 4.

"La posición del pueblo." Editorial in *El Comercio,* 1 March 1966, p. 4.

Potash, Robert A. *The Army and Politics in Argentina 1928-1945: Yrigoyen to Perón.* Stanford, Calif.: Stanford University Press, 1969.

*Presupuesto general del Gobierno Nacional de la República,* annual series. Quito, Ecuador: Talleres Gráficos Nacionales.

Price, Robert. "A Theoretical Approach to Military Rule in New States: Reference Group Theory and the Ghanaian Case." *World Politics* 13 (April 1971):399-430.

"Programa del Nuevo Orden Nacional." Mimeographed. Quito, Ecuador, 1963.

Putnam, Robert. "Toward Explaining Military Intervention in Latin American Politics." *World Politics* 20 (October 1967):83-110.

Pye, Lucian W. "Armies in the Process of Political Modernization." In *The Role of the Military in Underdeveloped Countries,* edited by John J. Johnson, pp. 69-90. Princeton, N.J.: Princeton University Press, 1962.

Quandt, William. *The Comparative Study of Political Elites.* Sage Professional Papers in Comparative Politics, no. 01-004. Beverly Hills, Calif.: Sage Publications, 1970.

Rankin, Richard. "The Expanding Institutional Concerns of the Latin American Military Establishments: A Review Article." *Latin American Research Review* 9, no. 1 (Spring 1974):81-108.

"Reforma agraria: entre el 'caos' y la justicia." *Nueva* 26 (January 1976):15.

"Respeto para las instituciones fundamentales del estado." Editorial in *Revista Militar de las Fuerzas Armadas Ecuatorianas* 4, no. 14 (May–June 1950):1–2.

Reyes, Oscar Efren. *Breve historia general del Ecuador.* 3 vols., 7th edition. Quito, Ecuador: Editorial "Fray Jodoco Ricke," 1967.

———. *Historia de la República, esquema de ideas y hechos del Ecuador, al partir de la emancipación.* Quito, Ecuador: Imprenta Nacional, 1931.

———. *Los últimos siete años.* Quito, Ecuador: Talleres Gráficos Nacionales, 1933.

Rodríguez Lara, Guillermo. Radio speech to the nation, quoted in *El Comercio,* 17 February 1972, p. 3.

Romero y Cordero, Remigio. "El Ejército en cien años de vida republicana." *El Ejército Nacional* 67 (1933):209–10.

Ronfeldt, David. "Patterns of Civil-Military Rule." In *Latin America in the 1970s,* edited by Luigi Einaudi, pp. 74–98. Santa Monica, Calif.: The Rand Corporation, 1972.

Ropp, Steve C. "The Military and Urbanization in Latin America: Some Implications of Trends in Recruitment." *Inter-American Economic Affairs* 24, no. 2 (Autumn 1970):27–35.

Ruddle, Kenneth, and Hamour, Mukhtar, eds. *Statistical Abstract of Latin America 1970.* Los Angeles: Latin American Center of the University of California, 1971.

Russell, D.E.H. *Rebellion, Revolution, and Armed Force.* New York: Academic Press, 1974.

Salazar Alvarado, Francisco. *Mensaje a la Asamblea General del Partido Conservador.* Quito, Ecuador, 1963.

———. *Mensaje a la Asamblea General del Partido Conservador Ecuatoriano.* Quito, Ecuador, 1961.

Sands, William F. *Our Jungle Diplomacy.* Chapel Hill: University of North Carolina Press, 1944.

Saunders, Thomas G. "Development and Security are Linked in a Relationship of Mutual Causality." *American Universities Field Staff Reports.* East Coast South America Series 15, no. 3.

Saxe-Fernandez, John. "The Central American Defense Council and *Pax Americana.*" In *Latin American Radicalism,* edited by Irving Horowitz, Josue de Castro, and John Gerassi, pp. 75–96. New York: Random House, 1969.

Schmitter, Philippe C. "Foreign Military Assistance, National Military Spending, and Military Rule in Latin America." In *Military Rule in Latin America: Functions, Consequences, and Perspectives,* edited by Philippe C. Schmitter, pp. 117–87. Beverly Hills, Calif.: Sage Publications, 1973.

———. *Interest Conflict and Political Change in Brazil.* Stanford, Calif.: Stanford University Press, 1971.

———. "Military Intervention, Political Competitiveness, and Public Policy in Latin America, 1950-1967." In *On Military Intervention and Military*

*Regimes,* edited by Morris Janowitz and Jacques van Doorn, pp. 425–506. Rotterdam: Rotterdam University Press, 1971.

———. "The Portugalization of Brazil? " In *Authoritarian Brazil: Origins, Policies, and Future,* edited by Alfred C. Stepan, pp. 179–232. New Haven: Yale University Press, 1973.

Schneider, Ronald M. *The Political System of Brazil.* New York: Columbia University Press, 1971.

Searing, Donald. "The Comparative Study of Elite Socialization." *Comparative Political Studies* 1 (January 1969):471–99.

Sellers, Robert, ed. *The Reference Handbook of the Armed Forces of the World.* Garden City, N.J.: Robert Sellers and Assoc., 1968.

Silvert, Kalman. *The Conflict Society.* New Orleans, La.: Hauser Press, 1961.

Skidmore, Thomas. *Politics in Brazil, 1930–1964: An Experiment in Democracy.* New York: Oxford University Press, 1967.

Smith, Peter. *Politics and Beef in Argentina: Patterns of Conflict and Change.* New York: Columbia University Press, 1969.

Solaun, Mauricio, and Quinn, Michael. *Sinners and Heretics: The Politics of Military Intervention in Latin America.* Urbana: University of Illinois Press, 1973.

"Solución política inevitable." Editorial in *El Comercio,* 29 March 1966, p. 4.

Stepan, Alfred C. *The Military in Politics: Changing Patterns in Brazil.* Princeton, N.J.: Princeton University Press, 1971.

———. "The 'New Professionalism' of Internal Warfare and Military Role Expansion." In *Authoritarian Brazil: Origins, Policies, and Future,* edited by Alfred C. Stepan, pp. 47–68. New Haven: Yale University Press, 1973.

———. *State and Society in Peru.* Princeton, N.J.: Princeton University Press, 1977.

Szulc, Tad. *The Winds of Revolution.* New York: Frederick A. Praeger, 1963.

Thompson, William R. *The Grievances of Military Coup Makers.* Sage Professional Papers in Comparative Politics 4, no. 01–047. Beverly Hills, Calif.: Sage Publications, 1973.

———. "Regime Vulnerability and the Military Coup." *Comparative Politics* 8, no. 4 (July 1975):459–87.

Tyson, Brady. "The Emerging Role of the Military as National Modernizers and Managers in Latin America: The Cases of Brazil and Peru." In *Latin American Prospects for the 1970's,* edited by David Pollock and Arch Ritter, pp. 107–30. New York: Frederick A. Praeger, 1973.

United States Agency for International Development. *Ecuador: Review of Financial Developments 1960–1969.* Airgram. Quito, Ecuador: Department of State, 1969.

United States Arms Control and Disarmament Agency, *World Military Expenditures 1971.* Washington, D.C.: Bureau of Economic Affairs, 1971.

Urrutia Suárez, Francisco. *Apuntes para la historia: la agresión peruana.* Quito, Ecuador: Editorial Ecuatoriana, 1968.

Velasco Ibarra, José María. *Conciencia o barbarie.* Medellín, Colombia: Editorial Atlántida, 1936.

"Vigencia de lo constitucional." Editorial in *El Comercio*, 23 December 1954, p. 4.

Villanueva, Víctor. *¿Nueva mentalidad militar en el Perú?* Lima, Peru: Editorial Juan Mejía Baca, 1969.

Villegas, Osiris Guillermo. *Políticas y estratégias para el desarrollo y la seguridad nacional.* Buenos Aires, Argentina: Editorial Pleamar, 1969.

Visitaduría General de la Administración. *El delito del 22 de diciembre y el constitucionalismo nacional.* Quito, Ecuador: Talleres Gráficos Nacionales, 1955.

von Behring, Mayor. "Evolución cultural de nuestro ejército." *Revista Militar de las Fuerzas Armadas Ecuatorianas* 2, no. 6 (February–March 1934):4–8.

Weaver, Jerry. "Assessing the Impact of Military Rule: Alternative Approaches." In *Military Rule in Latin America: Functions, Consequences, and Perspectives,* edited by Philippe C. Schmitter, pp. 58–116. Beverly Hills, Calif.: Sage Publications, 1973.

Wildavsky, Aaron. *The Politics of the Budgetary Process.* Boston: Little, Brown, 1964.

Wolpin, Miles. "External Political Socialization as a Source of Conservative Military Behavior in the Third World." *Studies in Comparative International Development* 8, no. 1 (January 1973):3–23.

Wood, David. *Armed Forces in Central and South America.* Adelphi Papers, no. 34. London: The Institute for Strategic Studies, 1967.

Wright, Freeman. *The Upper Level Public Administrator in Ecuador.* Institute of Administrative Studies, Central University, Quito, Ecuador: Editorial "Fray Jodoco Ricke," 1968.

Zolberg, Aristide. "Military Rule and Political Development in Tropical Africa." In *Military Profession and Military Regimes: Commitments and Conflicts,* edited by Jacques van Doorn. The Hague: Mouton and Co., 1969.

Zuvekas, Clarence. "Economic Planning in Ecuador: An Evaluation." *Inter-American Economic Affairs* 25, no. 4 (Spring 1972):39–69.

_____. "Ecuador: Selected Economic Data." Mimeographed. Quito, Ecuador: USAID, 1970.

_____. *The Ecuadorean Devaluation of 1970: Causes and Consequences.* State University of New York at Buffalo, Council on International Studies, Special Studies no. 33.

_____. "A Note on Capital Flight from Ecuador." Mimeographed. Quito, Ecuador: USAID, 1969.

## Supplementary Bibliography on Ecuador

Aguirre, Manuel Augustín. "Report from Ecuador." *Monthly Review* 13 (February 1962):456–60.

Barrera, Isaac J. "La política." In Unión Nacional de Periodistas, *Realidad y posibilidad del Ecuador,* pp. 139–44. Quito, Ecuador: Talleres Gráficos Nacionales, 1946.

Belfrage, Cedric. "El Ecuador en 1963: en la puerta hay un hombre armado." *Cuadernos Americanos* 137 (January–February 1964):31–47.

Blanksten, George I. "Ecuador: The Politics of Instability." In *Political Systems of Latin America,* edited by Martin Needler, pp. 69–90. Princeton, N.J.: Van Nostrand, 1964.

Borrero, Manuel María. *La revolución quiteña 1809-1812.* Quito, Ecuador: Editorial Espejo, 1961.

Brownrigg, Leslie. "Interest Groups in Regime Changes in Ecuador." *Inter-American Economic Affairs* 28, no. 1 (Summer 1974):3–18.

Bushnell, David. *The Santander Regime in Gran Colombia.* Newark: University of Delaware Press, 1954.

Castro Jijón, Ramón. "Breve apuntes sobre la historia de la escuela naval de Ecuador." *Revista del Colegio Militar Eloy Alfaro* 25 (June 1962):49–50.

Cevallos, Pedro Fermín. *Selecciones.* Biblioteca Mínima Ecuatoriana, México: Editorial J. M. Cajica, 1958.

*Codigo militar de la República del Ecuador.* Quito, Ecuador: Imprenta Nacional, 1908.

*Constitution of the Republic of Ecuador, 1946.* Washington, D.C.: Pan American Union, 1961.

Córdova, Andrés F. "La vida política ecuatoriana a través de la Constitución décima tercera." *Revista del Centro de Estudios Históricos y Geográficos de Cuenca* 7–8 (1936-1938):369–85.

Díaz, Antonio, "Cambios sociales de las clases dominantes del Ecuador." *Revista Mexicana de Sociología* 25 (May–August 1963):721–36.

————. "Los partidos políticos del Ecuador." *Política* (Caracas), 2, no. 28 (November 1963):105–16.

Galarza Arízaga, Rafael. *Esquema político del Ecuador.* Guayaquil, Ecuador: Editorial Alborado, 1963.

Grayson, George. "Populism, Petroleum, and Politics in Ecuador." *Current History* 68, no. 401 (January 1975):15–19, 39–40.

Guerrero, Carlos A. "El ejército y la política." *El Ejército Nacional* 11, no. 63 (1932):324–26.

Hassaurek, Friedrich. *Four Years among the Ecuadorians.* Edited by C. Harvey Gardiner. Carbondale: Southern Illinois University Press, 1967.

Howe, George. "García Moreno's Efforts to Unite Ecuador and France." *Hispanic American Historical Review* 16, no. 2 (May 1936):257–62.

Hurtado, Oswaldo. *Dos mundos superpuestos: ensayo de diagnóstico de la realidad ecuatoriana.* Quito, Ecuador: Instituto Ecuatoriano de Planificación para el Desarrollo Social, 1969.

Krieder, Emil and Key, E. Dwayne. "The Ecuadorian Sugar Conflict and the Variable Import Levy." *Inter-American Economic Affairs* 23, no. 2. (Autumn 1969):39–42.

Linke, Lilo. *Ecuador: Country of Contrasts.* 3rd edition. New York: Oxford University Press, 1960.

Llerena, José Alfredo. *Frustración política en 22 años.* Quito, Ecuador: Casa de la Cultura Ecuatoriana, 1959.

Loor, Wilfredo. *Estudios históricos-políticos.* Quito, Ecuador: Editorial Ecuatoriana, 1939.

McLeod, Jack; Rush, Ramona; and Friederick, Karl, "The Mass Media and Political Information in Quito, Ecuador." *Public Opinion Quarterly* 32 (Winter 1968-1969):575-87.

Maier, Georg. "The Impact of *Velasquismo* on the Ecuadorian Political System." Ph.D. dissertation, University of Florida, 1966.

――――. "Structure and Functioning of Ecuador's Chambers." *Specialia* 1 (1969):27-33.

Marchán Ramírez, Octaviano. *Los heroes ecuatorianos de 1941.* Ambato, Ecuador: Editorial Atenas, 1966.

Maynard, Eileen, ed. *The Indians of Colta: Essays on the Colta Lake Zone, Chimborazo, Ecuador.* Ithaca, N.Y.: Cornell University, 1966.

Melpoder, Anne E. "Personalism and Regionalism in Ecuadorian Presidential Elections, 1948-1968." Master's thesis, University of Florida, 1970.

Moncayo, Pedro. *El Ecuador de 1825 a 1875, sus hombres, sus instituciones, y sus leyes.* Santiago, Chile: Rafael Jover, 1885.

Nett, Emily. "The Functional Elites of Quito." *Journal of Inter-American Studies and World Affairs* 13, no. 2 (January 1971):112-20.

Orellana, J. Gonzalo, ed. *Resúmen histórico del Ecuador, 1830-1930, 1947-8.* Quito, Ecuador: Editorial "Fray Jodoco Ricke," 1948.

Palacios Sáenz, Carlos. *La conveniencia del régimen parliamentario en el Ecuador.* Biblioteca Mínima de Ecuatorianidad, no. 6. Guayaquil, Ecuador: Universidad de Guayaquil, 1947.

Pazmiño, Alfonso. "La cooperativa militar." *Revista Militar de las Fuerzas Armadas Ecuatorianas* 2, no. 6 (February-March 1934):83-86.

Plaza Lasso, Galo. *Problems of Democracy in Latin America.* Chapel Hill: University of North Carolina Press, 1955.

Puma, Carlos E. *Prismas militares: escenas de cuartel.* Quito, Ecuador: Talleres Gráficos del Colegio Militar, 1939.

Pyne, Peter. "Legislatures and Development: The Case of Ecuador 1960-61," *Comparative Political Studies* 9, no. 1 (April, 1976):43-68.

――――. "The Role of Congress in the Ecuadorian Political System and its Contribution to the Overthrow of President Velasco in 1961." University of Glasgow, Institute of Latin American Studies, *Occasional Papers,* no. 7, 1973.

Redclift, M. R. "Agrarian Reform and Peasant Organization in the Guayas Basin, Ecuador," *Inter-American Economic Affairs* 30, no. 1 (Summer 1976): 3-28.

Reyes, Jorge. "Los partidos como problemas." *El Comercio,* 11 November 1966, p. 4.

Saunders, John V. "Man-Land Relations in Ecuador." *Rural Sociology* 26, no. 1 (March 1961):57-69.

Szazdi, Adam. "Historiography of the Republic of Ecuador." *Hispanic American Historical Review* 44 (November 1964):503-50.

Terry, Adrian R. *Travels in the Equatorial Regions of South America in 1832.* Hartford, Conn.: Cooke and Co., 1834.

Torres Caicedo, Reinaldo. *Los diferentes estratos socioeconómicos del Ecuador: ensayos de cuantificación.* Quito, Ecuador: Junta Nacional de Planificación, 1960.

Viteri, Telmo. "Legislacion militar ecuatoriana, su origen, desarrollo, y evolución." *El Ejército Nacional* 3, no. 21 (1924):561-92.

Weil, Thomas; Black, Jan Knippers; Blutstein, Howard I.; McNorris, David S.; Mersereau, Mildred Gill; Munson, Frederick O.; and Parachini, Kathryn E. *Area Handbook for Ecuador.* Washington, D.C.: U.S. Government Printing Office, 1973.

Whitten, Norman. *Class, Kinship, and Power in an Ecuadorian Town.* Stanford, Calif.: Stanford University Press, 1965.

———. "Strategies of Adaptive Mobility in the Colombian-Ecuadorian Litoral." *American Anthropologist* 71, no. 2 (April 1969):228-42.

# Index

*Acción Revolucionaria Nacionalista Ecuatoriana* (ARNE), 41, 47, 56, 57, 66, 117, 152
Acosta Velasco, Jorge, 176–77
Africa, armed forces of, 22
Agency for International Development (AID), United States, 67
Agrarian reform: congressional barriers to, 156; of 1964, 66, 202 nn. 7, 8; of 1974, 182–83
Air force: officers of, compared to army officers, 94–96; organizational structure of, 23–24; pay of, 29; political role of, 23–24, 130, 197 n. 36; position of, 50–51, 176, 183–84; recruitment of, 25; size of, 21; training of, 20–21
Alba, Victor, 89
Alfaro, General Eloy, 15–16
Allende Gossens, Salvador, 4
Alliance for Progress, 55, 154. *See also* Reform
Anderson, Charles, 169
Anticommunism: and CIA, 56, 117; and U.S. military influence, 118; in Ecuador, 48, 56, 58, 61; in military, 8, 57, 117–21. *See also* Communist threat
Antimilitarism: after 1966, 144–45, 175; in early twentieth century, 16
Arbiter role definition: and coup behavior, 132–34; and public opinion, 113, 131; definition of, 131; shift toward, 135–45
Argentina, 11, 42, 88, 185, 219 n. 33; armed forces of, 25, 137; military professionalization in, 33, 163
Armed forces, Ecuadorian: budget of, 21–22; educational institutions of, 19–21; history of, 14–19; organizational structure of, 23–24; professionalization of, 30–34, 162–64; salaries, severance pay, and pensions of, 28–29, 32–33; service differences in, 21, 22, 23; size of, 21–22. *See also* Military coup d'état; Military officers; Military socialization; Recruitment patterns, military

Arosemena Gómez, Otto, 174–75
Arosemena Monroy, Carlos Julio: after 1966, 178, 181, 183, 184; and airport reception scandal, 59; and military junta, 144–45; banquet incident involving, 61; biographical sketch of, 55–56; *desgobierno* under, 58–63; foreign policy of, 56, 117, 199 n. 2, 209 n. 2; government of, 55–64, 133–34; political support for, 58, 154; relationship of, with José María Velasco Ibarra, 41, 48–52, 55, 199 n. 1
Arregui Viteri, Colonel Carlos, 59
Aulestia Mier, General Víctor, 42, 50, 59–60, 61, 178–79, 182, 184, 196 n. 23, 219 n. 43
Autonomous agencies, 1964 dispute over, 68

Bernbaum, Maurice, 60
Brazil: armed forces of, 26–27, 32–33, 164; military coups in, 201 n. 49; military government of, 89, 143, 186
Bucaram, Asaad, 64, 178–81, 219 nn. 34, 35
Burundi, 21

Cabrera Sevilla, General Luis, 61–62, 65–66, 67, 71
Caldera, Rafael, 6
*Calle, La,* 61
Capability to govern: civilian, 138–45, 162; impact of, on role definitions, 136–45, 162; military, 137–45, 162, 164
Capital flight, 48, 59, 66, 157–58
Castro, Fidel, 55, 58, 209 n. 1
Castro Jijón, Contralmirante Ramón, 61–62, 65, 71, 201 n. 3
Catholic church: anticommunism of, 48, 198 n. 6; schools of, and military attitudes, 93–94
Caudillos, nineteenth-century, 14–16, 163; decline of, 16–18
Center for Higher Military Studies (CAEM), Peruvian, 21, 59, 164

Central University: 1963 restructuring of, 66; 1966 military attack on, 71, 105; recruitment to, as compared to the Colegio Militar, 193 n. 53; riots and demonstrations at, 71, 109. *See also* Student demonstrations

Chambers of Agriculture, 49, 60, 156, 182. *See also* Land-owning aristocracy

Chambers of Commerce, 49, 60, 69, 70, 156, 175, 202 n. 16. *See also* Commercial oligarchy

Chambers of Industry, 60, 69

*Chatarra* scandal, 58, 123, 211 n. 26

Chile, 4, 137, 163

Chimborazo battalion, revolt of, 50, 91, 105–6

C.I.A. *See* United States Central Intelligence Agency

Civil-military relations: in Argentina, 6, 24, 33, 137, 163; in Brazil, 24, 201 n. 49; in Ecuador, 15–19, 32, 129–45, 149–59, 167–69

Civil wars, Ecuadorian, 15–16

Classic professionalist role definition: and coup decisions, 132–33; decline of, 137; definition of, 129–30

Class structure, 15–17, 142–43, 150–52; stability of, 169–72

Coalitions: civil-military, 154–56; formation of, 164–65; within military, 164–67

Coastal plutocracy. *See* Commercial oligarchy

Colegio Militar: and 1971 revolt, 177; cadets of, 33; curriculum of, 20, 192 n. 30; history of, 21; recruitment to, 24–27, 191 n. 22, 193 n. 53

Colombia, 195 n. 72

*Comercio, El,* 41, 114, 209 n. 19; attitude toward coups, 44, 64, 71, 116, 119; editorial ratings of government performance, 44, 53, 64, 73, 115, 180, 209 n. 21, 219 n. 31

Command and general staff school. *See* War academy

Commercial oligarchy: after 1972, 181, 183; and devaluations, 48, 176; in conflict with the military junta, 68–72, 144, 157–58; opposition of, to Arosemena, 55, 60–61, 63–64, 156–57; origins of, 15; political position of, 16, 18, 49, 53; political resources of, 70, 153, 156–58. *See also* Guayaquil, elites

Communist party of Ecuador, 47, 56, 60, 150

Communist threat: and Cuban revolution, 117, 119–20; and public disorders, 107; as a decision criterion, 8, 54, 62, 73, 79, 81, 85, 87, 117–19, 215 n. 6; exaggeration of, 117; institutional basis for fears of, 8, 119–21, 123, 126; military fears of, 57, 58, 63, 88, 92, 119–21, 159; military response to, 57, 66, 104, 119, 142–43

Concentration of Popular Forces (CFP), 40, 41, 64, 69, 152, 178

Confederation of Ecuadorian Workers (CTE), 49, 56, 61, 64, 154

Congress, Ecuadorian: after 1966, 145, 175, 179; and Arosemena, 58–59, 61, 62; and socioeconomic reform, 104, 156–57, 215 n. 23; and Velasco coup, 48–52, 198 n. 13; 1948–1960, 40, 41

Conservative party, 15, 18, 48, 55, 56, 57, 67, 82, 156, 184; in elections, 39, 41, 45, 47, 174; position of, in coups, 58, 59, 61, 69, 184

Conspiracies, 164–65, 200 n. 25; 1948–1960, 40, 41; 1963, 59–60, 164

Constituent Assembly, 1967, 145, 174; proposals for, 68

Constitution, Ecuadorian: definition of military role in, 51, 101–2, 207 n. 2; 1830, 15, 102; 1945, 59; 1946, 39, 101–2, 104; 1967, 104, 175, 178; on literacy and citizenship, 191 n. 24; on public order, 104; proposed reforms in, 67, 68–69

Constitutionalist front, 69–70, 144

Constitutionalist role definition: and coup behavior, 132–34; decline of, 59, 103–4, 119, 128, 135, 137–39; definition of, 130–31; origins of, 102, 103, 127

Constitutionality: and personal interests, 84, 101; and Velasco government in 1954, 42–45; and Velasco government in 1961, 49–52, 102; as a decision criterion, 54, 62, 79, 81, 83–86, 87, 101, 132–33, 208 n. 14

Cordero Crespo, Gonzalo, 47

Córdova, Andrés F., 174–75, 215 n. 11

Corporate indentifications, 125–28, 163, 170

Counterinsurgency: and communist threat, 8, 142; and developmentalist role definition, 132, 142–43; and internal security, 110, 142–43; and U.S. military training, 8, 141, 143

Coup decision-making, collective: changes in, 24, 168; patterns of, 164–67

Coup d'état. *See* Military coup d'état

Coup-motivating events. *See* Decision criteria for military coups

Coup positions of individual officers: frequency distribution of, 165–66; self-explanations of, 43, 63, 78–79

Cross-national research on military coups, 11, 87–88

Cuba: and communist threat, 57, 209 n. 1; armed forces of, 8, 172–73; conflict between, and the United States, 56; relations of, with Ecuador, 56–58, 182; revolution in, 159, 170, 172

Cuenca: revolt of 1962, 57–58; riots of 1961, 49

Decision criteria for military coups: and role definitions, 132–34; and theoretical framework, 3–4; communist threat, 8, 79, 81, 85, 87; constitutional norm, 79, 81, 83, 84, 85, 86; electoral threat, 79, 88, 180–81; hypotheses on, 6–9, 77; institutional interests, 7–8, 78–79, 81, 85, 87; 1948–1966, 86–87, 160; 1954, 83–84, 86; 1961, 84–85, 86; 1963, 85, 86; 1966, 85–86; 1970, 179; 1971, 179; 1972, 180–81; personal political orientations, 7, 79, 82–83; personal ties, 78, 81, 83, 84, 85, 87; public disorders, 7, 78, 81, 85, 87; public opinion, 6–7, 78, 81, 84, 85, 87; socioeconomic reform, 79, 83, 85–86, 87; underlying motives for, 125–28

Demonstrations. *See* Public disorders; Riots and demonstrations

*Desgobierno. See* Arosemena Monroy, Carlos Julio

Devaluation: 1961, 48, 153; 1970, 176

Developmentalist role definition: and coup behavior, 132–34, 143–44, 171, 180–81, 185; and high professionalization, 163–64; and national security, 141, 168; and the United States, 141; definition of, 131–32

Development plan, 66

*Dictablanda, La. See* Military junta

Division of El Oro, 23; political position of, 42, 51, 60, 62, 177

Ecuador, economy of: after 1972, 181–83; and balance of payments, 40, 48, 58, 59, 157, 175, 176; and export trends, 40, 41, 44, 45, 48, 59, 66, 68, 150–51, 153, 157, 175, 176, 181, 215 n. 7, 216 n. 27; and growth rates, 41, 45, 48, 59, 66, 68, 70, 150–51, 157, 159, 214 n. 2; and inflation, 40, 41, 45, 48, 59, 176, 181, 182; and political

tensions, 48, 150–59, 183; and recession of 1955–1963, 45–46, 151; oil boom in, 181–83; problems in, 45–46, 48, 151, 152, 157–58, 183; unemployment in, 45, 48, 215 n. 8

Ecuador, foreign policy of: and Cuba, 56–58; and East Europe, 58; and Organization of American States, 56; and the United States, 61. *See also* 1941 war with Peru; Rio Protocol; Two-hundred-mile limit; United States-Ecuadorian relations

Ecuador, government of: Council of State, 51; National Defense Board, 52, 210 n. 17; National Monetary Board, 156; National Planning Board, 67, 202 n. 6; National Security Council, 141–42; Supreme Court, 175, 178; Supreme Electoral Board, 57–58. *See also* Congress, Ecuadorian

Ecuadorian military. *See* Armed forces, Ecuadorian

Elections: as a factor in military coups, 8, 54, 64, 73, 88, 180–81, 185, 219 n. 34; congressional, 40, 41, 57, 58, 175; 1948, 39–40; 1952, 41; 1956, 45; 1960, 47; 1968, 174–75, 218 n. 2; 1972, 178, 180–81, 210 n. 20; pre-1948, 18, 191 n. 24

Elites. *See* Commercial oligarchy; Land-owning aristocracy

Escuela Aerea, 20

Escuela de Paracaidistas, 175

Escuela de Perfeccionamiento, 176

Escuela Militar, 17, 18–19. *See also* Colegio Militar

Escuela Naval, 20

Exports: and elites, 15; dependency on primary products for, 150–52, 158–59. *See also* Ecuador, economy of, and export trends

FEUE (Federation of University Students of Ecuador), 49, 56, 66

Finer, Samuel, 7

Fishing limits. *See* Two-hundred-mile limit

Flores, General Juan José, 15, 190 n. 9

Foreign military training, 20, 57; and coup behavior, 118–19; and role definitions, 140–41; in Argentina, Brazil, Spain, and Italy, 41, 66, 140–41, 199 n. 8; in the United States, 20, 65–66, 118, 141, 192 n. 35

Freile Posso, Colonel Guillermo, 61, 66–70

Frente Civilista, 183, 184

Frente Democrático Nacional (FDN), 47, 58

Gallegos Toledo, Camilo, 52
Gándara Enríquez, General Marcos, 60–62, 65–67, 71, 154, 155
García Moreno, Gabriel, 190 n. 9
General staff of the armed forces, structure of, 23
Guayaquil: decline of, 181; elites of, 48, 114, 143, 156–58, 178; 1959 riots in, 45–46, 109. *See also* Commercial oligarchy
Guerrilla movements: in Ecuador, 58; in Latin America, 209 n. 1
Guevara Moreno, Carlos, 40

Hidalgo politics, 15–16, 190 n. 7
High command: assignment to, 32, 197 n. 4, 199 n. 47; definition of, 23; position of, 42, 49–52, 57, 61–62
*Huasipungo,* 202 n. 8. *See also* Agrarian reform
Huntington, Samuel, 5, 10, 14, 156, 212 n. 51

Identifications underlying decision criteria, 125–28, 163, 170
Illiteracy, 27; and disenfranchisement, 191 n. 24; and military recruitment, 27
Indians, Andean, 15; recruitment of, 27–28
Industrialists, favorable policies for, 69
Institutional characteristics of military and coup behavior, 12, 14, 185. *See also* Armed forces, Ecuadorian; Professionalization
Institutional interests of the military: after 1966, 127, 144–45, 176–77, 179, 214 n. 55; as a decision criterion, 7–8, 78–79, 81, 85, 87, 121–24, 211 n. 31; under Arosemena, 59, 63, 122–23, 210 n. 25; under the military junta, 72, 123–24; under Plaza, 122; under Ponce, 45–46; under Valasco, 43–44, 48, 54, 121, 122, 138
Institutionalized coup d'état: and political development, 12–13, 169–73; and socioeconomic change, 12–13, 169–73; causes of, 24, 170
Instituto de Altos Estudios Nacionales, 142, 169, 192 n. 36
Internal security. *See* counterinsurgency
Interview sample, 77–78, 203 n. 2

Janowitz, Morris, 10, 89
Johnson, John J., 6, 10, 11

Junta Constitucionalista, 69–70, 144

Labor unions, 154. *See also* Confederation of Ecuadorian Workers; Strikes, labor
Lambert, Jacques, 32, 195 n. 74
Land-owning aristocracy: opposition of, to agrarian reform, 67, 114, 182–83, 202 n. 8; opposition of, to Arosemena, 60, 156–57; opposition of, to military junta, 67, 157; political position of, 49, 53; political resources of, 156–57
Liberal party, 15, 16, 18, 55, 67, 82, 114, 128, 150, 154, 156, 215 n. 11, 218 n. 7; in elections, 39, 41, 45, 47, 174; position of, in coups, 44, 58, 60, 69
Lieuwen, Edwin, 6

Mancheno, Colonel Carlos, and unsuccessful coup of 1947, 19, 102
Marginality. *See* Subproletariat
Mass participation: and legitimacy, 170; and military coups, 168, 170; under military governments, 171, 215 n. 16
Merchants. *See* Commercial oligarchy
Middle class, 125; in Ecuador, 126, 211 nn. 41, 42
Middle-class military: in Ecuador, 18–19, 125–28, 211 n. 43; theory of, 10
Military autonomy: and professionalization, 32–33; assertion of, 176–78; lack of, 18–19, 32–33, 191 n. 26, 195 n. 74
Military budgets: criteria for evaluation of, 123–24; military perceptions of, 121–24; trends in, 122, 124
Military coup d'état: and political catharsis, 169–73; and revolutionary change, 170–73; 1954, 41–44; 1961, 47–54; 1963, 55–64; 1966, 65–73; 1970, 175, 179; 1972, 145, 176–81; 1975, 181–84; 1976, 184; theoretical framework for the analysis of, 3–6, 11–12
Military government: after 1972, 181–84; and military self-confidence, 181; institutional, 93; reformist, 124, 171; research on, 185, 213 n. 46. *See also* Brazil, military government of; Peru, military government of
Military institution, reification of, 127–28
Military junta, 1963–1966, 65–73, 157–58; extrication plans of, 67, 68–69; *la dictablanda,* 68, 69, 83, 143; military opposition to, 69–73, 105, 143–44;

securing political support for, 154–55; socioeconomic reforms under, 66–72, 143

Military oath, 102–3, 212 n. 18

Military officers: economic and social status of, 17–18, 28–30, 137; opposition to politics among, 155–56, 171; perceptions of civilians by, 17–18, 162; personal political orientations of, 7, 79, 82–83; self-confidence of, 137–45, 162

Military revolts: Chimborazo battalion 1961, 50; Cuenca 1962, 57–58, 209 n. 12; War academy 1971, 176–77, 179, 218 n. 13

Military role expansion, 134–45, 168; and professionalization, 162–64, 168. *See also* Role definitions

Military socialization: content of, 17–18, 20, 102–3, 127–28; impact of, 19–20, 96, 128

Mobilization. *See* Mass participation

Modernization: impact on participation of, 152; trends in, 150–53, 169

Naranjo Campaña, Colonel Aurelio, 57, 59, 65, 68

National Arosemenista Movement, 58

National interests: and institutional interests of military, 7, 127–28; as a rationalization for coups, 9, 131

National security and development, 132, 141–45. *See also* Developmentalist role definition

National Velasquista Movement, 48, 67, 152, 178

Navy: organizational structure of, 23; political role of, 23–24, 206 n. 16; position of, 51, 182, 219 n. 42; recruitment of, 25; size of, 22

Nebot, Jaime, 42, 44, 178

Needler, Martin, 63, 89, 164–65

1941 war with Peru, 19, 142; impact of, on military, 19–20, 102, 127, 137, 163. *See also* Rio Protocol

*Nuevo Orden Nacional,* 59–60, 61–62, 201 n. 43, 218 n. 11

Nun, José, 7, 10, 89, 125–28

Oil exports: and economic conditions, 181; and multinational corporations, 181, 183; and state power, 181

Organization of American States: Punta del Este conference of, 56; sanctions of, against Cuba, 56

Parochial education and military conservatism, 93–94

Parra, Antonio, 47

Payne, James, 107, 208 n. 28

Perceived government performance and coup decisions, 79–82, 99

Personal backgrounds of military officers: age and rank in, 90–91; and coup behavior, 19, 89–96, 206 n. 23; and personal ties, 90–91; branch of service in, 94–96; education in, 93–94; military families in, 91–93

Personal political orientations of officers, 7, 79, 82–83

Personal ties and antagonisms: as a decision criterion, 43, 52–53, 72, 78, 81, 83, 84, 85, 87, 219 n. 37; collective impact of, 167

Peru, 25, 88, 182, 185; and border tension with Ecuador, 40; military government of, 144, 185; military professionalization in, 32, 33, 195 n. 72. *See also* Center for Higher Military Studies; 1941 war with Peru; Rio Protocol

Plaza, Galo, 39–40, 55

Plaza, General Leonidas, 15, 16

Political culture, 152

Political development: and mass mobilization, 170; and military coups, 169; and political institutions, 169; and socioeconomic reform, 170; in Ecuador, 150; theory of, 169

Political instability: and military intervention, 170; and social change, 171; in Ecuador, 15–16, 149, 158; in Latin America, 169, 190 n. 8; in Third World, 169

Political institutionalization: and military professionalization, 195 n. 85, 212 n. 51; and political development, 5, 169–70

Political institutions, Ecuadorian. *See* Congress, Ecuadorian; Political parties

Political participation: impact of, 152, 159, 169; trends in, 152–53, 169

Political parties, 18, 154–55, 215 n. 12. See also *Acción Revolucionaria Nacionalista Ecuatoriana;* Communist party of Ecuador; Concentration of Popular Forces; Conservative party; Liberal party; National Arosemenista Movement; Populism; Revolutionary Socialist party; Social Christian Movement; Socialist party

Ponce Enríquez, Camilo, 41–47, 68, 70, 174–75, 178, 181, 183, 184, 218 n. 20

Populism, 47, 151–54; and revolutionary change, 170–71. *See also* Bucaram, Asaad; Velasco Ibarra, José María

Praetorian politics. *See* Political development

Pratt, Colonel Charles, 60

Price, Robert, 10, 210 n. 6

Professionalism: and professionalization, 194 n. 69; classic, 9; new, 9. *See also* Classic professionalist role definition

Professionalization: and civil-military relations, 12, 32, 125, 166–68, 170; and institutional identification, 34, 96, 164, 170; and role definitions, 162–64; comparative levels of, 30–34, 194 n. 71; high levels of, 31, 162–64; low levels of, 163; minimal, impact of, 15–19; of Ecuadorian military, 15–19, 30–34

Public disorders: as a decision criterion, 7, 44, 52, 64, 71, 72, 78, 81, 85, 87, 104–10, 132, 179; concerns underlying, 106, 127; index of, 53–54, 72, 107–8, 199 n. 4, 208 n. 28; popular versus subversive nature of, 107, 109–10, 134

Public opinion: and arbiter role definition, 113; and public disorders, 109, 112, 114, 116; as a decision criterion, 6–7, 52–53, 62, 72, 78, 81, 84, 85, 87, 111 –16, 126–27, 179; perceptions of, 44, 54, 63–64, 112, 113–16, 159

Public order, maintenance of, 104, 130. *See also* Public disorders

Recruitment patterns, military: and perceptions of public opinion, 7; changes in, 17; compared to other countries, 25–27; of officers, 17, 24–27, 191 n. 20, 192 n. 38, 194 n. 55; of soldiers, 27–28

Re-election, presidential, military opposition to, 67, 69, 185

Reform: agrarian, 66, 114, 155; and counterinsurgency, 142–43; opposition to, 60, 114, 154, 159; socioeconomic, 65–66, 143, 155, 171; socioeconomic, as a decision criterion, 62, 79, 83, 85, 86, 87, 104, 179, 214 n. 47; tax, 66, 68, 69, 114, 155

Regional cleavages between coast and sierra, 58, 68; within military, 24–25

Retired officers: as a link to society, 7; in conspiracies, 165, 218 n. 11

Revolution: and military coups, 171–73,

217 n. 19; as a source of legitimacy, 170

Revolutionary Socialist party, 56, 60, 61

Revolutionary Union of Ecuadorian Youth (URJE), 56, 57, 58, 61, 154

Rio Protocol: opposition to, 70, 196 n. 5; provisions of, 19; renounced by Ecuador, 48

Riots and demonstrations: against military junta, 69, 70, 71; and working-class opinion, 7; Cuenca 1961, 49; Guayaquil 1959, 45–46; 1963, 56, 57; since 1966, 175, 184

Rodríguez Lara, General Guillermo, 177– 85, 195 n. 76

Role definitions, military: and coup decisions, 5, 9–10, 132–34, 160–62; and foreign training, 138, 140–41; and military government, 161–62, 185; and professionalization, 162–64, 168; arbiter, 131, 132–35, 139–40, 145, 161–62; causes of shifts in, 135–45, 162; changes in, 134–35, 161, 181; classic professionalist, 129–30, 132– 33, 137, 161–62; constitutionalist, 130–31, 132–35, 137–39, 161–62; developmentalist, 131–35, 140–45, 161–62, 168; types of, 129–32

Social backgrounds of military officers. *See* Personal backgrounds of military officers

Social Christian Movement (MSC), 41, 45, 47, 56, 58, 210 n. 3

Socialist party, 18, 39, 47, 55, 58, 60, 154

Solaun, Mauricio, and Michael Quinn, 87– 88

Sons of military officers: coup behavior of, 91–93; in Ecuador and in Brazil, 26– 27

Stepan, Alfred, 9, 89, 92, 213 n. 46

Strikes: businessmen's, 69, 70, 157; labor, 49, 58, 71, 183, 184

Structural causes of military coups: after 1972, 181–82; economic dependency, 149–52, 168; economic power of elites, 156–58; in theoretical framework, 5, 10–11; lack of legitimacy, 150, 159, 169–72; weak institutions, 153–56, 169–72

Student demonstrations, 48, 49, 70, 71, 105, 175, 215 n. 25. *See also* FEUE

Subproletariat, 151–52, 158; as basis for populist politics, 151–53, 155

Superior war college: Brazilian, 21; Ecua-

dorian, 21, 168, 169; Peruvian, 21; and high professionalization, 163–64
Swingman theory, 164–65
Systemic causes of coups. *See* Structural causes of military coups

Tariffs, import, 69, 70, 175
Terrorism, 210 n. 4; false incidents of, 60–61, 117. *See also* United States Central Intelligence Agency
Texaco-Gulf, 183
Thompson, William R., 87
Threatening elections. *See* Elections, as a factor in military coups
Two-hundred-mile limit: after 1972, 183; under Arosemena, 200 n. 38; under military junta, 67, 145

Underlying motives, 5, 10, 125–28. *See also* Identifications underlying decision criteria
United States: economic support for the military junta, 66; influence in Ecuadorian military, 118, 220 n. 28; military attachés, 60, 118; military doctrines, 8, 141; opposition to Arosemena and support for 1963 coup, 60, 118, 200 n. 28
United States Central Intelligence Agency: covert operations in Ecuador, 48, 56–57, 60, 61, 211 n. 27; false terrorism staged by, 117
United States-Ecuadorian relations: and Cuba, 48, 159; and banquet incident, 61. *See also* Two-hundred-mile limit
United States military, 5; as a model for Latin American militaries, 31, 118
United States military assistance program: missions in Ecuador, 9, 31; personnel

in Ecuador, 60, 118; training of Ecuadorian armed forces, 118
*Universo, El:* attitude toward coups, 44, 61, 64, 116; editorial ratings of government performance, 53, 63–64, 72–73, 115, 209 n. 21
Unsuccessful coups: importance of, 39; 1950, 40; 1954, 43–44; 1956, 45; 1975, 183–84
Urbanization: and mass participation, 151–53; and military attitudes, 94–95, 206 n. 15

Varea Donoso, Colonel Reinaldo, 41–45, 52, 61
Velasco Ibarra, José María: and *autogolpe* of 1970, 175; and 1946 dictatorship, 42, 196 n. 23; biographical sketch of, 41; 1944–1947 government of, 41; 1952–1956 government of, 41–45; 1960–1961 government of, 47–54, 132–33, 153–54; 1968–1972 government of, 174–79, 181, 215 n. 25; personal philosophy of, 41; treatment of military by, 41, 121–22
Venezuela, 6, 182; armed forces of, 89
Veto coups. *See* Elections, as a factor in military coups

War academy, 21, 23, 32, 33, 65; closing of, 40; curriculum of, 21, 103, 138, 192 n. 37, 219 n. 44; in 1961 coup, 51–52, 105; in 1972 coup, 177–79, 181; reopened, 121, 138, 156; revolt in 1971 at, 176–77

Yerovi, Clemente, 70, 72, 174

**Library of Congress Cataloging in Publication Data**

Fitch, John Samuel.
    The military coup d'etat as a political process.

    (The Johns Hopkins University studies in historical and
political science; 95th ser., no. 1)
    Based on the author's thesis, Yale.
    Bibliography: p. 221
    Includes index.
    1. Ecuador—Politics and government—1944–
2. Coups d'état. 3. Military government. I. Title.
II. Series: Johns Hopkins University. Studies in
historical and political science; 95th ser., no. 1.
JL3015.1948.F57    322'.5'09866    76–47381
ISBN 0–8018–1915–6